A FAITH

FOR THE GENERATIONS

VOLUME 1 IN THE ACSD MONOGRAPH SERIES

ACSD   Association for Christians in Student Development

A FAITH

FOR THE GENERATIONS

HOW COLLEGIATE EXPERIENCE IMPACTS FAITH

—————— **EDITORS** ——————

TIMOTHY W. HERRMANN, KIRSTEN D. TENHAKEN, HANNAH M. ADDERLEY, AND MORGAN K. MORRIS

Abilene Christian University Press

A FAITH FOR THE GENERATIONS
How Collegiate Experience Impacts Faith

Copyright © 2015 by Timothy W. Herrmann, Kirsten D. TenHaken,
Hannah M. Adderley, and Morgan K. Morris

ISBN 978-0-89112-344-6

Printed in the United States of America

All scripture quotations, unless otherwise indicated, are taken from the Holy Bible, New
International Version®, NIV®. Copyright ©1973, 1978, 1984, 2011 by Biblica, Inc.™ Used by permission
of Zondervan. All rights reserved worldwide.

Cover design by Marc Whitaker
Interior text design by Sandy Armstrong, Strong Design

For information contact:
Abilene Christian University Press
ACU Box 29138
Abilene, Texas 79699

1-877-816-4455
www.acupressbooks.com

15 16 17 18 19 20 / 7 6 5 4 3 2 1

The publication of this book has been sponsored by the
Association for Christians in Student Development.

ACSD Association for Christians
in Student Development

The mission of the Association for Christians in Student Development
is to equip and challenge members to infuse their Christian faith
into student development practice and scholarship.

TABLE OF CONTENTS

Acknowledgements

A volume such as this one cannot be produced without the help of a number of people, and this monograph is no exception. First we want to thank the Association for Christians in Student Development, especially the executive committee for their vision in commissioning a series of which this is the first volume. Past president Steve Beers, current president Kris Hansen-Kieffer, and scholarship chair Steve Ivester have been instrumental in bringing this project to fruition, and, without their support, this project could not have happened. Their collaboration was a significant encouragement to the editorial team. Perhaps more importantly, their actions provided continued evidence that the association is committed to promoting scholarship, contributing to the conversation regarding college student development, and providing thought leadership within the academy. This bold effort is both inspiring and laudable, and we are indeed grateful.

Next, we would like to thank Todd Ream, who coordinated the Taylor University Higher Education Symposium, *A Faith for the Generations: Explorations of How Collegiate Faith Impacts the Cultivation of Faith in the Decades to Come.* This monograph emerged from that event. Without Todd's energy, hard work, and innovative thinking, neither the symposium nor this volume would have been possible. We would also be remiss not to acknowledge the leadership of Taylor University, particularly President Eugene Habecker, for supporting this program and this monograph in many very concrete ways, especially by clearing the way for Taylor to host this symposium. Skip Trudeau, Taylor's vice-president for student development, also provided tremendous assistance in this project, particularly by initiating the early planning process and providing staff support.

Most importantly, we want to thank the authors of the various chapters. We believe that each chapter provides an important contribution to the discussion of how we may best nurture lasting, resilient, meaningful faith during emerging adulthood and especially beyond. The individuals who shared in this project were a joy to work with and repeatedly demonstrated that the faith they wrote about is the prime motivator for their efforts as well as the pattern that guides their work and their lives. Special thanks go to the symposium plenary speakers whose three chapters form the backbone of this volume. Christian Smith, Holly Allen, and Vern Bengtson have provided truly exceptional chapters and were extremely helpful in the formulation of this document.

And finally, to the members of ACSD, the practitioners who work so diligently, skillfully, and selflessly for the emerging adults at the center of this volume: thank you for the efforts and investments you make in these young lives. It is our sincerest hope that the material contained in this monograph will serve you well as you seek to serve students.

Timothy W. Herrmann, Kirsten D. TenHaken,
Hannah M. Adderley, and Morgan K. Morris

Upland, Indiana
April 2015

DEFINING THE TASK

TIMOTHY W. HERRMANN, KIRSTEN D. TENHAKEN,
HANNAH M. ADDERLEY, AND MORGAN K. MORRIS

Taylor University

In 2002, Alan Wolfe, in an insightful review essay on religion in American higher education, noted:

> One would be hard pressed to find a private college or university in the United States that cannot trace its founding to a religious denomination. One would be equally hard pressed, at least as far as America's elite universities are concerned, to find one that would identify faith as central to its current approaches to teaching, research, and student life. That is to say: No aspect of life is considered so important to Americans outside higher education, yet deemed so unimportant by the majority of those inside, as religion.

He went on to make the point that though higher education in its recent past had largely ignored religion, the picture was changing. Given the developments of the thirteen years that have transpired since the publication of his article, one might characterize Wolfe's prediction as understated. Just two years after this article appeared, higher education thought leader Alexander Astin asserted the centrality of the inner life in "Why Spirituality Deserves a Central Place in Liberal Education" (2004). In the intervening years, a host of books, articles, and conferences have addressed issues of spirituality and religion in American higher education. Prominent examples include *The Heart of Higher Education* (Palmer & Zajonc, 2010); *Sex and the Soul* (Freitas, 2008); *God on the Quad* (Riley, 2005); *Helping College Students Find Purpose* (Nash & Murray, 2010); and *Cultivating the Spirit* (Astin, Astin, & Lindholm, 2011). A simple search of the *Chronicle of Higher Education* database using the keyword "religion" yields 462 results for just the past three years. Clearly religion is *en vogue!*

While those who care about the place of religion in American life would be tempted to take heart at these developments, such a response might be unwarranted. Ironically, at the same time that attention to religion and spirituality in higher education has intensified, we have witnessed a decline in the religious engagement of American youth. Consider the following: the Pew Research Center (2012) reports a 20 percent population of "nones" in America. For those unfamiliar with this label, "nones" are those people (especially young adults) indicating no religious affiliation when surveyed. Of this number, two-thirds are men and mostly from European American or Asian American backgrounds. Nonreligious respondents are also more likely to be from families with more education and higher socioeconomic status. This description represents 20 percent of the nonreligious though only 13 percent of the general American population (Barry & Abo-Zena, 2014). Christian Smith (2005, 2009), a contributor to this volume and one of the most sought-after voices in this conversation, found that parental involvement far outweighed missions trips or youth group attendance in influencing their children's religious participation and practice during the transition to adulthood. Dunn and Sundene (2012) identified instability (vocational, relational, and physical) and rapidly shifting values as disruptive to emerging adults' spiritual journeys. So while we might be encouraged that the academy is increasingly open to considering the place of religion and spirituality in American life, we must conversely be troubled by the fact that this new openness does not seem to be yielding positive results in the lives of emerging adults. This fact calls to mind, and perhaps renders ominous, another of Wolfe's (2002) predictions in the previously noted commentary: that "the young are likely to set the future course of religion in America."

So, that is why we are here. The purpose of this monograph is to facilitate a discussion of how Christian educators can accomplish their work with students, create conditions on their campuses, and influence the academy in a manner which helps our students to embrace the life of Christ for their own well-being, the benefit of their neighbors, and the sake of the kingdom. While the value of such a conversation is likely not in question for most readers, how this task should be approached and the ultimate ends of our efforts are matters of legitimate debate. Thus, it is our hope that the chapters that follow will help you as you seek to make a difference in your institutions and in the lives of the emerging adults with whom you work.

The essays included in this monograph cover a variety of topics related to the theme originally addressed at the 2014 Taylor University Higher Education Symposium: *A Faith for the Generations: How Collegiate Experience Impacts Faith*. After this brief introductory chapter, the monograph—as did the symposium—begins with an interview with Christian Smith, previously noted as a key voice in the current dialogue regarding emerging adult spirituality. This interview is not only insightful, but it also creates an excellent context for what follows in subsequent chapters.

In Chapter Two, Perry Glanzer reports on recent research that helps us better grasp the manner in which faith informs our students in their development and articulation of a sense of purpose. Those of us who work with students, and particularly those who value matters of faith, understand the tremendous diversity represented in their religious experiences. Though many find belief and commitment relatively straightforward matters, many others do not. If we are truly open and willing to hear what students are think and feel, and what they believe or do not believe, some will share stories of significant pain and struggle—and even loss of faith. Hannah Schundler, in Chapter Three, describes her research with students who experience significant spiritual struggle on faith-based campuses. A reading of her work makes it clear that in order to nurture real faith, such institutions must embrace their students' real doubts.

In recognition that faith is indeed a journey and that as educators we are fellow pilgrims as much as (or perhaps more than) we are knowing guides, Holly Allen, in Chapter Four, helps us to consider just what it means to walk "with emerging adults on their spiritual journey." Her treatment discusses religious culture among emerging adults as well as respectful and meaningful ways in which educators may engage that culture.

As in any realm of human endeavor, the way we frame or talk about our educational practices has an important shaping influence on our efforts and ultimately on what our students gain from such experiences. In Chapter Five, Micah Weedman argues that the manner in which we frame missions or service experiences has great effect on the eventual student learning and formation that results.

In what could be considered a continuation of the conversation begun in Allen's chapter, Guy Chmieleski, in Chapter Six, speaks to the importance of mentoring, its common obstacles, and ways in which mentors can be empowered and encouraged.

In Chapter Seven, Bill Kuhn explores a question that underlies the efforts of all who desire to nurture student faith: "What is the experience of spiritual formation in the lives of traditional, undergraduate college students?" He applies a phenomenological, narrative approach to try to answer this question and to discern themes of college student spiritual formation. As the monograph moves from Chapter Seven to Chapter Eight, readers are asked to shift their attention from a focus on the importance of a lived experience to a focus on the importance of religious particularities and theological dogma. Specifically, Stephen W. Rankin challenges aspects of the work of Sharon Daloz Parks and others. Even the most devoted Parks advocates (and I confess myself to be one) will find his challenges to be thoughtful and perhaps even corrective.

If the spiritual landscape of emerging adulthood is changing, so are our perspectives on the manner in which we are to work with college students. In Chapter Nine, Aaron Morrison considers how understandings of the campus minister's role relate to church affiliation. In Chapter Ten, Mark Husbands provides a wonderfully rich description of how to foster education in a manner that nurtures resilience or "grit." In addition to a convincing discussion of the theological underpinnings of this approach, he describes the Emmaus Scholars Program at Hope College, a model that surely merits imitation.

The book closes on a hopeful tone from what might seem an unlikely voice in a publication focused on emerging adulthood. Noted gerontologist Vern Bengtson reports on his research and offers an encouraging picture of adults reclaiming and reinvigorating the faith of their youth. His chapter is an important reminder of "keeping the end in mind" as we work with students and seek to nurture their cultivation of real, resilient, life-altering faith in Christ.

We are grateful to have the opportunity to share the work and thoughts these authors have offered, and we look forward to continuing this important conversation and important work with you.

References

Astin, A. W. (2004). Why spirituality deserves a central place in liberal education. *Liberal Education, 90*(2), 34–41. Retrieved from http://files.eric.ed.gov
/fulltext/EJ682573.pdf2004

Astin, A. W., Astin, H. W., & Lindholm, J. A. (2011). *Cultivating the spirit: How
college can enhance students' inner lives.* San Francisco, CA: Jossey-Bass.

Barry, C. M., & Abo-Zena, M. M. (2014). *Emerging adults' religiousness and
spirituality: Meaning-making in an age of transition.* New York, NY: Oxford
University Press.

Dunn, R. R., & Sundene, J. L. (2012). *Shaping the journey of emerging adults:
Life-giving rhythms for spiritual transformation.* Downers Grove, IL:
InterVarsity Press.

Freitas, D. (2008). *Sex and the soul: Juggling sexuality, spirituality, romance,
and religion on America's college campuses.* New York, NY: Oxford
University Press.

Nash, R. J., & Murray, M. C. (2010). *Helping college students find purpose: The
campus guide to meaning-making.* San Francisco, CA: Jossey-Bass.

Palmer, P. J., & Zajonc, A. (2010). *The heart of higher education: A call to renewal.*
San Francisco, CA: Jossey-Bass.

PEW Research Center. (2012). "Nones" on the rise. *Religion and Public Life.*
PewResearchCenter. Retrieved from http://www.pewforum.org/2012/10/09
/nones-on-the-rise/#_ftn4

Riley, N. S. (2005). *God on the quad: How religious colleges and the missionary
generation are changing America.* New York, NY: St. Martin's Press.

Smith, C., & Denton, M. L. (2005). *Soul searching: The religious and spiritual life
of American teenagers.* New York, NY: Oxford University Press.

Smith, C., & Snell, P. (2009). *Souls in transition: The religious and spiritual lives
of emerging adults.* New York, NY: Oxford University Press.

Wolfe, A. (2002). Faith and diversity in American religion. *The Chronicle of
Higher Education.* Retrieved from http://chronicle.com/article/FaithDiversity
-in/15089

1

EMERGING ADULTHOOD AND RELIGIOUS FAITH

A Conversation with Christian Smith

TIMOTHY W. HERRMANN

Taylor University

Christian Smith is the William R. Kenan Jr. Professor of Sociology and Director of the Center for the Study of Religion and Society at the University of Notre Dame.

The following exchange was the opening event for the 2014 Taylor University Higher Education Symposium. The conference theme, *A Faith for the Generations: Explorations of How Collegiate Faith Impacts the Cultivation of Faith in the Decades to Come,* was intended to prompt a conversation about how those in Christian higher education might more effectively prepare their students to develop a rich, sustained, and deepening faith after college. In organizing the symposium, the conveners concluded that the best way to *start* a conversation was *with* a conversation. This article edition of that conversation is offered with the hope that it will stimulate further dialogue about the important topic of faith in emerging adulthood. In an effort to optimize clarity and flow, the conversation was edited to fit this format.

TH—What is emerging adulthood and how might it be considered different than what we have formally considered young adulthood?

CS—The concept of emerging adulthood comes from Jeffrey Arnett's work. Emerging adulthood is its own phase of the American life course, somewhere between being a teenager, or an adolescent living at home, and being a full-fledged adult. But there is a difference between emerging adulthood and young adulthood—young adults are already adults, but young in age, and emerging adults are still developing into adulthood. Emerging adulthood is a unique phase of life with its own characteristics. Now what do we mean by this?

If people interview or survey Americans and ask what it means to be adult in this culture, most Americans say that an ideal adult is someone who has a real job or career—not just something they are bouncing around or trying on. Adults have a real place to live that is their own, they are married or seriously cohabitating, and they are starting to have children. The idea of emerging adulthood in former eras, or the transition from being a teenager in high school to being a real adult, was much shorter and simpler.

Now any of these categories risk oversimplifying—and if any of you are historians, you know things are always more complicated than this—but a variety of social, cultural, technological, and economic changes since the 1960s and 1970s have all worked together to stretch out the period of time between emerging adulthood and adulthood, making it longer and more complex. Jeffrey Arnett now considers the formal period of emerging adulthood as being between age 18 and 29, for a total of 11 years.

There are definitely exceptions to this time period though. Some people, for example, marry their high school sweethearts and get jobs right out of college, moving them into adulthood earlier in life. Some people wait well into their 30s to really figure out who they are, what they are going to be, who they are interested in, where they are going to live, what they are going to do for a living, and so on. So there is wide variance here, but conceptually we are talking about emerging adulthood as basically being "postponed settling down."

A variety of factors have contributed to the increasing length and complexity of the period of emerging adulthood. The expansion of higher education and the globalization of the economy, for example, contributed to increasing numbers of people going to graduate school, and therefore, more young people are being students rather than working real jobs. Additionally, since the 1960s, there has been a huge delay in the average age of first marriage for both men and women. The availability of contraceptives has changed the meaning of sex and relationships in today's culture. Over the decades, all of these changes have together resulted in the emerging adulthood phase of the American life course where it takes a long time before people become real adults.

This change in emerging adulthood comes with both positive and negative effects. One positive effect is that now people don't get immediately stuck in a job that they have to work for the rest of their life but that may not be appropriate for them. There is a lot of time to explore, start over, and try something new. Emerging adults have the freedom to learn and adjust—which is, I would say, a good thing in general. But it also comes with transience, uncertainty, and a feeling of never being rooted anywhere. Emerging adults do not know what they are really going to do or when they are going to have to move again. So there is a lot of anxiety and rootlessness that can build up for five, ten, or twelve years for some. This lengthy transition at a crucial time in people's lives results in what is now conceptually understood as emerging adulthood, or basically a "postponing" of becoming what most people consider to be a real adult.

TH—In your research you found that only 9 percent of emerging adults noted having a concern for God's perspective on how they live their lives. How can those who desire to nurture meaningful, resilient, and enduring faith commitments among emerging adults begin to address this apparent disinterest in an active, relationally-based faith in God?

CS—Starting with what I just said about postponed settling down and combining it with a couple other factors, the dominant challenge in the religious and spiritual lives of emerging adults is evident. In many societies, but especially in American society, being a faithful, practicing, publicly engaged person of faith is strongly associated with real adulthood, and therefore, with family formation. In the United States, the connection between family and religion is extremely close. It is really powerful how many churches, for example, are set up to be oriented around a particular version of family. So for most emerging adults—not all, but for most—there is a general sense that even though they may be interested in God or religious faith, they see it as something they will commit to later in life. Emerging adults anticipate that when they have to settle down and become a spouse or parent, they will become more serious about religion. The nature of emerging adulthood does not lend itself to encouraging strong, committed, invested faith.

So just for one example, most versions of Christianity have some kind of strong ecclesiology—to be a good Christian, you should be a part of a church and probably seriously involved in a church. The nature of emerging adulthood has very strong themes of transience where everything is kept open or up in the air. A self-reinforcing cycle of structural conditions encourages emerging adults to keep all their options open and to not make any commitments. So the idea of really getting involved with a church and committing to building some roots just doesn't fit with emerging adulthood. The very structure and culture of emerging adulthood mitigate against being involved in a church, which sort of throws a wrench into the idea of being a serious Christian.

The other thing about emerging adulthood that undermines religious commitment is that emerging adults spend time with other emerging adults. Emerging adulthood is highly age-stratified, and there is not a lot of integration with and connection to people of different ages. At work, they may have to deal with people of different ages, and at school they may have professors, but those are not considered real relationships—they are just professional interactions. In real life, emerging adults hang out with people of their type—which, again, is in contrast with the idea of Christian community, where the living and the dead, the unborn, the whole community of faith shares life together. Emerging adulthood doesn't naturally lend itself to that type of community, which perpetuates the lack of serious religious faith and practice among emerging adults.

TH—What are the characteristics of moralistic therapeutic deism and what have you studied that led you to the conclusion that this phrase defines the faith of American youth?

CS—I spent a summer with a lot of colleagues interviewing teenagers all over the country about their view and practice of religion and spiritual life. Over the course of the summer, it increasingly dawned on me that most of the Christians are actually not Trinitarian. The idea of Jesus is almost nonexistent—they talk about God very easily, but not Jesus or the Holy Spirit or the Trinity. Not only are they not theological, but operationally there is just a God. Then it dawned on me that the nature of this God is pretty disconnected from their ordinary lives, which started to feel like deism more than the classic Christian God who is personal, involved in history, and involved in developments of human life.

I then realized that their God's basic purpose is to solve people's immediate problems and make people feel good—which is where the therapeutic part of the term came in. In talking about therapy I'm talking about a cultural sensibility that life is about my happiness, my satisfaction, and me feeling good. And yet, their beliefs weren't absolutely morally relativistic—there would be this moralistic edge to things. So in the phrase "moralistic therapeutic deism" by "moralism" I mean an ungrounded sense that certain things are just right or wrong or good or bad. Nobody could quite explain why they were right or wrong or good or bad—they didn't fit into a larger narrative that made any sense—but even without an ability to explain why, they had a clear understanding of some things that would be totally wrong.

Eventually, it dawned on me that the de facto functional religion of most American teenagers, whatever their denomination, is moralistic therapeutic deism—and there are five core beliefs of moralistic therapeutic deism. A God exists who created the world, so it is theistic and creationistic. The purpose of life is to be happy and satisfied. God wants people to be nice, kind, and fair to each other—which is sort of the sum total of God's will. People should be nice to each other, which is what the Bible and every religion teaches—so all religions are essentially the same. Finally, good people go to heaven when they die. So heaven is for good people and almost everybody is good—you have to be a horrible person not to go to heaven.

In all of this, Jesus doesn't show up, so I decided that moralistic therapeutic deism is a functional religious faith for people who live in a highly pluralistic society. It binds people together who are otherwise very different, and it helps people, especially teenagers who experience significant turmoil, to cope with their lives. Moralistic therapeutic deism is a simplistic religious faith, but life doesn't really work that way. So as teenagers carry this faith into their twenties, it starts to break down and become more complicated, because the twenties are too much of a challenge for moralistic therapeutic deism. This faith is still operating in the background for a lot of people though—essentially communicating that God is probably what life is about.

TH—*In* Souls in Transition, *you wrote that "emerging adults are not only less religiously committed and involved than older adults, but also tend to be less involved in and committed toward a wide variety of other non-religious social institutional connections, associations, and activities." What are some of the practical implications of this lack of commitment?*

CS—There has been a strong age effect since at least the mid-twentieth century, where, after one leaves home, religious involvement almost completely plummets and then creeps back up again in the twenties and the thirties. This same age effect is evident with voting, volunteering, and being members of organizations. In general, emerging adults are not integrated into various voluntary institutions of society. When emerging adults become real adults, then they feel like they ought to become more connected. In the meantime though, emerging adults are generally disconnected—they spend time with people their own age and do not integrate into society. Emerging adults are not involved in church, politics, civic life, or community organizations because they are generally socially isolating.

TH—*Have you noticed any connection between the lack of religious commitment and the lack of involvement in these other kinds of civic activities?*

CS—In general, for the whole adult population, people that are more involved in church are more involved in everything. So there is a positive correlation between being a church member and being connected to everything else—either people are joiners or they are not joiners. The same correlation will likely be true of emerging adults too, but because of this life course phase, emerging adults are generally minimally connected.

Because this phase of life is crucially formative for people as they are developing their identities, it is a problematic time for them to be so disconnected from so many things. Another way to describe that is to say that it is a dangerous thing to let people, emerging adults in this case, be socialized by their peers.

This socialization by peers is directly correlated to the absence of an adult presence in the lives of many emerging adults. This absence is not necessarily any one group's fault though—when people are in different stages of life, it is not easy to blend those seasons. Places like church are where such blending can happen—because the church is one of the last non-age stratified voluntary institutions in the United States—but if twenty-year-olds aren't going to church, then the church can only be minimally helpful, which perpetuates the problem among emerging adults of a lack of connection and blending.

TH—How would you describe emerging adult morality?

CS—Most emerging adults, regardless of their ability to articulate this, seem to existentially feel caught by having been told their entire lives not to judge another person's system of beliefs. They have learned to be tolerant and accepting—which has some virtue, I think, but is completely naïve as it has played out. Emerging adults have never been trained or given the intellectual tools to figure out how their tolerance doesn't descend into complete relativism where anything anybody believes is fine.

So the operating background model is moral individualism, where everyone simply decides for themselves, based on their own subjective, intuitive sense or experiences. Each person is authorized to determine what is right or wrong, and nobody else can question that, because it would be considered as questioning the integrity of another person's personhood. Consequently, emerging adults are caught between their strong leaning towards relativism and their awareness that not everything can be right or wrong.

Very few emerging adults are true, absolute moral relativists. Again, most have a sense of right and wrong, but the adult world has not given them the tools to figure out how to have moral commitments and convictions without being judgmental or intolerant. I think it is definitely possible to work out, but it takes formation, modeling, and teaching that emerging adults are not getting in public schools. Emerging adults are not immoral people any more than other adults are, but the culture of emerging adulthood doesn't know how to choose anything other than moral relativism and moral individualism.

The most morally committed people describe their morality in two primary ways but both use the same key phrase. They claim to know what the truth is, saying "for me" this is right or wrong. One version of "for me" is used by those who believe something to be true of them and true of everybody, but they describe such belief as their individual conviction so as not to create conflict. The other version of "for me" is used by those who believe something to be true only for them, and someone else could believe something completely different. That latter version of morality is moral individualism.

TH—Can you describe the six major religious types among emerging adults?

CS—In order to understand the religious and spiritual lives of emerging adults well, this diversity of religious types must be taken seriously. Often we describe the typical experiences or behaviors of emerging adults, but there is actually incredible variance among their religious and spiritual lives. One religious category of emerging adults is called *committed traditionalists,* and these people were raised in a committed religious family. They know what they believe and are committed to practicing these beliefs. For these emerging adults, religion forms their identity and their life. Another group of people are in a category called *selective adherence,* and they were raised in a religious tradition but are now evaluating what they believe and what they don't believe. These emerging adults haven't abandoned their religiosity, but they are not completely committed to it.

A third group of emerging adults are the *spiritually open*. In an overt sense, there are few spiritual seekers among emerging adults, but there are some emerging adults who were raised nonreligious but felt somewhat left out of something. Maybe their friends were going to youth group or other people in English class knew some biblical reference while they were completely clueless. These emerging adults sense they missed out on something that most of their peers had, but they are not actively seeking. They are not hostile, and they are not religious, but they are curious—so they are more likely to engage in a conversation than the emerging adults in the first two types.

A fourth type, representing a large percentage of emerging adults, is called the *religiously indifferent*. These emerging adults are not hostile toward religion, but they are not interested. Religion holds no meaning, and therefore, these emerging adults are indifferent. As referenced previously, emerging adults anticipate that when they have kids, they will take them to Sunday school and "figure out" religion, but until then, they are postponing adulthood and, therefore, they are indifferent toward religion.

Another group of emerging adults is called the *religiously disconnected* and have no connection to religion whatsoever—they have never been to church and they don't know anyone who is religious. Finally, about 10 percent of emerging adults are *irreligious*—they have rejected religion and are actively hostile. These emerging adults were either raised nonreligious and have become more militant or they were raised religious and have now rejected religion.

Because of the significant diversity among these six types emerging adults, conversations about religion or spirituality require varied understandings of who emerging adults are. People working with emerging adults must adopt a posture of asking questions in order to engage in a fruitful and productive conversation. The qualitatively distinct diversity among the religious and spiritual lives of emerging adults needs to be recognized so as to avoid over simplifying their beliefs.

TH—How can we encourage our students to seriously embrace the truth of the gospel, even in its exclusive aspects, when moral individualism so often seems to lead to moral relativism?

CS—There are certainly implications of this morality for Christian higher education. Initially, Christian colleges have an advantage in working with emerging adults, because these colleges begin with a normative commitment to a particular perspective. There always exists a commitment and a worldview at work, and at a Christian institution, these commitments and worldviews are at least somewhat concrete. Christian colleges have commitments; they stand in particular traditions; and they are trying to work out education, intellectual life, and society. I think that is a huge advantage.

I would say, too, that Christian colleges have an advantage working with emerging adults based on the extent to which they remain committed to true liberal arts education and not just technical education or practical degrees. The long-term development of a liberally educated society is crucial, and this model ensures that students are the real product of higher education.

It is important that students who come to a Christian college are able to get a solid theological education, so that when they graduate, they will have learned about the Christian story. Students should also have an opportunity to expand their horizons, not just generally and intellectually, but with regard to what Christianity is and who the church or the community of God may include. These two things can be realized at a Christian college and are very important in nurturing faith and other commitments among emerging adults.

Finally, research shows that relationships between faculty—including student development professionals—and students are crucial. Interpersonal relationships with faculty who they bond with, can talk with, and who are mentors to them are among the most formative experiences for students. Therefore, who the faculty members are, what the institutional mission represents, and what the student-to-faculty ratio is among other things, are subtle cultural characteristics that make a significant difference for many students.

I think also that colleges have incredible potential to form most of their students, but to make the formation really work, it requires a rough consensus about a vision. From the admissions office where they give tours to high school students, all the way through the faculty and the people in the dorms, to the person who speaks at the convocation, there should be an institutional culture that understands what they are committed to doing. With a culture where everyone is committed to a specific vision, opportunity for powerful formative influence arises. It requires an institutional culture where everyone is pulling the rope in the same direction though. Therefore, it is increasingly necessary for faculty and administrators at Christian colleges to be explicit about and consistent with their commitments. When such a vision or mission is realized, there is more power to form students into adulthood.

THE HEART OF PURPOSE

The Major Difference behind Students' Answers
to One of Life's Biggest Questions

PERRY L. GLANZER

Baylor University

Former Harvard President Derek Bok (2011) recently wrote, "One of the least examined and yet most fundamental questions about undergraduate education" concerns "how students acquire the values and convictions that help to give meaning and purpose to their lives" (n.p.). This lack of attention to the development of students' purpose seems a bit odd because purpose has been associated with many of the positive outcomes sought in higher education, such as academic self-efficacy, motivation for academic achievement, generally successful educational experiences, and clarity regarding one's future occupational plans (Bronk, 2014).

One particularly understudied area concerns the role that students' religious or nonreligious identity plays in purpose development (Bronk, 2014). Recent work among emerging adults and college students has provided us with some evidence that significant differences exist among students based upon religious or nonreligious identity (Astin, Astin, & Lindholm, 2011; Braskamp, Trautvetter, & Ward, 2006; Bronk, 2014; Small & Bowman, 2012;

Smith, Christoffersen, Davidson, & Herzog, 2011; Smith & Snell, 2009). Yet, as Astin et al. (2011) noted regarding students' quest for meaning and purpose, "How particular aspects of these students' religious faiths may specifically serve to enhance quest inclinations warrants further focused study" (p. 36).

This chapter reports on a recent research effort to explore students' perceptions of the influence of their particular religious or nonreligious identity and worldview on their development of purpose. The study relies upon findings from an analysis of two different qualitative datasets of 185 interviews with young, emerging adults.[1]

One goal of the interviews was to explore the purposes students identify and the connections between these choices and their religious or nonreligious worldviews.

The Choice of Purpose

In her recent book, *Purpose in Life: A Critical Component of Optimal Youth Development*, Kendall Cotton Bronk (2014) identified six common life purposes that individuals choose: religion, family, career, political and/or civic activities, and artistic pursuits. While an examination of the 185 student interviews confirmed the presence of these purposes, it also revealed additional items Bronk did not identify. These twelve purposes as well as illustrative quotes from the interviews are listed below:

- Career (e.g., "Well, I know I want to be a nurse. I'm in nursing school and I know I probably want to get a postgrad degree in nursing.")
- Happiness (e.g., "I mean ultimately I just want to be happy.")
- Service and/or love (e.g., "I always felt like my purpose was to help people.")
- Family (e.g., "Have a family, kids, grandkids.")
- Friends (e.g., "I'd have to say family and friends.")
- Creative accomplishments (e.g., "Making things. That's kind of broad, but I'm a studio art major, so I like to create interesting things.")

---

[1] For background information and notes concerning the research methodology used, see the Methodology section at the end of this chapter.

- Experiences (e.g., "Learning new things, seeing new places.")
- God (e.g., "My biggest purpose is to love God and bring glory to Him.")
- Religion (e.g., "My religion.")
- Change the world for good (e.g., "I want to use my knowledge and ability to try and better life for somebody else.")
- Material goods or money (e.g., "I would like to make a lot of money and not have to worry about making car payments or worrying about insurance or when I buy a house—mortgages, and just, you know, being financially secure. I think that's a big purpose for me.")
- Civic involvement (e.g., "I want to serve others through leadership roles.")

As the quotes indicate, some students focus upon only one purpose. Many students, however, combine these purposes in a wide variety of ways. In fact, one way to make sense of how students talk about these purposes is to think of them as *ingredients* for the good life. In some cases, students combine only two of the ingredients. As one student stated, "My purpose is to excel in my career and somehow use that career to help other people." Indeed, this kind of combination was common when students understood their purpose as the motivation for their career. As this student noted,

> The main point that I have behind my career choice is that I want to
> work in aerospace, specifically with space flight because I feel that
> I want to help humanity get into space and push out the bound-
> aries more.

A significant minority of students add together three or more different purpose ingredients. Certain ingredients, such as friends, happiness, material goods, and family, were especially prone to combinations. Indeed, not one respondent listed friends as the sole purpose, although this student came close:

> Making my friends happy. . . . Um, there's a, in my brother's graduating
> class, the valedictorian, I barely remember his speech, I barely remem-
> ber anything, but this has stuck with me. If you can't be happy yourself,

the best thing to do is make other people happy. . . . So I try to make my friends as happy as possible.

As in this case, the mention of happiness would often be combined with other things, "My friends and my family and just being around happy, uplifting atmospheres, so that's what gives my life meaning." In addition, very few respondents articulated their purpose primarily in terms of achieving material possessions.

Usually, those mentioning material possessions included other purposes as well, such as the following student: "To own my own house, have kids, [and] get married, like everyone else. Be well off." As in this case, family quite often proved to be a purpose listed along with other purposes: "I definitely want to be married, and like I said, the graphic design thing, I'm dying to go into that. I can't wait to graduate and just enjoy life, that's very important right now." Similarly, as one religious student noted, "I would definitely say my family and my religion; they kind of, and they also actually go like together because my parents resonate with very strong, religious backgrounds and so I think this is very strongly rooted in me."

As can be seen with all of these quotes, the combination of the different types of ingredients varied considerably, and, in some cases, students would order the ingredients under one overarching ingredient. For example, one student noted, "Overall, for me, it's like God and through Him I can be happy, I can, like I have meaning to my life and—I mean then there's also like my family and my friends. But like the utmost thing would be God."

In this case, God proved a common ordering purpose. Similarly, happiness often served as an overarching purpose: "Having a family, a nice family, a good job, nice cars, [and a] nice house. Just really being accomplished. . . . Having those things would make me happy." It should be noted, however, that not everyone prioritized their list of purpose ingredients or even came up with a purpose.

In each of the interview datasets, a third of students claimed not to have found their purpose (e.g., "I don't really have a sense of purpose."). Some considered themselves purposeless because they reduced purpose to one single ingredient, their future career. Since they were not settled upon a major or job, they believed they lacked purpose. The following interviewee illustrates this category:

> Yeah, I guess I'm still trying to figure out exactly what I want to do as far as a career path, that's the main thing that I'm struggling with right now, as far as what I want to do for a career basically.

Yet, others realized that purpose extended beyond school, career, or even their family, as this student noted:

> I mean, I don't know what my purpose per se in life is yet, but, you know, I want to be happy. I want to have a family. So that's what I'm striving for. I'm trying to get a degree so I can get a good job. Just do the typical thing, you know, buy a house. Do what everyone is supposed to do so.

The nature of these purposeless students and their search clearly related to something beyond a simple quest for a career or a longing to have a family. Moreover, while both religious and nonreligious students confessed to not having a purpose, a disproportionate number of purposeless students did not identify with a religious identity. This finding raises a question regarding what larger perspectives and outlooks guide students' choices about purpose. The answer to this question relates to the heart of purpose, something that can only be captured by listening to students' stories.

The Heart of Purpose

Meredith attends a public university on the West Coast. She states, "I was born Christian and baptized and everything." However, she claims, "As I got older and through high school and college, I've definitely kind of stepped away from it." Today, she does not identify with any religious identity. She attributes this de-conversion to the fact that "I'm very big into math and very big into science and so I think, oh, this is going to sound kind of mean, but I'm not kind of as blind." Science has provided her with true light.

> I think really very extreme religious people are kind of blinded by their faith and are unable to see like really big scientifically proven truths. And so I don't want to say it helps me like see better metaphorically, but I think in terms of some people it does.

According to Meredith, science has also helped her to develop self-reliance, which becomes a major theme in her interview:

> I think it really just makes me more self-reliant . . . I'm moving forward toward my own future goals and what I can do, instead of what I can do for God. I don't know if that makes me selfish, but I guess that's what I do to make myself a better person and to help me and to help people surrounding me instead of like doing something for a deity that may—that probably doesn't exist.

Self-reliance in many ways proves to be the hallmark of her outlook on life. When asked what makes life meaningful, she replies, "School and kind of the opportunity it's giving me to advance my life." In particular, she appreciates "the idea of becoming an adult and being self-sufficient and having a full-time job and really just being able to go out there and be my own person."

Not surprisingly, this general idea about what makes her life meaningful also informs her more specific purpose. At first, she defines it more generally: "I mean ultimately I just want to be happy." What this means, though, also translates into what might make her self-reliant:

> I want to enjoy my life and not have to worry about, and this does sound materialistic, but I would like to make a lot of money and not have to worry about making car payments or worrying about insurance or when I buy a house—mortgages, and just, you know, having to be financially secure. I think that's a big purpose for me.

Oddly, this whole vision contrasts with the lessons she notes that her parents instilled in her. She says they taught her, "There's the whole money can't buy happiness thing"; however, she counters with "but it can get you pretty damn close." She also adds,

> At least my mom has taught me a lot about, you know, your family can help you sometimes and it's okay to rely on them and that they'll still be there for you and to not kind of discount them.

However, based on her purpose, Meredith would appear to have discounted this lesson.

Does she have any discussions about her purpose in college? For example, are there classes or assigned readings? She admits, "No. Not really. As a math major, we don't talk about life that much; we talk about numbers." When asked if she has had conversations with faculty, she notes that she did have one inspiring math teacher, but their relationship and conversation only addressed professional matters. She has had conversations with friends about this issue in college. Oddly, these conversations seemed to undermine her goal of being self-reliant:

> I think they really helped to know that I'm not alone. Like I'm not the only one who's kind of struggling with this stuff and so it's easier to know that I'm not alone and we can kind of rely on each other and be able to vent to each other when we just have no idea what we're doing with our life.

Marsha, a student from an evangelical college, shares some similarities with Meredith. She told us, "I was baptized as a baby, and I just never really got it." She also rebelled for a time against her parents taking her to church. "I remember for a period of time I was like 'Why do we have to go to church? That's stupid nobody else does.' And my dad's like, 'That's what we do, we go to church as a family on Sunday, and this is what we do.'" Despite the lack of an in-depth answer to this question, she admits her rebellion was not necessarily against God or occasional church attendance: "I never was like, 'I never want to go to church, I hate God' . . . you know, never really had that." Eventually, Marsha began to own her faith at a fairly early age:

> I didn't really come to own my faith until I was in ninth grade. In junior high, I went through confirmation, and I thought it was the stupidest thing, and I was so upset that I had to skip dance class to be there. But confirmation Sunday, which is the beginning of June, I say that's my first encounter with Christ. I was standing up at the front of my church, and looking at the cross, and like, "Oh wow, this is real, this is more than going to church on Sunday morning. It's more than just being nice or not cussing or whatever."

What provoked this thought? It was not the confirmation classes. "I was a horrible, horrible confirmation student. I slept in class, wrote notes in class; I was lucky I was there, I didn't pay attention." Marsha's reflection had more to do with a particular event that helped bring her to that point:

My freshman year of high school, I attended a three-day high school retreat. It was a girls' weekend called Chrysalis, and it's a ministry I'm still involved with . . . high school students of all denominations attend, and it's seventy-two hours of you hear talks and meditations and you sing and you eat meals. And it's just a lot of fun. No phones, no clocks, no computers, no anything but God, and that weekend is, I like to say, the reason I'm at [this university]. That's where I met my friend Stephanie who went here. That's where I realized that I can have a relationship with Christ, that's not something I had ever known or realized or internalized before.

This retreat also changed her whole outlook toward her life.

Going through junior high . . . I always cared a lot about what other people thought about me and presenting myself in a very composed and put together way. And, and I still have that in my life . . . going to Chrysalis and really learning that, my faith is my own, and that God loves me deeply and that he wants to have a relationship with me, . . . and just realizing that I don't have to do it all on my own, and that I am a daughter of the King, and that he has a plan for my life, and there's so much freedom in that. I don't have to be put together; I don't have to do it on my own. I don't have to be the "It Girl."

Marsha felt worn down by the pressure of trying to self-author her life in front of a large audience from which she sought approval. She did not want the strain of that kind of "freedom." Instead, she found freedom in what she viewed as God's design and story. This outlook has shaped her purpose in deeply religious ways:

My purpose in life is to glorify the Lord, and he is orchestrating the things in my life. I feel like I'm here because this is where he's called me, and the relationships I've had are because of the things, he's wanted to teach me through those friends right now.

This outlook emerges from a theological view of who she is as a person and how God created her: "I believe that we are created in the image of God, and that he has designed us for his glory and his purpose." Fulfilling who she believes she is created to be brings her a unique kind of freedom, "It's not confining. It's freer, if anything. There's direction and purpose in living to a higher calling and living for a higher purpose." In this respect, Marsha believes she has found a "grand" or "higher" purpose.

The stories of Meredith and Marsha represent the common divide we found when examining the narratives students set forth to justify how they thought about purpose. While the 185 interviewed students came from diverse student populations at a variety of religious and secular colleges, no particular religious or nonreligious identities (e.g., atheist, agnostic, nonbeliever, etc.) accounted for the primary conceptual divide among interviewees. What did account for the major divide was whether or not students believed in God.

The "Freedom" of Non-Theists

Meredith represents the common characteristic we found among the non-theistic interviewees, whether they described themselves as atheist, agnostic, culturally Jewish, nonreligious or something else. They loved the freedom to create their own purpose. Monica, a self-described "spiritual but not religious" student from a liberal arts university, provides a typical example of this subset. She started by contrasting her current outlook about meaning and purpose to how she believes a theistic outlook would influence her perspective: "I wouldn't think as critically about my meaning and purpose because I would think, 'Okay, I can rely on someone else for that. God has a purpose for me and I'd just have to listen to God.'" In contrast to what she saw as the constraining nature of theism, Monica valued the freedom to author her own life meaning and purpose:

> And I think that's important to me, knowing that my meaning and purpose in life has nothing to do with anyone else . . . that it's all my decision and not like God has a plan for me and it will see itself out because it's his plan and not mine, so therefore it has to happen—I just have to wait and see. But I can't wait and see if it's my own plan.

These two aspects of Monica's outlook—the criticism of religious approaches and the exaltation of the freedom to choose their purpose—characterized virtually every nontheistic interview.

Indeed, nonreligious students often defended their approach by attacking what they see as the dependent, constrained, or disempowering outlook of the religious believer. Dennis, a former Catholic, claimed,

> I think religious people, although they would really like to think freely, I think the fear of hell is a big obstacle to thinking freely a lot of the times. Belief in an absolute final word of God that can't be changed, I think that's an obstacle, too, to thinking without any preconceived notions.

Brooke, an atheist attending a Catholic university, called religious belief a "crutch." Anne, a nonreligious student at a regional university claimed, "I don't want to be stereotypical here, because I don't mean to do that. But I think it tends to be if you're religious then you kind of have this 'meant to be' mentality." Jeremiah, a nonreligious Jewish student at a secular liberal arts college, claimed, "I think religion can sometimes be—I don't want to say a copout, but an easy way to find purpose, because, I mean, the meaning of life is essentially spelled out in most religious doctrine." Chase, an atheist liberal arts student at a Lutheran college, claimed of his earlier religious worldview:

> Whereas before I think morality was more simplistic because you had a book and you could look it up, you know, now you're taking responsibility for more morality and you're being forced to question whether what you're doing is right.

Since the nonreligious students renounced or doubted belief in any sort of deity and associated religious doctrines, they felt free to create their own story. As Tyson, a public research university student, noted, "I've kind of made my own purpose and I kind of like that, being able to control why I was here." Brooke claimed, "I think I definitely feel more liberated and stuff." In some cases, the freedom was from a particular religious belief. Albert, a student at an Ivy League school, commented,

> I would say, in the instance that there's no book to tell you what to do, there's no clear rules, but I'm definitely, I think, happier because I was always very afraid of hell when I was religious, and it's very disturbing.

Cheryl, an atheist, maintained that she did not "look to one place to find where the meaning of life is because the meaning of life is all around us."

This strong belief in their ability to self-author their own meaning and purpose finds resonance with a common theoretical understanding of purpose development during this stage in life (Baxter Magolda, 1999, 2001, 2004).

The Burden of No Religious Belief

What exactly then is the new meaning of life? The nontheists were not quite in unison regarding that answer. Some, like Meredith, turned to achievement and material ambitions, but others hoped to help others. What they had in common was that they prized the freedom to create their own purpose. Yet, the freedom often left them without clear direction regarding their purpose. They also admitted to being unsure about where they would turn for answers.

As a result, these students constantly fluctuated between celebrating their freedom and recognizing the problems and difficulties this freedom created. The difficult work involved in building one's purpose from scratch instead of starting with some general architectural guidance from religious traditions proved burdensome. Indeed, one nonreligious respondent, Darren, used this building metaphor:

> Religion generally provides some sort of starting point for that sort of discussion. Without a religious view, I would just sort of start at nothing and just try to build it all by myself and through discussion with others, which I think can be both a detriment and an aid in trying to figure things out, I guess.

Gregory, who claimed to follow a "religion of the self," stated,

> I guess I personally feel very liberated that I sort of can control my own destiny . . . but then again I do have to find a purpose, right? I do have to find a philosophy that I feel comfortable living. . . . So it doesn't make it that much easier.

Katie, a nonreligious student at a secular liberal arts college admits,

> Not having anything to identify with on a spiritual level at least, you kind of have to guide your own values and sometimes it's maybe difficult to remember exactly what you want to stick true to, like what your priorities are.

What also appeared to add to this struggle was that these students lacked communities linked to their philosophical or nonreligious identity that cultivated conversations about purpose. While a few did mention their involvement in secular humanist clubs, these groups did not seem to fulfill this sort of role. As one Ivy League student noted regarding his experience in one such club:

> I wouldn't say we talked about the meaning of life . . . questions for a meeting might be "Is America a Christian nation?" or we might discuss a certain argument for the existence of God, or around the holidays we'll have a themed one like the origins of this holiday and is it becoming more or less religious.

In this case, the secular humanist club appeared to focus more upon responding to certain religious views than building a substantive secular humanist identity.

Overall, these students saw themselves as taking the difficult "road less traveled," or to use a metaphor other than the building or road image, they wanted to be artists who create their own story and draw their own life maps. However, for these students, starting from a blank page proved challenging. The perceived reward for this challenge is the sense of authenticity to themselves and lack of alienation from a tradition. Jeremiah, a nonreligious student, admits regarding his perspective:

> [It] probably made it harder for me to find the meaning of life, but I think it'll also give me a truer meaning of life—like a definition of a meaning of life that better fits the way I feel, the things I believe, as opposed to some described doctrine.

Yet, Kathryn, a student at a secular liberal arts college, celebrated her freedom while also realizing that she may need to return to a tradition, although on her own terms:

> It's not like my opinions should be tied down to anything. They can really go in whatever direction I want. If I want to go to another religion, I could, which I don't think I will. I think eventually I'll probably go back to Judaism just for the comfort of it and the tradition. I like being raised with a tradition like that, and so I would want to pass that on to my children eventually. But I don't know if I will go back to

necessarily believing in God, and I think I believe more in the community it forms and the traditions that are made, rather than some divine being looking over me.

Overall, what emerges from our interviews is that being nontheistic primarily contributes one major thing to one's search for purpose: a sense of freedom. However, nontheism may also heighten the difficulty of finding substantial substantive guidance to help with the search.

The core of the struggle for these students was their doubt about whether a grand purpose even existed. They concluded, as this student noted, "I don't feel like I was put here on earth for any particular reason." In other words, these students rejected any view relating to an objective meaning or purpose to life. One student stated,

> You know when people talk about meaning of life, they try to impose some kind of ideal—when I say that there is no essential meaning of life, that's what I mean; I mean that there is no ideal to live up to.

Another nontheistic student shared a similarly pessimistic view about the nature of purpose, as well as the possibility of making a big difference in life.

> I'd say it's something I'm still figuring out because I'm not sure. The sense of purpose is a thing that I think—I don't necessarily agree with the concept because I just don't think anybody is truly like necessary or anything. I think that if I accomplish things that help other people, that's great. But I also don't think that I can make a large difference in the world, and I feel that way about most people.

Anne, an atheist, provides another example. She claims, "I would like to think that I have a purpose," yet, she goes on to admit:

> I don't know, I'm kind of up in the air because the thought of something that is meant to be your purpose—I don't know—that's an interesting concept in my mind, but I can't decide if that's something that actually exists, so, I don't know.

Anne considers herself agnostic about purpose—at least in any larger metaphysical sense. She is not sure if it is something one can discover. She does, however, have what she terms "a bucket list": "I definitely want to complete the things on that. I want to travel a lot. I wanna like get a good job so that I can support a family. You know things like that." What she resists is a belief that her life might be part of some kind of larger story. "I wasn't born and then I'm meant to do this. I don't believe that kind of a thing."

The Grand Purpose of Theists

Julie, like Marsha, represents a theistic contrast to the examples above. She has taken a wandering road toward discovering her purpose, as she recounts:

> I started when I was five, and I told my dad I was going to be a banker just like him. And then I was going to be an artist, then a musician, then . . . I mean I've been so many things that I want to be.

She came into the university undecided about her major and briefly chose journalism. Her Christian faith played a part in helping guide her toward a different purpose:

> I guess last summer, it was a time of just real reflection for me on where I'm going, what I want to do, and you know what God has planned for me, and I just realized, you know, I've always been really engaging myself in the world around me, like I've never been content to not know what's going on, like I read the news every day diligently and I have for years, and I was thinking that journalism would be obvious. I like the news so much, but then I realized the job of a journalist is really as an onlooker and someone who's kind of looking in from the outside and, in some ways, even finding what's going wrong, so really a negative sort of viewpoint. But then I realized that I really want to be the one on the inside, the one who's doing something and making change. So that sort of led me to international studies.

Still, a conference sponsored by the office of spiritual life at her university shaped this view of her vocational purpose:

> We put on "Be the Change" conference this past semester, and that was, it was very cool for me because the theme of the week was sort of how God can use your gifts, and before that I had really not seen how my career plans could fit into God's plan for me.

Julie's realization of how her gifts fit into God's larger narrative gave her specific life direction.

I really see myself as somebody who can bring justice in the world and safety to people who desire justice, and this is new. I mean it's something I really just have kind of come on in the last year or so, but just a real passion for, you know, bringing a better life to people, and bringing better quality of life.

The speakers at the "Be the Change" conference helped her see this new passion in a whole new light, as she explained:

You know, what one of the speakers really communicated was that doing research into the peoples of the world—which is what I wanted to do, do research and analysis on international affairs—gives people who want to help them such a clear picture of how to do that. Because if people don't know what their needs are, then they don't know how to help them. And if they don't know how to help them, then they just come in and start slapping a Band-Aid on everything they see and no lasting change is enacted. And that, for me, was sort of a "Wow, okay, so this is a way that I can actually be using what I want to do for God," you know, and making a real difference in the world with what I want to do. So that's a long answer.

For Julie, she suddenly saw a convergence between what she perceived as her personal desires and gifting for God's purposes in her life and the world.

Like Julie, the theistic students (as opposed to the nontheistic students) affirmed the idea that one discovered—and not merely created—meaning and purpose. As Jacob, a student at a Jewish university, proclaimed, "Of course there's meaning. As a religious person, there's got to be meaning. There's got to be purpose, I should say, because that's how I'm defining it. There's got to be purpose." For theists, belief in God and God's revelation helped situate life in a greater narrative or picture. In other words, this group of students would much rather locate themselves in a grand narrative or painting than create a smaller individual story or illustration to support their purpose. Using the illustration metaphor, Julie summarized what she believed was the advantage of her Christian faith while also describing the burden the nontheist outlook would impose:

It's given me a very clear, "This is what I'm meant to do," and that's sort of the outline, and then I color in between the lines. I think someone who didn't have that, it would be a lot more confusing and intimidating to try to come up with the whole image and the colors in between.

Students used a variety of metaphors to communicate the support religion provided. The following students, in particular, used road or direction language:

- Your purpose in life is supposed to be directed towards like God's higher purpose, and so I like to think that hopefully I'm heading down that road, and I'm making choices that aren't just good for me but are good for like the plan that God has for my life and how that affects other people. (nondenominational Christian)
- I think God has a purpose for all of us. And I think that gives life meaning; searching for that purpose gives life a direction. (Jewish)

In contrast to the nontheists who felt constrained by belief in a God who provides a larger story, the theists saw it as freeing, similar to the freedom found in obtaining a map when one is lost.

While not always articulated, the basis for this theistic view appeared to rest upon the belief that God designed humanity. Therefore, if God designed humans, we fulfill our created end by following his plans and purposes. This student articulated the outlook directly:

> I believe that we are created in the image of God, and that he has designed us for his glory and his purpose, and he didn't need to create us, he didn't need us but he made us for his joy and his glory. And so I think that, it's not confining it's more free, if anything. There's direction and purpose in living to a higher calling and living for a higher purpose.

As the student noted above, the conception that following God's plan or direction is somehow constraining does not apply to these students because they are fulfilling their original design. Moreover, God's plan provides a sense of grandeur. It is "higher" and bigger than one's self.

Conclusion

The fact that theists and nontheists differ in how their worldview informs their understanding of purpose should not be surprising. Various surveys and measures of purpose have repeatedly indicated that religious respondents consistently demonstrate greater purpose (Bronk, 2014; Smith, 2009).

In the interviews examined above, some reasons emerged for this religious/ nonreligious distinction regarding the contribution of identity to purpose. Nonreligious individuals find the major advantage of their approach to be a singular one: it grants them a sense of freedom to pursue whatever ends they desire. Yet they face the challenge of choosing those ends without the help of historical religious traditions and the evaluative frameworks those traditions provide. This perceived handicap may provide one reason why studies consistently find the nonreligious less likely to have a personal sense of purpose. Even the nonreligious claim that their views create some difficulties for purpose development.

In contrast, as Mariano and Damon (2008) suggest, spirituality and religion function in helping theistic students develop purpose by providing an identity that connects them to a larger story, cause, and community. In addition, this narrative provides a cognitive plan larger than one's own perspective that is then looked to for making sense of the world. As Mariano and Damon (2008) claim, it "invests young people's goals with value and meaning, which in turn, contributes to these goals becoming inspiring purposes" (p. 218). The interviews suggest that students' goals became meaningful for them because they play a role in a larger story or narrative about life. Some individuals may become teachers or doctors because helping people feels good; however, those who strongly believe that God exists and is working in the world find not only a cognitive explanation but also a cohesive story that gives meaning to a life destination. In this regard, the way that religion and purpose combine has something to do with what Bronk (2012, 2014) observed. Religion provides an identity that connects a larger story to the highest ideals of the self.

Overall, both nonreligious and religious identities offer something different regarding the question for purpose. For the nonreligious, their identity offers them freedom. However, they also admit that this freedom can be a handicap because they do not have certain theological or communal resources to aid their quest. The religious find in their identity and associated traditions a larger metanarrative about God's plan and the future that helps to support, guide, and make sense of their quest for purpose.

Methodology

The interviews that form the basis of this article come from two different groups. The first group of seventy-five students came from a randomly selected national sample of college students who had previously responded to a larger, nationally representative survey of 2,500 students by the Gallup® organization. The second group of 110 students was taken from interviews at a diverse group of ten universities. The ten different colleges and universities were chosen to ensure a wide variety of ideological, philosophical, and religious perspectives and to discover if the unique missions of particular universities, such as various forms of religious institutions, contribute something to the university's institutional activities in support of purpose development (Braskamp et al., 2006). Consequently, institutions with the following identities were included: Baptist; Catholic; Evangelical, Jewish; Latter-Day Saints; Lutheran; a secular, regional college; a secular, private, Ivy League research university; a secular, public research university; and a secular, liberal arts college.

After obtaining IRB approval from the primary investigator's institution, we obtained permission to interview students from their universities. All recruitment occurred through on-campus communication channels such as official student lists, student newspaper advertisements, on-campus advertising, e-mail forums, or relational networks. Initial contacts and appointments were all made through e-mail.

In all of the cases, we sought diverse representation regarding gender, ethnicity, and religion, when applicable. In all, we interviewed 85 females and 101 males. Regarding religion, they identified as follows: sixty-four Christian or some form of Protestantism, twenty Catholic, sixteen Jewish, eleven Latter Day Saint, sixteen nonreligious, eleven agnostic, ten atheist, ten spiritual, seven Buddhist, two Unitarian, four Muslim, one Hindu, one Unification Church, and one None.

The interviews were semi-structured in that while the interviewers had a list of research questions, we would often take time to explore possible avenues that we had not anticipated. Interviewees were paid either $30 or $25 upon the successful completion of an interview depending upon the interview set.

To code the interviews, the research team used an inductive approach to analyze the responses since our desire was to generate frameworks from the particulars of student responses, rather than to impose theory upon them. To do this, we used a two-cycle coding process through which descriptive categories could emerge (first cycle) and then be combined into thematic categories (second cycle) (Saldaña, 2013). In the first cycle, we used a holistic coding process to identify broad categories of response. In holistic coding, data is examined in "chunks" to determine a summative word or phrase that represents the meaning of the passage. Following the holistic coding process, we performed a second round of coding that then pulled these disparate parts together to identify patterns and elements of greatest salience. To do this, we used an axial coding approach (Saldaña, 2013). In our second cycle process, we re-examined the first cycle subsets within the largest "meta-code" categories and recoded them into either existing codes or new subcodes. We then identified common categories that described groups of similar codes within these subsets. The findings detail the nature and characteristics of these subset categories by focusing upon the various ways that interviewees' parents, friends, teachers, and other adult mentors, as well as other experiences (e.g., religion/nonreligion, schooling) had upon adolescents' development of purpose.

References

Astin, A. W., Astin, H. S., & Lindholm, J. A. (2011). *Cultivating the spirit: How college can enhance students' inner lives.* San Francisco, CA: Jossey-Bass.

Baxter Magolda, M. B. (1999). *Creating contexts for learning and self-authorship: Constructive-developmental pedagogy.* Nashville, TN: Vanderbilt University Press.

Baxter Magolda, M. B. (2001). *Making their own way: Narratives for transforming higher education to promote self-development.* Sterling, VA: Stylus Press.

Baxter Magolda, M. B. (2004). Self-authorship as the common goal of 21st century education. In M. B. B. Magolda & P. M. King (Eds.), *Learning partnerships: Theory and models of practice to educate for self-authorship* (pp. 1–35). Sterling, VA: Stylus Press.

Bok, D. (2011). Back jacket quote for Astin, A. W., Astin, H. S., & Lindholm, J. A. (2011). *Cultivating the spirit: How college can enhance students' inner lives.* San Francisco, CA: Jossey-Bass.

Braskamp. L. A., Trautvetter, L. C., & Ward, K. (2006). *Putting students first: How colleges develop students purposefully.* San Francisco, CA: Anker Publishing Company.

Bronk, K. C. (2014). *Purpose in life: A critical component of optimal youth development.* New York, NY: Springer. doi:10.1007/978-94-007-7491-9_6

Mariano, J. M. & W. Damon. (2008). The role spirituality and religious faith play in supporting purpose in adolescence. In R. M. Benson, R. W. Roeser, and E. Phelps (Eds.), *Positive youth development and spirituality: From theory to research* (pp. 210–230). West Conshoshocken, PA: Templeton Foundation Press.

Saldaña, J. (2013). *The coding manual for qualitative researchers,* (2nd ed). London, UK: Sage.

Small, J. L., & Bowman, N. A. (2012). Religious affiliation and college student development: A literature review and synthesis. *Religion & Education, 39,* 64-75.

Smith, C., Christoffersen, K., Davidson, H., & Herzog, P. S. (2011). *Lost in transition: The dark side of emerging adulthood.* New York, NY: Oxford University Press.

Smith, C., & Snell, P. (2009). *Souls in transition: The religious and spiritual lives of emerging adults.* New York, NY: Oxford University Press.

3

SPIRITUAL STRUGGLE WITHIN A FAITH-BASED INSTITUTION

HANNAH SCHUNDLER

Gordon College

In recent years, the topic of college student spirituality has been receiving much attention in developmental literature and higher education research. This interest follows decades of neglect (Astin, 2004; Love & Talbot, 1999). Educators are recognizing not only the importance of spirituality and meaning in holistic development but also the growing interest in spirituality among college students. The topic of spiritual struggle or loss is one area of spirituality that is significantly relevant for student affairs professionals in institutions committed to the promotion of faith development.

Spiritual struggle or loss can be understood as a prolonged crisis period in which an individual is unable to commit to a set of beliefs or convictions. Research has shown that students in faith-based institutions are not exempt from spiritual struggle and crisis. In fact, according to some recent studies, students at faith-based institutions are actually more likely to experience spiritual struggle than their peers at other types of institutions (Bryant & Astin, 2008). There is great potential for spiritual growth in faith-based institutions, where most individuals are engaged in an ongoing process to define the importance of spirituality and faith in their lives. However, students who struggle to reconcile questions of faith, meaning, and purpose, also face potential for spiritual loss and alienation within the community.

This chapter presents data from a qualitative study on the experience of spiritual struggle within a faith-based institution. This phenomenological study examined factors that contribute to spiritual struggle within a faith-based institution, the experience of students who spiritually struggle within the faith-based community, and the institutional elements that support or challenge students during this developmental "crisis." The final section discusses implications for educators at faith-based institutions who are committed to supporting students at all stages of faith development.

Literature Review

Bryant and Astin (2008) define spiritual struggle as "intrapsychic concerns about matters of faith, purpose, and meaning in life" (p. 2). According to this scale, spiritual struggle involves: (1) questioning religious or spiritual beliefs; (2) feeling unsettled about beliefs; (3) wrestling with difficult topics, such as suffering and death; (4) experiencing anger toward God; and (5) being disillusioned about one's religious upbringing.

Parks (2000) uses the metaphor of a "shipwreck" to describe experiences that "rip into the fabric of life" and cause a "collapse of self, world, and 'God'" (p. 28).

Most major world religions recognize struggle as an expected and even essential part of the journey (Pergament, Murray-Swank, Magyar, & Ano, 2005). Additionally, many developmental theories (Erikson, 1980; Marcia, 1966) identify crises that, if overcome by the individual, lead to growth. Theories of spiritual development articulated by Fowler (1981) and Parks (2000) both recognize the presence of crisis in the faith development process.

Spiritual struggle among college students is relatively common, especially during a developmental period when individuals are exploring their beliefs and identity (Erikson, 1980). A national survey (Astin, 2004) indicated that two-thirds of students questioned spiritual or religious beliefs at least occasionally and 68 percent felt unsettled about spiritual or religious matters to some extent. One survey (Johnson & Hayes, 2003) revealed that 26 percent of college students experience considerable distress due to religious and spiritual problems.

Bryant and Astin (2008) identified correlates of spiritual struggle and found that it was associated with being a religious minority, being female, attending an Evangelical or Catholic university, converting to another religion, being on a spiritual quest, and majoring in psychology. In another study, significant spiritual or religious distress was correlated with confusion about beliefs, loss of a relationship, sexual assault, homesickness, and suicidal thoughts and feelings (Johnson & Hayes, 2003). Parks (2000) highlights many of the same life crises that can lead to "metaphorical shipwreck" in college students but also identifies abstract crises, such as "defeat of a cause, betrayal by a community or government, or the discovery that an intellectual construct is inadequate" (p. 28). Both circumstantial and existential factors can contribute to "shipwreck" and a time of questioning and uncertainty about spiritual or religious beliefs, meaning, and purpose.

While former studies (Bryant & Astin, 2008) emphasized some of the physical and psychological consequences of spiritual struggle, other research (Parks, 2000; Pargament et al., 2005; Rockenbach, Walker, & Luzader, 2012) demonstrates positive outcomes of spiritual struggle that occur as a student explores, reflects, and makes meaning following the struggle. Parks (2000) identifies the "gladness" (p. 29) that one experiences after surviving the metaphorical "shipwreck" (p. 28); this "gladness on the other side of shipwreck arises from an embracing, complex kind of knowing that is experienced as a more trustworthy understanding of reality in both its beauty and terror" (p. 30). The shattering of one's faith can precipitate "transformation" (p. 29) and a fuller and more complete understanding of self, the world, and God if one perseveres through the struggle.

Spiritual struggle is not uncommon among college students; 18 percent of students in the UCLA study reported that they frequently questioned spiritual beliefs, and 16 percent felt unsettled about beliefs "to a great extent" (Bryant & Astin, 2008, p. 12). However, research indicates that students reach different conclusions or commitments following the crisis. Fisler et al. (2009) identified four outcomes of spiritual struggle at a public institution: "recommitment" to original spiritual beliefs; "readjustment," which identifies a shift in authority; "blending" by synthesizing new ideas with former beliefs; and "loss of faith" (pp. 266–267).

Students at faith-based institutions also experience spiritual struggle and uncertainty during the college years. This topic of spiritual struggle or loss is arguably more critical for faith-based institutions because a huge component of their mission is to encourage and foster spiritual growth and development. This chapter will examine factors that contribute to spiritual struggle, the experience of students who spiritually struggle, and institutional elements that support or challenge students during spiritual struggle.

Methodology

This qualitative study used a phenomenological approach to examine the topic of spiritual struggle within the context of a faith-based institution. The participants for this study were six upperclass students or recent graduates from a small, faith-based, liberal arts university in the Midwest. The researcher recruited three female participants and three male participants for this study with the assistance of university faculty and student affairs staff who have regular interaction with students. Faculty and staff were asked to identify and contact students or recent graduates who experienced spiritual struggle during their time in college. The researcher conducted individual interviews with each participant, which were transcribed, analyzed, and coded to find emerging themes.

The researcher used the identifiers of spiritual struggle described by Bryant and Astin (2008) for the recruitment process. As mentioned above, this scale defines spiritual struggle as (1) questioning religious or spiritual beliefs; (2) feeling unsettled about beliefs; (3) wrestling with difficult topics, such as suffering and death; (4) experiencing anger toward God; and (5) being disillusioned about one's religious upbringing.

Results

All six participants in the study were raised in conservative, Protestant families. During the interviews, the participants described the centrality of church and Christian teaching in their upbringing and described the way Christian beliefs and practices shaped and guided their parents' actions and decisions. As Sebastian pointed out, "I grew up in a Christian home, my parents are both Christian, went to church every Sunday, my dad was [a church leader] . . . I like grew up going to church like three times a week."

Some of the participants commented on the lack of alternative viewpoints or perspectives in their lives with regard to religion and faith during their upbringing. They only realized the insularity of their upbringing after going to college. Natalie pointed out:

> I guess I grew up with religion like everywhere . . . Yeah, it was, I don't think that I really realized it like at the time, but I was very like surrounded by it and I just like thought that was how everyone is. This is where everywhere is. But that's, I mean, not true.

While describing his very conservative upbringing, Matt commented that he only knew two individuals who "were not Christians, but those were the only people I knew and they were kinda off in a way."

Christian beliefs and ideals also influenced the participants' educational and social lives during childhood and adolescence. Five of the six participants were active members of their youth groups, with Christian friends as a primary peer group before college. Matt and Mariah attended private Christian schools from kindergarten through the end of high school. Ashley was homeschooled in a Christian home and then attended a Christian high school. Paul spent part of his childhood abroad while his parents served as missionaries. Religion and faith played a major role in participants' lives prior to college, shaping the social and for some, academic environments of the participants and their families.

Re-examination of Religious Beliefs and Framework

The strongest theme to emerge in this study was the identification of college as a place to re-examine religious beliefs and convictions. Paul even entered college with the assumption that "college is where you do the grand questioning." The participants discussed the realization early in college that their beliefs and convictions had been shaped by a strong religious upbringing, which led them to question the reasons and extent to which they held those beliefs themselves. Mariah pointed out:

> I think it just came to a point where I had looked back at my life was just like, wow, I've literally just been bombarded with Christianese my whole life, and bombarded with religion, and stuff like that, and so I think it came to a point where I was like, ok, so this is everything that I've been told about like, who I am as a Christian and like just everything I've been told about who God is and what Christianity is, but like, what do I actually believe based on my experiences or like lack of an experience?

The realization that she had been surrounded with Christianity her entire life caused Mariah to ask questions about her identity and her personal beliefs.

Other participants identified experiences in college that led them to re-examine their own personal beliefs and convictions. Natalie's semester abroad caused her to question the beliefs of her white, middle-class, American upbringing. As she pointed out, "I got to talk to people [abroad] a lot about how they see things. And it was just interesting to me that they see the world in a very different way than I had seen the world." In response to some conversations that revealed different cultural assumptions and truths, Natalie commented,

> I wonder if I think that because I was born in America, and so I started thinking about all of these things and I like I wonder if all these other values I have are because of where I lived and grew up and if I grew up here would I have different values?

Natalie's exposure to other values and beliefs caused her to analyze the social constructs that impacted her own religious framework.

Matt described the experience of being in a new environment in college and stated, "It was only in the absence of family, friends, and church constantly reinforcing ideas that I was even able to conceive of the possibility of God not being real in a serious way." The college experience allowed Matt to explore questions of faith and identity away from his family and home church. Paul pointed out that "being in an academic setting allows you to think in a more sort of academic way . . . that's what was necessitated for me to actually bring up these larger thoughts."

Most of the participants began to experience questions and spiritual struggle during the first two years of college, partially due to a new environment, as well as space away from their upbringing in which to ask challenging questions. Ashley's case was slightly different, as she delayed early questions about faith and practice until later on in her college career. During the first few years of college, she adopted many of the faith practices of her peers; however, during her senior year, she began to question the extent to which she desired to maintain the faith practices she had adopted. She commented, "It didn't really become apparent until senior year that I wasn't really sure if I actually believed everything I guess my life had kind of become."

All six participants discussed the personal or intellectual factors that prompted them to question or challenge their formerly held beliefs and convictions. In Sebastian and Natalie's cases, specific circumstances prompted new questions about faith and God. For Sebastian, the deaths of a few friends and family members in high school and college sparked anger and questions about God's goodness and justice. He began wrestling with these questions before college but continued to feel unsettled about them as he experienced more personal tragedy in college. After experiencing the deaths of two close friends and family members, Sebastian felt very angry and frustrated toward God and recollected, "I was like, well, forget this God, you are taking everyone I care about and cares about me away." In Natalie's case, a cross-cultural experience prompted questions about the degree to which her faith beliefs and personal identity had been shaped by her cultural lens. She describes how her study abroad experience

> gave me a chance to re-evaluate like, who do I want to be? And take away my parents and my family and my friends all from back home and just like ignore that for a little while and say . . . "Am I who I am because I want to be? Or because people are telling me to?"

Upon returning to the university campus, Natalie continued to wrestle with these questions about identity and faith.

Ashley, who had delayed some early questions about faith and practice, experienced spiritual struggle during her senior year in college in the midst of many simultaneous transitions. Regarding the spiritual questions she and her friends experienced, she commented:

I think a lot of questions started coming about because I was a senior; had a bad summer; friend groups were changing; my living situation was changing; on top of that, in a few months everything was going to change . . . with so many things changing, so many things seem really uncertain and [the struggle] just kind of came at that time because that was the stage of life we were in.

During a time of transition filled with questions and uncertainty, Ashley began to reflect more on her faith and ask, "Is this even what I want my life to be, is this even what I believe?"

In Matt and Paul's cases, the reexamination of former beliefs was not prompted by specific circumstances but rather by new questions or knowledge that did not fit their old paradigm. Matt, who grew up in a very fundamental church and family, recalls reading statistics early in college about different faith practices, as well as low religiosity, in certain parts of the world and wrestling with questions of hell and eternal damnation. He describes how the conception of hell he had while growing up—"fire and brimstone, burning torture, that sort of thing"—led him to ask questions about God and religion. As he began to research and read more by non-Christian writers, he began asking, "How there could be good people who weren't Christians?" These new questions caused Matt to assess many of his preconceived ideas and convictions. He states:

Like someone pulled a string, so many of my unique Christian beliefs, as well as beliefs gained as a Christian on the age of earth, on evolution, use of Genesis, reliability in the history of the Bible, on views of the gospels, on the origin of the universe, on the origin of humanity, on sin, nature, morality, purpose, Jesus, God, on religion in general, on knowledge, on epistemology, on evidence, on eternal life, on hell, on heaven, on happiness, and joy and hope, on secular worldviews . . . on hedonists, on unselfishness, on empathy, on sex, on sexuality, on character, on identity, on hell . . . on so many more began to unravel.

As Matt's paradigm and understanding of the Christian faith began to falter, he realized he must re-examine his belief and identity regarding this vast range of topics. He did not compartmentalize his spiritual struggle from his worldview and personal beliefs but recognized a need to rethink his beliefs in light of a changing framework. After an extended period of searching, in which God felt very silent, Matt concluded he had lost his faith and no longer subscribed to Christianity. Because Matt chose to abandon his old paradigm, he realized that:

> I had to build a new world to live in. The afterlife, ideas of divine love, providence, and communications, [the university's] Christian community, none of these things provided comfort or support anymore. Slowly my habits, my patterns of thought, and my hopes and dreams all began to change.

Matt confronted realities and new truths that did not synthesize with his old paradigm, which led to an intense period of spiritual struggle and the eventual resolution in a completely new paradigm and spiritual identity.

Paul also wrestled with the question of hell and new questions that created dissonance with the framework of his upbringing. Growing up with an interest in science, Paul had learned to compartmentalize his faith convictions with questions of scientific evidence and evolution. Speaking about his understanding of faith and science upon entering college, Paul states, "So at that point, up until then, I'd done a good job of compartmentalizing the two . . . and not really wanting to let the two collide because I was afraid of what might happen." Once in college, Paul decided to "let those walls kind of collapse and see what happened" in an effort to maintain intellectual integrity with faith. Paul described how many peers did not engage large difficult questions about evolution, free will, or eternal damnation, and instead had the mindset that "I don't understand and [those topics] seem really bad but just, give it to the Lord, I mean, Christianity has to be right." Paul found himself playing devil's advocate, both to his friends, but more importantly, to himself. College became a time to search for a model that accounted for intellectual truths and nuance.

All the participants discussed a re-examination of religious beliefs in college that was prompted by circumstances or a new environment. This re-examination caused participants to ask questions about their own beliefs as well as about their individual identity.

Frustration toward Religious Culture on Campus

The participants all expressed some degree of frustration or unease toward the religious culture on their campus. In the midst of spiritual struggle, participants felt frustrated with their friends, classmates, and chapel speakers for accepting faith without engaging with uncertainty or doubt. Mariah described her frustration toward the spiritual atmosphere on campus that she identified as "fake" and "cheesy," while Paul identified the spiritual atmosphere as intellectually "disingenuous" at times. Mariah felt "annoyed" with the Christian community and said the religious culture on campus was both "cheesy" and an "overload of like Christianity and restraints."

Paul primarily expressed a frustration toward a lack of intellectual integrity in the belief systems of many peers and friends within the college community. He expressed surprise that despite the fact that many of his peers were "really, really smart, some people that are doing great things . . . people who have been on [cross-cultural missions trips]," faith was very "simple" to them. Larger questions about evolution, hell, free will, and other difficult topics did not seem to faze or affect many of his peers. Many of these peers clung to the beliefs of their upbringing and did not challenge themselves or wrestle with the complexities of faith and the world.

Selective Openness Regarding Spiritual Struggle

None of the participants shared their spiritual struggle or questions with the majority of people in their social or academic spheres but instead chose to confide in a select few friends, faculty members, or counselors in the campus counseling center. The participants were not outspoken individuals on issues of doubt or struggle but rather wrestled with their questions and uncertainties with a very small group of trusted peers and mentors. As Matt explained, he initially did not tell his professors about his loss of faith because there was

> a lot of uncertainty with coming out with something which is not generally approved by the community around you, especially when you hear bad stories from the Internet and elsewhere about going to hell, or being kicked out of their parents' home, disowned, that sort of thing;

so you have to evaluate. You end up evaluating these things in your head over and over again.

Matt's fear of rejection and other perceived consequences prevented him from being honest with peers and contributed to his withdrawal from others in the community. He told a counselor and a professor about his spiritual struggles but did not share with his peers.

The other participants talked more honestly with select friends about their spiritual frustrations and struggles. Some described seeking out like-minded friends who shared some of the same questions and frustrations. Ashley pointed out that during the time of spiritual struggle, her "friend group changed a little bit and included some people who . . . appeared more cynical about life in general but also about Christianity." Mariah also pointed out that she befriended "the bad students" on campus who experienced similar struggles and frustration with the campus community. Paul said that although he never explicitly shared his specific struggles until after graduation, he noticed he "seemed to befriend the misfits . . . at least social misfits, deemed by probably the majority of . . . campus, because in my mind, those were the people that really had questions that you know, didn't have this puritanical view." Although Paul did not talk explicitly with peers about his struggles, he did have more honest conversations with various professors regarding his spiritual questions and struggles. The participants all found a small network of trusted individuals to share and discuss their questions and spiritual frustrations.

Despite their security in sharing with this small group of individuals, the participants all discussed the need to hide their spiritual struggles from the greater campus or residential community. Sebastian discussed how he invested in the social life on campus but disengaged from the spiritual atmosphere. Although he had shared his honest thoughts and frustrations with some close friends, he said that "unless I got really close to someone I never really told them about stuff. And so . . . I have a lot of surface-level friends, and so like, that was kind of how I, I still stayed in the [university] community." Natalie also described "keeping relationships at a surface level" in order to allow others to assume she had retained certain beliefs.

Some participants described the sense that they pretended to believe things in order to appeal to the campus community. Natalie continued to stay involved with small groups and other spiritual aspects on campus, but she did not disclose any of her deeper questions and struggles. She participated in Bible studies but would "sometimes say things that I don't even know if I believe; but I'm like, if I still believed the things I say that I believed, then I would say these things." Later, she admitted that she worried about how others would respond to her questions or uncertainties about spiritual beliefs. After discussing this fear, she stated, "I avoid that problem by actually pretending to believe the things if I need to." Matt echoed this idea and also used the verbs "pretend" or "play along" to describe his participation with peers in a spiritual setting. He commented:

> It's kind of like I'm frozen where I was a Christian back in high school and early [college] . . . I can't really say what I actually think and, lots and lots of pretend. . . . I can't let people know. Um, I have to play along.

This idea of maintaining a certain image or withholding deeper thoughts or uncertainties in the campus community was evident in all interviews.

Perception and Reality of Community Acceptance

The participants noted that although there was a commonly held perception that the institution was open to spiritual questions and struggle, this perception did not translate to reality in their experiences. This gap between perception and reality was often mysterious to the participants themselves, and they found it difficult to pinpoint why this gap existed, even as they described it. Mariah found the gap to be evidence of hypocrisy, and stated, "I mean, people say all the time, like, 'Not everyone [at this university] is a Christian,' but it's like, we don't act like that. We act like everyone is a Christian." Her frustration was that some clichés or mantras of Christians on campus did not line up with individual attitudes toward spiritual doubt and questioning.

Others identified this gap at a broader structural level. Both Natalie and Paul found the institution to be open to questioning and critical thinking, especially in comparison to the churches of their upbringing. Their experiences with professors and courses demonstrated the openness of the institution to questioning and critical thinking. However, they still perceived the student body as more narrow-minded or closed off to questions. Natalie noted:

> theoretically in my mind [the institution] is a very open place and open to questioning and open to people questioning. Like, I know people talk about there being atheists who come here—I don't know any—but a place where people won't judge you for asking questions but will like appreciate that you're asking the questions. Um, but I guess I still sometimes, like, as an institution I think that might be accurate, but even around some students I feel like maybe it's just like—I don't know—I feel like I am afraid of being judged, even though—I don't know—it doesn't seem like that would be the case at [this institution]; it still is an issue somehow.

Paul said that the "overlying theme of [the institution] seem to be more welcoming of questioning." However, this contrasted with his observation of the "simple" faith of his peers that was "unwavering," even in the midst of questions or topics that posed a threat to this paradigm. Discovering the existence of this gap between the perception of the institution as an open place and the actual experience of students with questions and doubts was very illuminating and could lead to further research.

Support from Faculty and Staff

All the participants identified faculty or staff members within the university who supported and/or challenged them during their spiritual struggle. Participants identified both personal and intellectual ways in which professors provided support. Ashley identified several staff members who were "all really understanding people instead of being judgmental." She commented, "It was helpful to be able to talk with someone who wasn't like a best friend or something, that they kind of have an outside opinion." Matt also identified a faculty member who "is very understanding" and "did probably 99 percent listening" to his various questions and struggles. Sebastian shared his story and spiritual struggles with his hall director, who reassured him that "doubting is a great part of your faith." Regarding that conversation, Sebastian commented "that was a big—that statement—just hit me and I was like, well, that's good; at least I am in a decent place right now." The simple assurance that spiritual doubts are healthy and normal changed Sebastian's perspective on his current state.

Participants also discussed intellectual ways in which professors challenged them in their thinking. Paul commented that the fact that some professors at the institution were able to integrate their faith with scientific theories such as evolution was a support to him because this posture demonstrated that "integrity is being pursued, and we're not going to shy away from the tough questions just because they force us to reconsider things." Natalie remembers a time when a professor critiqued a chapel message given earlier that day. She recalls, "I was like, you can do that? I didn't know that was a thing . . . what they say isn't always true?" This professor demonstrated the importance of thinking critically about faith and the absorption of truth. Natalie also identified the ways in which this same professor challenged her to continue wrestling with spiritual questions, rather than resigning herself to apathy or a position of being "undecided." Matt and Paul also identified professors who were open to intellectual conversations about faith and spiritual struggles. The participants found faculty and staff members helpful for both personal and intellectual support during times of spiritual struggle.

Implications for Practice

The re-examination of spiritual beliefs and identity parallels developmental changes that occur when individuals transition from adolescence to adulthood. For traditional college students, this transition between adolescence and adulthood occurs at the beginning of the college experience. For college students on a residential campus, this occurs not only at the beginning of college but also in an environment away from parents, family, and other support networks. Drawing from development theories (Erikson, 1980; Marcia, 1966), the participants in this study faced a "crisis" that required them to ask questions about their religious beliefs, convictions, and upbringings. With the exception of one participant, none had committed to a new spiritual identity but instead continued to search and wrestle with beliefs and identity.

The work of Parks (2000) describes the challenges of faith and meaning making during young adulthood. After identifying various personal or intellectual factors that create dissonance in one's faith, she comments that "this kind of experience can suddenly rip into the fabric of life, or it may slowly yet just as surely unravel the meanings that have served as the home of the soul" (p. 28). The participants in this study identified the factors that ripped into their "fabric of life" and rendered their initial faith paradigms and ways of making meaning insufficient and incomplete. This realization caused participants to explore and search for new frameworks that addressed new questions and new truths. One participant articulated this concept when he stated, "I had to build a new world to live in." Parks states that if individuals are able to "survive shipwreck" or the unraveling of faith paradigms, they will never return to former ways of knowing but will instead experience "gladness in an enlarged knowing and being, and in a new capacity to act" (p. 29). Parks's theory and research identify the changing landscape of faith in the lives of young adults and the challenges that precipitate a re-examination of belief.

For some students, new intellectual ideas and development during the college years conflict with spiritual beliefs or convictions, leading to a period of spiritual struggle, uncertainty, and doubt. However, as the participants noted, other students may enter college with a foreclosed view of faith. These students are less willing to engage questions or ambiguities that may challenge or alter prior faith commitments. If one of the primary goals of a faith-based institution is to cultivate a mature and resilient faith for a lifetime of religious commitment, then educators must discern how to best prepare both students who spiritually struggle and those who cling to a foreclosed view of faith. Educators must seek to support students experiencing spiritual struggle but also cultivate an environment on campus that fosters questions and a maturing of young adult faith.

First, the curriculum within faith-based institutions should provide students with ways to integrate increased knowledge with previous faith beliefs. Faculty members should not be afraid to ask hard questions or even wrestle with challenging questions and topics themselves. Students in the sciences may particularly experience some of these intellectual and spiritual challenges as they attempt to synthesize scientific ideas into traditional beliefs about creation and the Bible. Foundational general education courses may provide opportunities to engage some of these questions in an interdisciplinary way. The general education curriculum requirements should allow students at all developmental stages to engage with questions of faith in an intellectually challenging way that honors integrity and intellectual honesty.

Second, faculty and staff members must create learning environments and learning activities that appropriately challenge and even deconstruct faith convictions and concepts. The purpose of challenge and deconstruction is not to shatter or destroy a young adult's faith, but rather to introduce nuance and the ability to reflect more critically on faith beliefs and convictions. Educators at faith-based institutions have a unique opportunity to refine and strengthen the faith convictions of young adults in a nurturing but also intellectually stimulating environment. For traditional-aged students, the college years bridge adolescence and emerging adulthood and provide opportunities for students to develop self-awareness, maturity, and internalized commitment to an identity. Faculty and staff members must remember that part of their role is to prepare students to face ambiguities and complexities within a life of faith. Educators do not prepare students by preserving the brittle and unchallenged faith of their upbringing. Instead, educators best serve students by helping them develop a resilient, mature, and dynamic faith.

Challenge and deconstruction, when coupled with support, can help students grow in their own understanding and internalization of faith. Faculty and staff must design various learning experiences that create a healthy dissonance and critical reflection of faith. For example, cross-cultural learning experiences, especially in partnership with churches or Christian ministries, provide students with a lens of the worldwide church. This type of experience can remind students that faith practices and traditions differ by culture, and that human beings express adoration and faithfulness to God in various ways.

Another learning experience that provides reflection and examination of faith convictions involves engagement with individuals who hold different perspectives on faith and action. Opportunities for this type of engagement exist in a large group setting, such as chapel, as well as individual interactions. Additionally, a student body that reflects the diversity of the church, in terms of race, ethnicity, socioeconomic status, and denominational affiliation, creates an environment in which students learn from differences as they worship and follow the same God.

As much as students benefit from engaging different Christian perspectives, students may also develop greater intellectual and spiritual maturity through discussion and dialogue with individuals outside of the Christian faith. Service learning opportunities and cross-cultural experiences provide avenues to engage with individuals from different faith backgrounds and perspectives. The invitation of speakers or individuals from different religious traditions to campus can also provide forums to dialogue about meaningful and challenging topics. The opportunity to listen to other opinions and articulate one's own questions, beliefs, and perspectives is an incredibly valuable experience. Although these interactions may introduce uncertainty or new questions into students' lives, especially those who have not engaged such perspectives before, students can wrestle with these new ideas and ambiguities in a safe and nurturing environment. If part of the role of a faith-based institution is to prepare students for faithful action and engagement in an increasingly pluralistic world, educators must take some risks within the faith-based institution to expose students to incongruent and challenging perspectives.

Third, faculty and staff members can help students understand that doubt and struggle are normal parts of the faith process. Spiritual struggle is an expected part of the Christian faith journey, as evidenced by the lives of the apostles and other Christian leaders throughout time. However, students may not have previously experienced doubts or uncertainties in their faith. The topic may not have been addressed or encouraged within their families or churches. Faculty and staff members can support students by reassuring them of the normalcy and even expectation of spiritual doubts and uncertainties in a life of faith. As the saying goes, "The opposite of faith is not doubt but certainty." However, students may not recognize the inherent nature of doubt in faith. In appropriate settings, faculty and staff members could also serve students by sharing times of doubt or uncertainty in their own spiritual lives. Finally, faculty and staff members can demonstrate, both through word and action, that questions and struggles are part of a life of intellectual and spiritual integrity.

Parks (2000) reminds educators and students that a static and unchanging faith is not only unrealistic but also intellectually dangerous. She states:

> Commitment to truth requires a questioning curiosity and ongoing and rigorous examination of one's most elemental assumptions. In the face of new understanding, one may come to perceive an earlier experience of faith or religious belief—an earlier way of making meaning— as now outgrown or otherwise irrelevant. . . . A richer perception of faith, however, enables us to recognize that fidelity to truth may indeed require changing a particular set of beliefs—and yet be important to the ongoing tasks of finding a more adequate faith. (p. 18)

If faith is a way of making meaning of self, world, and God, it must be capable of engaging with new challenges and intellectual development. As finite humans, we will never fully comprehend or understand the mysteries of God. We will always have questions. Faculty and staff who "live the questions" (Rilke, 2013, p. 24) and model a life that explores and wrestles with ambiguity can support students with difficult and often unanswerable questions about God.

Fourth, faculty and staff can support students by simply demonstrating care for their spiritual and intellectual well-being. Whether this care manifests itself in conversation with students or in thoughtful and open feedback to student reflection papers, students benefit when they see that faculty and staff members care for them. This unconditional care, even toward students with spiritual doubts and uncertainties, provides a respite and safe haven for students during challenging and difficult seasons. In the study, many participants perceived that faculty and staff members were more open and accepting of spiritual struggles than their peers were. Faculty and staff members can support students in very helpful and sustaining ways simply by demonstrating an unconditional care, regardless of the students' spiritual state.

Finally, educators must help students find ways to reconcile new beliefs with old perspectives. When students begin to re-examine their religious framework, they often recognize ways in which this framework is insufficient. This realization understandably contributes to resentment or disillusionment toward the formative faith structures of their upbringing. Students experiencing spiritual struggle and a re-examination of prior beliefs may perceive the religious beliefs of their previous churches, pastors, and even parents as immature, naïve, or ignorant. While this tension is expected as individuals reconcile their former beliefs with new ideas and concepts, educators must help students—and perhaps parents— navigate this change. Educators must find ways to communicate to parents, when appropriate and necessary, that the goal of the faith-based institution is to help students develop a mature and lasting faith. The intention of providing challenging learning experiences is not to shatter or destroy faith but rather to help students internalize their Christian faith. While students may not recognize the benefit of their upbringing during times of spiritual struggle, educators can support students and parents through prayer, empathy, and a desire to cultivate a richness of faith and identity in students.

Conclusion

The college years are a critical time for students to make meaning, ask questions about self, identity, and God, and develop a philosophy or paradigm to guide and shape their beliefs and behavior in the world. Traditional-aged college students experience intellectual and cognitive development in this transition between adolescence and adulthood as well as an increase in independence and autonomy from parents and other former structures of support. New perspectives, ideas, experiences, and individuals within the college environment serve to challenge the preconceived ideas and convictions of students and cultivate more holistic and nuanced ways of understanding the world. While these factors can lead to incredible growth and maturity, educators must realize the potential vulnerability and fragility of faith and belief during these years. Students at any institution, including faith-based colleges and universities, may experience spiritual struggle and uncertainty during these years. Some research (Bryant & Astin, 2008) has indicated that students at faith-based institutions are *more* likely to experience spiritual struggle.

The presence or absence of spiritual struggle during the college years introduces different challenges for educators who hope to nurture mature faith commitments in young adults. Educators should not fear the presence of spiritual struggle in the lives of their students, nor should they give easy answers to placate questions and uncertainties. The experience of spiritual struggle during the college years fosters an opportunity for students to test and refine adolescent faith convictions. Educators best support students by helping them grapple with new questions and seek new ways of knowing. The absence of spiritual struggle may signal a need for educators to challenge preconceived faith notions. Again, the purpose is not the destruction of adolescent faith but rather the maturation of faith that prepares students for future challenges, tragedies, and questions inherent in a life of faith.

If educators at faith-based institutions hope to develop students personally, intellectually, and vocationally to respond effectively to their callings in the world, the college must be a place that values intellectual integrity, spiritual maturity, and a nuanced framework from which to engage complex realities. The curriculum and the co-curriculum must offer students opportunities to examine their intellectual and spiritual framework in light of new questions and knowledge and wrestle with incongruities and inconsistencies. Within a nurturing community that supports and challenges students, individuals are encouraged to reflect on life's big questions, a process necessary in the building of a more nuanced, mature, and ultimately more resilient faith.

Faith-based institutions must effectively support and challenge students experiencing spiritual struggle. Educators must remember that struggle and "crisis" offer great opportunity for the student's personal, intellectual, and spiritual growth. The unraveling of former paradigms and frameworks precipitates a period of searching and eventual commitment to a new way of knowing and understanding. This new way of knowing and understanding allows for nuance and ambiguity, which is present in all of life. While the outcome of spiritual struggle is unpredictable, educators must foster a nurturing community that facilitates the students' ability to approach challenge, uncertainty, and "crisis," so that they may grow toward greater understanding, meaning, and faith.

References

Astin, A. W. (2004). Why spirituality deserves a central place in liberal education. *Liberal Education, 90*(2), 34–41.

Bryant, A. N., & Astin, H. S. (2008). The correlates of spiritual struggle during the college years. *The Journal of College Education, 79*, 1–27.

Erikson, E. H. (1980). *Identity and the life cycle.* New York, NY: Norton.

Fisler, J., Agati, H. A., Chance, S. M., Donahue, A. E., Donahue, G. A., Eickhoff, E. J., . . . Foubert, J. D. (2009). Keeping (or losing) the faith: Reflections on spiritual struggles and their resolution by college seniors. *The College Student Affairs Journal, 27*, 257–274.

Fowler, J. W. (1981). *Stages of faith: The psychology of human development and the quest for meaning.* San Francisco, CA: Harper & Row.

Johnson, C. V., & Hayes, J. A. (2003). Troubled spirits: Prevalence and predictors of religious and spiritual concerns among university students and counseling center clients. *Journal of Counseling Psychology, 50*, 409–419.

Love, P., & Talbot, D. (1999). Defining spiritual development: A missing consideration for student affairs. *NASPA Journal, 37*, 361–375.

Marcia, J. E. (1966). Development and validation of ego-identity status. *Journal of Personality and Social Psychology, 3*, 551–558.

Parks, S. D. (2000). *Big questions, worthy dreams: Mentoring young adults in their search for meaning, purpose, and faith.* San Francisco, CA: Jossey-Bass.

Pergament, K. I., Murray-Swank, N. A., Magyar, G. M., & Ano, G. G. (2005). Spiritual struggle: A phenomenon of interest to psychology and religion. In W. R. Miller & H. D. Delaney (Eds.), *Judeo-Christian perspectives on psychology: Human nature, motivation, and change* (pp. 245–268). Washington D.C.: American Psychological Association.

Rilke, R. M. (1929). *Letters to a young poet* (Rep. ed. 2013). New York, NY: Penguin Books.

Rockenbach, A. B., Walker, C. R., & Luzader, J. (2012). A phenomenological analysis of college students' spiritual struggles. *Journal of College Student Development, 53*(1), 55–75. doi:10.1353/csd.2012.0000

4

WALKING WITH EMERGING ADULTS ON THE SPIRITUAL JOURNEY

HOLLY C. ALLEN

Lipscomb University

Emerging adults are navigating a culture that finds Christianity too narrow and judgmental. For this and other reasons, many eighteen-to-thirty-year-olds are walking away from church—though not necessarily from their faith. Our task is to find ways to join twentysomethings during these crucial formative years as they enter the workforce, forge adult identities, revisit childhood beliefs, and re-story their lives.

Emerging adults often desire authentic intergenerational relationships as they enter adulthood; they need those older and wiser to listen as they voice doubts and fears, negotiate peer and hierarchical relationships, and integrate who they were with who they are becoming. As we facilitate these differentiation and individuation processes, we are living out the commitment to connectedness and community to which Christ calls us.

Bringing the generations back together in our faith communities is a central passion in my life. As I have studied intergenerational issues, I have become aware of the absence of Millennials in churches, and I have a particular and personal reason to study emerging adults. Two of our three children are Millennials: Daniel is currently thirty-one and single; Bethany, twenty-nine, married this past summer. In their journeys over the past several years, Daniel and Bethany have followed some of the common emerging-adult trajectories that are described in this chapter. On the other hand, our older son, David, a GenXer, married just out of college; he and his wife, Karen, had four babies in six years—all before they were thirty. Because David and Karen followed a very different pattern than many current emerging adults, my husband and I were not prepared for the new pattern of young adulthood lived by our two younger children. As parents, we have been experiencing this new pattern with them, so my current research is helping me understand the emerging adulthood process.

As I anticipated addressing the questions of the Taylor University Higher Education Symposium and this subsequent monograph, particularly the role that college experiences continue to play in faith development in the years after college, I constructed and distributed the survey below.

SURVEY

1. Looking back on your college years, how are your college experiences still impacting your faith and/or spiritual development? Please include both positive and negative trajectories.

   Along the way you may wish to offer examples from the settings mentioned below:

   Particular course work
   Particular people (professors, coaches, staff, roommates, etc.)
   Extracurricular (clubs, sports, choir, drama, band, etc.)

2. How would you describe your arc of faith since you left college?

3. How would you describe where you are now in your faith/
   spiritual journey? (e.g., Spiritual life? Involved with a church?
   Participating in socialjustice/benevolent/ministry?)

   Age: _____

   Gender: _____

   Dates you attended college (e.g., 2001–2006): _____ to _____
   Type of college/university: (if more than one, indicate and
   show years of attendance there)

   public/state university
   community college
   private school (nonreligious)
   private school (Christian or other religion)

I sent the survey to the emerging adult children of my friends, and the
friends of my emerging adult children, asking them to complete it if they
were willing, and to send it to others if they would (a basic snowball sample
technique). I received about two dozen responses from people ranging in
age from twenty-four to thirty-three. About one-third attended public universities; a handful attended private, nonreligious universities, and about
half attended Christian universities.

One key purpose of the Taylor Higher Education Symposium was to
explore how collegiate experience impacts the cultivation of faith in the
decades after college. The survey offered an opportunity to consider the
perspectives of some who had relatively recently experienced college. Some
of the respondents found their college experiences to be generally positive

and beneficial for their spiritual growth and development. For example, Trent, twenty-four, who attended a private Christian university, wrote:[1]

> I grew up in a Christian household and thought I had a stronger conception of faith than most other college students. However, looking back, I see now that my beliefs and understanding of God were both hollow and narrow. It was not until my later years in college that I developed a true, tangible sense of faith. I experienced somewhat of an identity crisis during my first two years in college, as I was trying to figure out who I was and where my passions lay. During this time, I sought the answers to my questions through my studies, my peers, and my extracurricular activities. My studies provided intellectual stimulation, while my friends and participation in activities such as pledging and band gave me social confirmation. Together, these things were catalysts for my personal growth, in which I underwent a process of spiritual maturation. In my later years at the university, I became heavily involved in a church and a volunteer organization while also working two jobs and taking my most challenging coursework. During these years, I learned and cultivated a deep appreciation for my God-given abilities, and it was this time that my perspective of life transitioned from the pursuit of self-indulgence to the desire to worship the Lord through my words and actions.

Devon, thirty-one, also found his college experiences to be beneficial to his spiritual growth:

> My year at a small Christian university was very helpful in my spiritual journey because, at that time, I was returning to following Jesus after a couple of years of being away from the Lord, and it was very helpful to be around a lot of devout Christians in an atmosphere where Jesus is exalted (e.g., chapel twice a week). After one year there, I transferred to a public state school because the small Christian school did not offer the major I decided to pursue. This was a very different experience, but I got plugged in right away with a campus ministry there; I sought that out initially, but once there, they pulled me right in. This group of Christians met so many of my spiritual/social/emotional needs during my college years (and up through my graduate studies). I know that this group kept me on track spiritually, but I probably underestimate the spiritual benefits I received from it. We met on Tuesday evenings

---

[1] Names of respondents were changed, and any reference to a particular school was removed.

every week for a devotional. I made friends in this group, and it gave me a social outlet. It constantly reminded me of who I am (a follower of Christ), and to shine the light of Christ on campus. Without this group, I may have made friends whose social activities centered around drinking and partying, or I may have just been lonely and depressed and spiritually weak.

Both Trent and Devon are living their lives as followers of Christ, actively involved in faith communities.

For some of the participants who responded to the survey, college experiences had a less positive effect on their life of faith. For example, Emma, twenty-eight, who attended a private Christian university, said:

I feel that my experiences in college had a significant impact on my faith journey. During my time in college, my thinking in many aspects of my life was challenged. I was a vocational missions major and very much enjoyed studying the Bible and missions. I had excellent and supportive Bible professors, but I began to see how little I knew and understood the Bible. There seemed to be contradictions in the Bible that I did not understand, and my professors could not explain them. The more I studied the more I became uncertain about aspects of Christianity as I had seen it in churches and Christians. As I studied the radical life Christ called his followers to, it became clear that this was not what I or most others I knew were living out daily. In college, I also became much more aware of the severe and overwhelming needs of so many people in the world. I began to understand how small and insignificant a change I could make towards helping others and the world. Many church activities I had spent so much of my life doing seemed unrelated to helping others. My life in America seemed very privileged and selfish and nothing like what Jesus asks for his disciples to be. All of these conflicting thoughts contributed to me not attending church for the first time in my life my junior and senior years of college. I felt too hypocritical attending church when I did not understand so much of the Bible, and the passages I did understand I felt I was too poorly representing in my life. I graduated and a few months later began attending church again. When I chose to return to church, I still did not understand how to live a Christian life or understand much of the Bible. I still do not. I never lost my faith in God, but felt too conflicted about my life and the lives of other Christians not being able to live out the way of Christ. I decided to attend church again because I believed I should try. Seven years later, I am still trying, and often failing, to be more like Christ.

Josh, twenty-five, attended a private, nonreligious university. Josh wrote:

> Most of my friends in college were non-religious, so I suppose that still impacts the way that I experience faith and spirituality. Namely, I don't think there's much of a place for it in the public sphere (this is probably compounded by my coursework in political science). During college I developed a lot more skepticism, and since leaving have been trying to move back into the faith; it has not been easy, though, as I haven't found any communities that I feel like I belong in. Young adult programs and Bible studies are either filled with people that I can't relate to or who don't have the time to commit to really getting to know each other. Groups for older adults don't seem to want to accept me because I'm much younger, don't have kids, etc. It's very lonely; and as a result I think my faith has been generally eroding since leaving school. I don't see a lot of people like me who have strong faith.

These four stories are representative of other survey responses. The impact of peers, faculty, extracurricular experiences, coursework, campus ministries, and mission trips, as well as the role of chapel, was sometimes positive, sometimes negative in the lives of those who responded.

Crucial Place

The college and post-college years are a crucial period in the human life cycle. This is the period when "one begins to care for oneself, deal with one's own and others' sexuality, search for meaningful work, and negotiate and renegotiate relationships to parents, peers and communities" (Cushing & McGoldrick, 2004, p. 249). Since Jeffrey Arnett's 2004 book *Emerging Adulthood,* much has been said on the unique characteristics of this particular generation of twentysomethings. Two features most commonly mentioned are that they are taking longer to grow up and embrace the typical tasks of adulthood—such as work, marriage, and children—than generations before them and that they are leaving the church in higher numbers than the generations preceding them (Kinnaman, 2011; Smith, 2009).

Emerging adults are marrying decidedly later than previous generations: in 1960, the average age of first marriage for men was twenty-two, for women, twenty; in 1990, the average age of first marriage for men was twenty-six, for women, twenty-three; in 2013 the average age at first marriage for men was twenty-nine, for women, twenty-seven (Barkhorn, 2013). In general, emerging adults believe that settling down (marrying and having children) is for later, maybe around thirty (Smith, 2009).

Twentysomethings tend to occupy several jobs before they settle into a career. Several factors may be contributing to this current phenomenon:

- The job market has been very poor since 2008.
- Young people of this generation are staying in school for many more years; partly because they are unable to find jobs in their area of interest or expertise, they go to college or they go to graduate school.
- Boomer parents have been more willing to support their children into mid- and later twenties; they are paying not only for college, but graduate school, or even doctoral work; or they are supplementing income from poorly paying jobs, and they are allowing children to move back home more frequently than in past generations.

All of these factors have contributed to current twentysomethings postponing some of the traditionally accepted roles of young adults.

The second common generalization about emerging adults is that they are leaving organized religion in higher numbers than young adults did in the past. According to the General Social Surveys which have been conducted since 1972, 23 percent of people ages eighteen to twenty-nine are unaffiliated, compared to 12 percent of eighteen to twenty-nine-year-olds who were unaffiliated in the 1970s and 1980s ("Religion Among the Millennials," 2010). The Pew Research Center's Forum on Religion and Public Life offers similar statistics. According to these figures, 25 percent of Millennials are unaffiliated. Thus, they are significantly more unaffiliated than members of Generation X were at a comparable point in their life cycle (20 percent in the late 1990s) and twice as unaffiliated as Baby Boomers were as young adults (13 percent in the late 1970s) ("Religion Among the Millennials," 2010).

Kinnaman (2011) frames the question somewhat differently, though he is getting at the same construct. The Barna Group (Kinnaman's research organization) has devoted its resources and energies to understanding "the departure of young adults from church life when they leave home for college or enter the workforce after high school or college" (Barna & Kinnaman, 2014, p. 96). In *You Lost Me* (Kinnaman, 2011), the discussion is framed around emerging adults who at one time were part of a faith community, and *Churchless* (Barna & Kinnaman, 2014) revisits that data, indicating that seven out of ten young people drop out of church life; some of these 70 percent are "nomads," some are "exiles," and some are "prodigals" (p. 98).

Nomads are the most common; they represent four out of ten young people from Christian backgrounds. Nomads try on various worldviews, lifestyles, and pathways open to them, "majoring on experiences and relationships rather than on truth and restraint" (Barna & Kinnaman, 2014, p. 97). Nomads tend to challenge the way things have been done in all institutions—family, government, and civic organizations—not just churches. Many nomads still call themselves Christian, though they exhibit little or no involvement with a local church (Barna & Kinnaman, 2014; Kinnaman, 2011).

Barna and Kinnaman's (2014) analysis of their research found that two out of ten young adults are exiles: "lost between church culture and the wider culture [they feel] called to inhabit and influence" (p. 97). They find it difficult to integrate living in a complex, post-Christian, nuanced world while retaining their faith—though exiles may still call themselves Christian. They want to follow Jesus *and* be relevant to the wider cultural marketplace. Some are not able to live congruently in both worlds and eventually may become prodigal. Nomads and exiles still identify for the most part as Christian, though they may not attend a local church. Prodigals have left not only the church; they have left their faith. About one out of nine young adults who grew up Christian are currently prodigal according to Kinnaman's research (2011; Barna & Kinnaman, 2014).[2]

One of the questions addressed in this symposium was: How can we create good places for these wandering twentysomethings to reconnect, to once again choose what we might call the abundant life in Christ? In

---

[2] Barna and Kinnaman also point out that three of ten emerging adults remain active in their faith, participating regularly in a faith community.

order to speak to that question, we should become aware of the cultural world these emerging adults inhabit as well as some of the consequent outlooks, views, and traits of many twentysomethings that relate to their religious choices.

Who Are Emerging Adults?

Christian Smith's 2009 work, *Souls in Transitions: The Religious and Spiritual Lives of Emerging Adults*, offers an in-depth look at the worlds of younger emerging adults.[3] Smith describes the eighteen- to twenty-three-year-old participants in his study as quite optimistic. Reflecting this optimistic outlook, Jeffrey Arnett (2004) says that when emerging adults describe their future, they see "lifelong, harmonious happy marriage; happy, thriving children; and satisfying and lucrative work" (p. 222). Sharon Parks (1986) adds another dimension to this optimism, saying that young adults want their faith communities to be ideal, that is "pure, consistent, authentic, and congruent" (p. 96). If emerging adults seek and cannot find this authentic and pure faith community, "they may become disillusioned and abandon church or faith or both" (Simmons, 2011, p. 31). This particular dynamic is reflected in both Emma's and Josh's responses to the survey.

This new generation also values tolerance. In fact, tolerance may be the most monolithic descriptor of this generation. Smith (2009) notes several common characteristics of emerging adults that capture various facets of tolerance including: "everybody's different," "it's up to the individual," "more open-minded," and "all cultures are relative" (pp. 48–51). Closely related to the value of tolerance is the idea that choice is good; that is, "if I chose it, it is good," or "if you chose it, it is good [for you]."

---

[3] Smith, who directs the National Study of Youth and Religion (NSYR), has been conducting longitudinal qualitative and quantitative research since 2003, following the same cohort of 3,000–3,500 young people who were thirteen to seventeen during the first wave of the research project; sixteen to twenty-one during the second wave; eighteen to twenty-three in the third. Smith and his colleagues have now concluded the fourth wave with the participants as twenty-four- to twenty-nine-year-olds and are in the process of analyzing the data. About 2,500–3,000 were surveyed by phone for each wave and 250 to 300 were interviewed in person. Several major books have resulted from this research; the most relevant for our purposes are *Soul Searching: The Religious and Spiritual Lives of Teenagers* (2005) and *Souls in Transitions: The Religious and Spiritual Lives of Emerging Adults* (2009).

Other common characteristics of emerging adults that impact, intersect with, or influence their spiritual journeys are that they typically seek mentors, appreciate story/narrative, and express deep interest in social justice issues. Relationships are particularly important to them, as well as community, with the added stipulation that they desire *authentic* relationships and *authentic* community.

Another piece of the puzzle that can help us understand twentysomethings has to do with faith development issues. What is going on *developmentally* in emerging adults regarding faith issues? What language can help us understand the arc of faith development in emerging adults?

Most emerging adults are still grappling with the perennial issues of identity and differentiation. Erik Erikson (1963) in his theory of psychosocial development says that identity vs. role confusion is the crisis that defines adolescence—that is, ages thirteen to nineteen. Perhaps for much of the twentieth century, identity and differentiation issues were typically dealt with during adolescence, but today most twentysomethings are still navigating these necessary rites of passage to adulthood. For those raised in Christian homes, owning one's faith is a crucial aspect of identity and differentiation. Key questions include: Who am I? What is my foundational identity? Am I Christian merely because my parents are Christian? Do I really believe what I thought I believed as a child and as a teen?

This process is complicated for the current generation by the pervasive cultural values of tolerance and choice because these ideals, if held as ultimate, inherently conflict with the exclusive claims of Christianity. Emerging adults are finding it difficult to align cultural and Christian beliefs, a task which has always been an integral part of identity and differentiation issues but is much more complex today. Erikson (1978) says that fidelity should emerge when the stage of identity vs. role confusion is navigated successfully. Fidelity is "the ability to sustain loyalty freely pledged in spite of inevitable contradictions and confusions of value systems" (p. 125).

Cushing and McGoldrick (2004) believe that the differentiation of self is "a quintessential task of young adulthood," defining differentiation as "a state of self-knowledge and self-definition that does not rely on the acceptance or rejection of others" (p. 237). However, what has contributed to self-definition and identity validation up to this point (e.g., sports, beauty, or even being a good youth group kid) may not continue as the vehicle for successful functioning in the adult world (Graham, 2004, p. 226).

Several well-known theorists have studied faith development per se in youth and young adults; while some aspects of previous faith development theories fit well with current emerging adults, other insights do not work as well for this generation.

James Fowler's (1981) theory is probably the best-known theoretical perspective on faith development. Fowler sorts faith development into six stages (plus a pre-stage for infants and toddlers). Most of the adolescents and many of the adults in Fowler's original study were in stage three, which Fowler labeled the synthetic-conventional stage. This stage is described as follows:

- a personal and largely unreflective synthesis of beliefs and values
- characterized by conformity; one's whole identity wrapped up in this perspective
- little critical reflection; those who differ are seen as "the other"
- authority derives from the top down and is invested with power (Fowler, 1981).

In the past, most adolescents were content in this stage, and in fact, many adults remained in this stage throughout their lives (Fowler, 1981). Today, most emerging adults (and many adolescents) are catapulted out of this stage due to the cultural context and the complexities of living in such a broken world, both inside and outside the church. When this happens, young adults may find themselves grappling with reality in Fowler's fourth stage, the individuative-reflective stage. While in this stage, persons may begin to:

- realize that the world is far more complex than stage three allows
- take personal responsibility for their beliefs/feelings
- detach from their defining group

Stage four can involve a period of demythologizing; it can be heavily existential, where nothing seems certain but one's own existence. It can be a stage of angst and struggle, and disillusionment may reign. Those who stay in this disillusioned place too long may become bitter and suspicious, losing trust in churches and people. Emma (from the earlier survey) seems to be in Fowler's stage four.

In the past, most of those who dwelt in the individuative-reflective stage for a season eventually came to a new and settled ownership of faith. However, the twentysomethings I have come to know who are wrestling with faith issues, church issues, and congruence issues are taking much longer to navigate this stage. These individuals are dwelling here, not for a few months, or even a year or two, but sometimes for a decade trying to align their current lives and beliefs with some version of their former faith. It is a painful process, and, as we are seeing, it does not always yield to Fowler's next stage.

Fowler (1981) calls the fifth stage conjunctive faith, and those in this stage exhibit:

- willingness to examine myths, taboos and standards from childhood and youth
- openness to persons and groups that are different from ourselves
- allegiances beyond "tribal" gods and "tribal" taboos
- acceptance of paradox

In some ways, this stage does not seem to fit what is happening after stage four with emerging adults. In fact, current twentysomethings often begin stage four quite able to examine the myths and taboos from childhood, to receive people of other groups, and to recognize that paradoxes permeate our world. Interestingly, many of my nineteen-year-old college students identify with stage five, believing they have already moved through the difficult stage four. I am not convinced that this is so; however, Fowler's research was conducted in the 1970s; perhaps the trajectory for current emerging adults will not reflect the journey of the participants in Fowler's study.

John Westerhoff's (1976) styles of faith seem to fit the journeys of this generation somewhat better, especially as he recognizes that persons may revisit various styles at different times in their lives. A synopsis of Westerhoff's faith styles includes the following:

- Experienced faith (early childhood): received and accepted faith
- Affiliative faith (childhood; similar to Fowler's synthetic-conventional stage): this is the style of belonging, with the attitude that this is what "we" believe, what "we" do
- Searching faith (adolescence, twenties, or later, or never): time of doubts, questions; are the stories true? Is this what I believe? Characterized by critical thinking; may be revisited several times in life. [I think many of our twentysomethings are here; they are hoping to find faith communities that are safe places to voice doubts, to ask real questions.]
- Owned or mature faith (adulthood, or maybe never): ability to live with faith in the face of paradox; tested faith. Beliefs are held with integrity and compel the person to act on them, living lives in congruence with beliefs. [I do see many twentysomethings attempting to live congruent lives with their faith, but the tenets of their faith are still forming—as perhaps is so for all adults.]

Also in the 1970s, another theorist, William Perry (1970), studied intellectual and ethical development in college students; he called the childhood stage *dualism*. Persons in this stage believe that most everything is either right or wrong and typically depend on an authority to make the ethical judgment. Of course, some teens, emerging adults, and even mature adults may dwell in this stage. Most move into a period of *multiplicity* where they recognize that there are a multiple, acceptable possibilities. These individuals then move to a place of *relativism,* "the acceptance that the world is inherently ambiguous, complex, and unknowable" (Love, 2002, p. 363), before eventually moving to adult *commitment* to specific beliefs and values (though open to change). Though Perry's work was not focused on faith development per se, it is closely related, as it considers how persons come to commitment about their beliefs and values.

Sharon Parks (1986, 2000) constructed another version of faith development in the 1980s, building on Perry and Fowler. Parks added a stage (which she calls a *form*) between adolescence and adulthood that she calls "probing commitment." Parks (2000) places this form before Fowler's stage four (individuative-reflective), and it is similar to Perry's initial commitment in relativism, before adult commitment (Love, 2002). In this period of probing commitment, Parks says young adults are trying on beliefs, values, or lifestyles to see if they fit, something like test-driving a car. Brian Simmons (2011) gives several illustrations of this period of probing faith. Simmons describes a former student who had stopped going to church; when Simmons asked why, the student said: "I wanted to see what would happen" (p. 48). Another student visited a variety of churches quite different from her denomination, saying: "I'm checking out the other options . . . sort of like dating before getting married" (Simmons, 2011, p. 32). Another who had been taught drinking alcohol was wrong, began to drink—frequently— and she said, "The sky didn't fall" (Simmons, 2011, p. 49).

Bailey Gillespie (1988) calls this young adult period a time of "reordering faith," that is, "restructuring, relearning the life of faith, retesting and sorting out their feelings of religion" (p. 178). Testing beliefs can be good; in fact, doing so is probably necessary to own one's faith. However, staying in this place for too long is unsettling and can prompt some to simply walk away. Why are emerging adults staying in this testing, probing, questioning place for so long?

The Long Transition

According to Christian Smith (2009), for emerging adults, coming to full committed faith can be compromised by several causal mechanisms. One pervasive issue is the difficulty twentysomethings have managing multiple transitions and new adult responsibilities; they often feel overwhelmed. One twenty-eight-year-old recently shared on Facebook:

Recycle.
Cook fresh vegetables.
Get to work on time every day.
Business casual should be stylish but not look like you buy your clothes at H&M.
Don't spend too much money on clothes.
Volunteer on weekends. Don't eat too many carbs. Have a hobby.
Read good books. Get plenty of sleep. Spend time with friends.

Work-work-work-work-work-work-work-work-work.
Meet new people. Maintain Chinese. Do yoga. Try
new restaurants.
Save money. Buy good quality inexpensive furniture.
Watch poignant films. Call family. Get a haircut.
Have nice-looking hair but don't blow dry every day.
Work-work-work-work-work-work-work-work.
Don't wear yourself out.
Be emotionally available for your fiancé.
Men make it further in my profession, so work harder.
But don't work harder, work smarter.
Keep your commitments. Don't overcommit yourself.
Don't put things off. Keep a personal journal. Think big.
Imagine a greater future for yourself. Live in the present.
Choose the right insurance. Plan for retirement.
Enjoy life now. Don't work too much.
Don't get stuck in the middle of the career ladder. Maintain regu-
lar car maintenance.
Don't drive, bike. Buy a bike.
Don't spend too much money.
WHAT??? HAVE I FOUND A CHURCH?
ARE YOU KIDDING???

(used with permission by the author)

Besides coping with the time-consuming and all-encompassing tasks of constant transitions and new responsibilities, emerging adults encounter other obstacles to their faith journeys and in particular their commitment to a faith community. One ubiquitous influence is the strong cultural message of tolerance as the highest good and the related messages that all choices are equal, that all beliefs are equally valid, and that all cultures are relative (Smith, 2009). In light of these pervasive cultural "goods," churches begin to appear problematic—that is, intolerant, exclusive, judgmental, and unwelcoming to doubters (Barna & Kinnaman, 2014; Kinnaman, 2011).

And last, many twentysomethings are living lifestyles that conflict with the religion of their youth. For example, they are partying, hooking up, having sex, and cohabiting; though some may compartmentalize their beliefs from their lifestyle, and others may broaden their understanding of Christianity to include their new behaviors, still others are choosing to walk away, perhaps temporarily, perhaps forever (Setran & Kiesling, 2013; Smith, 2009).

How To Respond

Given these significant obstacles to owning a mature faith, is it possible to make a persuasive case to emerging adults for the value of life in community? Most seasoned believers recognize that transformation from nonbeliever to new believer and from new believer to mature believer happens best in community; and eighteen to thirty-year-olds need to be participating in faith communities as much as any other believer perhaps more so. According to Barna and Kinnaman (2014), nomads and exiles have not left their faith—they have just left the church. Can we make a compelling case for the value of church life to these wanderers?

The biggest difficulty we face is that it is difficult to impact twentysomethings because (1) *they* are rarely among us in our churches, and (2) *we* are rarely with them—in *any* venue.

Something New

I have experienced something in the last few months that contradicts the pervasive message that twentysomethings are dropping out of church in unprecedented numbers. My husband and I moved to Nashville, Tennessee, very recently; since we arrived, we have observed that several churches are attracting *hundreds* of twentysomethings. We have been visiting two of these fresh, amazing, and vibrant faith communities, Ethos and Midtown, both of which have multiple gathering locations. Over the several weeks that we were visiting these various venues, I was preparing to speak at the Taylor University Higher Education Symposium about emerging adults and their faith, so I took the opportunity to ask some specific questions of those who worship with Ethos and Midtown. Week after week, during the "meet and greet" break before worship began and following the worship service, I asked the young men and women who were near me, "Why are you a part of this faith community? What draws you here?" Additionally, I often lingered to chat with the ministry staff, and in those conversations,

I asked, "What draws these students and twentysomethings here? What are they looking for? What are they finding?"

I received permission from those I spoke with to use their names and share what they said. Here are some samples. I asked several people "What draws these students/young adults?" Elliot, a staff member at Midtown, offered:

> Our authenticity; there is no religiosity. We speak and talk like this all the time; we're accessible. It's life conversation, not Sunday conversation. We are the opposite of Christian Smith's moralistic, therapeutic deism. There is no show. And humility; this is the real me, and I have stuff. We are on same level.

Dave, another Midtown staff member, added:

> A safe place to ask questions and to doubt. We don't appear to be a particular denomination—that is, not connected to the religious establishment, where everything is over-professionalized. They see that we are not pastor-centric—they aren't attracted to the superstar model of a pastor. And our worship is not a performance—there is no stage; we call no attention to those who facilitate our singing. There is a call into life here—who we are and who we will be. We tell the truth here, about what is and what can be.

Finally, a female college student at Midtown had this perspective:

> The preaching is honest, gripping, real. I sense that the ministers struggle with real issues just like all of us. And I can tell that the ministry team look out for each other.

I heard similar things at Ethos. Rachel, a staff member there, said,

> Freedom to find—or help create—ministry. A very simple church structure—Sunday worship and small groups. Around that, room to initiate and create and experiment.

Cyrus, another member of the Ethos staff, answered:

> They feel welcome and received where they are. Don't have to fit a mold. Don't have to be at some particular place, socially, morally, or theologically. And they value our authenticity. We are pretty real here. No BS.

Lastly, a male college student at Ethos shared what drew him there:

> I feel safe here. I can just be me. I can ask any question I want and no one will be shocked. It's okay to ask questions—even if you are not sure you believe.

Key themes that appear in these brief samples were repeated in almost every conversation I had with students or staff. These themes included authenticity, simplicity, and humility; a sense of empowerment; and "real" relationships. Perhaps most importantly, participants felt welcome and received where they were, even with their doubts. To this last point, the mission statement on the Ethos website reads:

> Ethos is a church located in the heart of downtown Nashville, TN. Whether you are a devoted follower of Jesus, a skeptic giving this whole church thing a shot, or somewhere in between—you are welcome here. At Ethos we will never assume that you have your life together, if you won't make that assumption about us. We are a group of imperfect people, loved by a perfect God . . . We hope Ethos will become a place where you find life in Jesus Christ. (http://www.ethoschurch.org/about/)

One Conviction, One Observation: Two Choices

One conviction and one observation have led me to two viable choices. The *conviction* is that the generations need to be together; that is, all generations—infants to octogenarians, and *this includes twentysomethings*. The *observation* is that twentysomethings are sparsely represented in traditional churches. In light of this conviction and this observation, I find that I have two choices.

The first is to go where twentysomethings are; in my case, that means Ethos or Midtown. My husband and I have committed to doing exactly that in Nashville. The reason is that we know that these young adults need older people to walk with them. We know this experientially: we helped lead a church plant in the mid-1990s. We were in our late thirties, and we were almost the oldest in the church. In four years, the church grew to include hundreds of college students and graduate students, some young families . . . and one fabulous, much older couple. Leading this young, enthusiastic church was an amazing but difficult journey; we had lots of ideas and lots of energy, but not much wisdom or discernment about which ideas were actually doable; and of course, we had few financial resources. After four years, the church hit an extremely difficult patch; we desperately needed older and more experienced church leaders to walk with us. But they were not there, and the church floundered. I learned *experientially* the importance of having all generations in a faith community, and since that time, I have found other support for the understanding that I learned so painfully in that place. My book (with Christine Lawton Ross, 2012) *Intergenerational Christian Formation: Bringing the Generations Together for Ministry, Community and Worship* (2012) offers biblical, theological, empirical, sociological, theoretical, and practical support for the importance of bringing all the generations back together.

In particular, research on religious socialization informs this discussion. A key point of religious socialization studies is that Christian commitment is formed and strengthened as individuals *develop relationships* and *actively participate* in faith communities that teach, model, and live out the communities' beliefs. Smith (2005) takes that point somewhat further by saying that these communities must be *cross-generational*. David Kinnaman agrees. In the conclusion to his 2011 book *You Lost Me,* which examines why emerging adults are leaving Christian churches, Kinnaman describes three things he has learned from fifteen years of research. The first is that "*intergenerational relationships in faith communities are crucial*" (p. 203, emphasis mine). Kinnaman's conclusion aligns closely with Smith's insight as well as the premise of my book: that intergenerational Christian communities uniquely and profoundly nurture Christian faith and development.

Therefore, in light of my conviction, one good choice is to join the twentysomethings where they are; and for me at this time, it is Ethos in Nashville. The problem with this choice for others with similar convictions is that many communities do not have an Ethos or a Midtown. The twentysomethings may not be attending traditional churches, and indeed they may not be part of a faith community at all. Thus, the second choice is to discover ways to welcome these wandering young adults into our more traditional churches. Both Josh and Emma (in the earlier-mentioned surveys) indicated that they had made some effort to visit various churches but had not felt received, or welcomed, or had not found what they were looking for. We must ask: "How can we welcome them? How can we offer to twentysomethings some of what they are seeking in our less edgy faith communities?" I submit a few suggestions below.

(1). Explicitly welcome emerging adults at each gathering, for example: "We are particularly blessed to have among us our twentysomethings who are learning what it means to be part of the adult world. We want you to know that those of us who are older have been through these tough years and are here to support you. We are willing to mentor you as you figure out the financial world, learn to live with roommates or to live on your own, negotiate the work world of bosses and co-workers, and generally take responsibility for your decisions and your lives. We are here and want to bless you as you move through these challenging years, and we are glad you are with us today to worship with us."

(2). Voice acknowledgement of the unique challenges of this crucial stage of life. For example, offer opportunities to discuss what many emerging adults are experiencing and feeling: differentiation and individuation, Fowler's (1981) individuative-reflective stage, Parks' (1986, 2000) probing commitment, Westerhoff's (1976) searching faith, and Gillespie's (1988) reordering faith. Discuss the differentiating process, noting that it does not mean leaving behind all that one has known; *differentiating* from family and church of origin does not have to be done alone; it can be accomplished in connection with others, in community.

Other conversations could acknowledge the overwhelming nature of emerging adulthood and the willingness of this community to offer wisdom and discernment to aid twentysomethings as they adjust to the adult work world, cope with financial responsibility, and navigate a sexually charged environment. Our son Daniel moved to Houston four years ago at the age of twenty-seven; fairly quickly, he found a faith community and vibrant group of young single professionals, but he continued to call and ask us questions—about car maintenance, investment choices, life insurance, buying a house, furniture, etc. Eventually, we recommended that he talk with older adults in the congregation for local recommendations—which he did, and he found a plethora of wonderfully helpful middle-aged and older adults who were happy to offer insights and practical advice to him.

(3). Listen. Let these twentysomethings know that you seek their ideas, their input, and that you want to hear their voices. Empower them to start ministries. A year or so ago, some young women at Ethos wanted to begin a ministry with prostitutes in the downtown area of Nashville. The young leadership of Ethos gave their blessing, and an astonishing ministry was initiated. Emerging adults have amazing amounts of energy and countless ideas; traditional churches need that energy and those ideas. Listen. Empower.

(4). Be authentic; be transparent. This young generation craves authenticity. Of course, older generations have witnessed the damage too much transparency can cause, but that should not hinder us from sharing more openly (but wisely) with those coming along behind. We should admit our struggles and acknowledge our flaws. We need to tell our stories—share our joys, our failures, what God has been doing in our lives, and how we have endured. This generation is actually interested in the stories of older people; they are also actively seeking mentors. Hearing our stories will build connecting bridges by which these mentoring relationships can form.

(5). Invite questions. Make it known that this church is a safe place to discuss doubts, real doubts about God, his existence, his role in the world, the exclusivity of Jesus's claim, the problem of evil in the world. There are other adults—not just young adults—who have questions and will be grateful to know that their questions can be addressed in an atmosphere of love and acceptance—even if there is disagreement. Invite emerging adults to join you as they sort out who they are and what they believe; let them know that you value their journeys, and that you want to walk with them and share their spiritual journeys.

(6). Offer the presence of God. Barna and Kinnaman (2014) close their book *Churchless* with a very moving piece about what faith communities offer that no other community can. They indicate that young adults can meet most of their needs in any number of venues, but only faith communities offer the very presence of God. In fact, when twentysomethings decide to visit a new faith community, Barna and Kinnaman (2014) say they are not really looking for a church—they are "looking for an encounter with God, or if not that explicitly—they are looking for his essence which is love" (p. 193). It will not matter if you welcome them, listen to them, and invite their questions, and it will not matter if you are authentic and can discuss young adult faith development articulately—if the powerful presence of God himself is not with you.

Conclusion

One of the recurring themes in Smith's book *Souls in Transition* is that some of the emerging adults who participated in the study are finding communities of faith to aid them as they recover from poor life choices made in their teens and early twenties. Smith (2009) tells the story of Andrea, a twenty-one-year-old whose nonreligious childhood was followed with teen years characterized by promiscuity, drug and alcohol abuse, poor relationships with family members, and trouble with the law. At the time of the interview, Andrea is attempting to pull out of her damaged past and has found a faith community where she regularly attends Sunday worship as well as weekly classes to learn about Christianity. She also actively participates in a life group—a small fellowship group in which people "of various ages discuss recent sermons, read the Bible, share what is going on in their lives, and pray together" (Smith, 2009, p. 171). Though Andrea has not yet committed, she says that she is learning and that she wants to know more. She says,

> I like the people at my church and their beliefs. I'm learning something, and it gives me a sense of belonging somewhere . . . where I feel secure, at church. So I feel an interest in going because I know I'll need people, and church is kind of a real close group of people. (Smith, 2009, p. 173)

The process of becoming Christlike in one's attitudes, values, beliefs, and behaviors—that is, Christian formation—does not happen alone. As Andrea's story illustrates, emerging adults need faith communities. In these cross-generational communities, they can begin to realize that some choices are better than others, all choices are not equally good, and tolerance as a premier, stand-alone value is not comprehensive enough.

Smith (2009) says that "religious beliefs, relationships, and practices often offer [Andrea and others] helpful resources for getting their lives back in order" (p. 85). In intergenerational faith communities, Smith (2009) indicates, these recovering twentysomethings find people who care about them, belief systems that help them set boundaries regarding what is healthy and unhealthy and right and wrong, and new relationships with men and women across the generations who can function as role models and provide accountability.

They also find God.

References

Allen, H. C., & Ross, C. L. (2012). *Intergenerational Christian formation: Bringing the generations together for ministry, community and worship.* Downers Grove, IL: InterVarsity.

Arnett, J. J. (2004). *Emerging adulthood: The winding road from the late teens through the twenties.* New York, NY: Oxford University Press.

Barkhorn, E. (2013, March 15). Getting married later is great for college-educated women. *The Atlantic.* Retrieved from http://www.theatlantic.com/sexes/archive/2013/03/getting-married-later-is-great-for-college-educated-women/274040/

Barna, G., & Kinnaman, D. (2014). *Churchless: Understanding today's unchurched and how to connect with them.* Grand Rapids, MI: Baker.

Cushing, B., & McGoldrick, M. (2004). The differentiation of self and faith in young adulthood: Launching, coupling, and becoming parents. In F. B. Kelcourse (Ed.), *Human development and faith: Life cycle stages of body, mind, and soul* (pp. 236—250). St. Louis, MO: Chalice Press.

Erikson, E. H. (1963). *Childhood and society* (2nd ed.). New York, NY: Norton.

Erikson, E. H. (1978). *Adulthood.* New York, NY: Norton.

Fowler, J. W. (1981). *Stages of faith: The psychology of human development and the quest for meaning.* San Francisco, CA: Harper.

Gillespie, V. B. (1988). *Experience of faith.* Birmingham, AL: Religious Education Press.

Graham, A. (2004). Identity in middle and late adolescence. In F. B. Kelcourse (Ed.), *Human development and faith: Life cycle stages of body, mind, and soul* (pp. 223—235). St. Louis, MO: Chalice Press.

Kinnaman, D. (2011). *You lost me: Why young Christians are leaving church . . . and rethinking faith.* Grand Rapids, MI: Baker.

Love, P. G. (2002). Comparing spiritual development and cognitive development. *Journal of College Student Development, 43*(3), 357–373.

Parks, S. (1986). *The critical years: Young adults and the search for meaning, faith, and commitment.* San Francisco, CA: Harper Collins.

Parks, S. (2000). *Big questions, worthy dreams: Mentoring young adults in their search for meaning, purpose, and faith.* San Francisco, CA: Jossey-Bass.

Perry, W. G., Jr. (1970). *Forms of intellectual and ethical development in the college years: A scheme.* New York, NY: Holt, Rinehart, and Winston.

"Religion Among the Millennials." (2010). Retrieved from http://www.pewforum.org/2010/02/17/religion-among-the-millennials/

Setran, D. P., & Kiesling, C. A. (2013). *Spiritual formation in emerging adulthood: A practical theology for college and young adult ministry.* Grand Rapids, MI: Baker.

Simmons, B. (2011). *Wandering in the wilderness: Changes and challenges to emerging adults' Christian faith.* Abilene, TX: Abilene Christian University Press.

Smith, C., with Denton, M. L. (2005). *Soul searching: The religious and spiritual lives of American teenagers.* Oxford, UK: Oxford University Press.

Smith, C., with Snell, P. (2009). *Souls in transition: The religious and spiritual lives of emerging adults.* Oxford, UK: Oxford University Press.

Westerhoff, J. H., III. (1976). *Will our children have faith?* New York, NY: Seabury Press.

5

TOWARD A THEOLOGY OF IMMERSION

A MacIntyrean Critique of Missions
Language at One Christian University

MICAH B. WEEDMAN

Belmont University

I want to begin with a story about a recent graduate of Belmont. We will call him Eric. Eric texted me one afternoon and asked to meet for coffee the next day to discuss plans for after graduation. When we sat down to chat, he began immediately with the declaration, "I want to move to Jackson." He was referring to Jackson, Mississippi, and I quickly remembered that he had been on one of Belmont's spring break immersion trips to the Spencer Perkins Center for Reconciliation in Jackson. The Perkins Center was founded alongside Voice of Calvary ministry by John Perkins and thus is located in one of the birthplaces of the Christian Community Development movement (along with Lawndale Community Church in Chicago).

I did not, and still do not, know Eric very well, but I knew his girlfriend well enough to know that she was taking a teaching fellowship in an inner-city school in Nashville. So, in good pastoral mode, I immediately dismissed his desire to move to Jackson and surmised that he and Amy had just broken up. So I began, ever so pastorally, "Well, okay. What prompted this? And what does Amy think about this?" I do not know what I expected—tears maybe, a confession perhaps, and a chance to dispense some wise advice. "She's totally on board." "Really?" I asked, pastoral expertise dripping from my words. "I thought she was staying here in Nashville to teach." Eric confirmed that she was and that they had talked at great length. When she finished her fellowship in Nashville, she hoped to join him in Jackson and secure a teaching job there.

At this point, I ditched the pastoral concern and jumped straight to the logistics. "Have you thought about a timeline," I asked. "Next week," he answered. "Then you have a job?" "No," he answered, "but I'm pretty sure that the Perkins Center will let me volunteer there for a while." "You know that they don't pay you for that, right?" I asked. He looked at me coolly. Clearly, this was not going quite the way he thought it might. So, I backed up and tried to straighten out my own confusion.

"Let me get this straight: you are moving next week to Jackson, Mississippi, a town that you are not from, in order to volunteer at a place that you visited for a week just a few months ago. You don't have a job there, and you don't have any friends. But you are going to do it anyway, because you really want to use the degree you got in audio engineering technology from the best AET program in the world in order to help the Perkins Center straighten out its music studio so that local kids can record rap and gospel music there."

Eric, less cool now: "Exactly. And I want you to help me make it permanent."

In this chapter, I explore the potential formational aspects, especially regarding vocational discernment, of what we at Belmont call immersion trips. First, I demonstrate how our shift in language—from "missions" or "mission" trips to "immersion" trips—came about as a result of a certain problematizing of "missions" language inherent in our increasingly diverse student body. Second, I further problematize missions language using Alasdair MacIntyre's notion of a practice. After that, I institute immersion as a constitutive practice for Christian higher education, relating it to key Christian practices like catechism, pilgrimage, and liturgy while situating them within the educational mission of the university. Finally, I conclude with the theological implications, in hopes that we might develop a "theology of immersion."

Before I get into the main arguments of this chapter, though, I confess that some disclaimers are necessary. First, when discussing Belmont's language shift to "immersion trip," I do not mean to suggest that we are either unique or original in doing so. In fact, like any good student development or campus ministry professional, I quite blatantly stole this idea from other institutions, including Santa Clara University, a Roman Catholic school in California and Hope College, a Reformed Church of America school in Michigan. Second, my point here is not to problematize all "missions" language within theology, missiology, or the wider church. I am dealing quite directly with Belmont's own context, which I will explore. Third, what I hope to offer here is not rooted in any hard research or analysis—quantitative or qualitative—but is instead operant at a nearly purely conceptual level. I begin with a review of the ways these kinds of trips shape college students.

Service Learning and Leadership: Literature Review

That community service experiences and college student leadership development are related is hardly a new suggestion; in fact, the literature on this relationship is broad. Astin and Sax (1998) showed that participation in service programs increased student measures in thirty-five different personal and interpersonal development areas, including leadership skills. Dalton and Petrie (1997) performed a qualitative study of students in service learning programs that demonstrated how participation in these programs increased student leadership participation as well as the development of leadership skills. Eyler and Giles (1999) performed comprehensive studies of service learning programs to evaluate student learning and found that, among other outcomes, student participants in service learning programs developed leadership skills as well as a desire to effect social change in political and organizational environments. College graduates concluded that service opportunities were among their most valuable learning experiences and that they were able to assume more leadership positions in these classes than in traditionally taught classes. Other studies have confirmed these findings (Giles & Eyler, 1994; Gray et al., 1998; Keen & Keen, 1998; Knee, 1999; Mabry, 1998; McElhaney, 1998; Peterson, 1998; Raskoff, 1997; Vogelgesang & Astin, 2000; Wade & Yarborough, 1996; Wielkiewicz, 2002, 2000; Zawacki, 1997).

Additionally, service experiences in college have been shown to have a positive impact on the personal and moral development of students (Astin & Sax, 1998; Astin, Sax, & Avalos, 1999; Boss, 1994; Eyler, Giles, & Braxton, 1997; Eyler & Giles, 1999; Giles & Eyler, 1994; Gray et al., 1998; Keen & Keen, 1998; Kendrick, 1996; Markus, Howard, & King, 1993; Ostrow, 1995; Peterson, 1998; Rockquemore & Schaffer, 2000; Vogelgesang & Astin, 2000; Wade & Yarborough, 1996).

A number of studies have demonstrated a link between service learning and leadership developed in both secondary and undergraduate students. For example, Pleasants et al. (2004) have shown that service learning helps motivate students' wider learning by giving them "direct knowledge of, and an active interest in, the area being studied" (p. 16). This level of engagement is important for several reasons. In the context of the specific target of this study (the Duke University Talent Identification Program's Leadership Institute), service learning spoke directly to the mission of the entire program. A core part of the mission of the Talent Identification Program is leading high-achieving students to "opportunities of community and civic engagement" (Pleasants et al., 2004, p. 17). Service learning not only fulfills that goal directly but also allows students to both "construct meaning" and gain a sense of perspective on what community and civic engagement means by offering their own direct problem-solving skills and project management to the task at hand.

Likewise, service learning offers a great deal of flexibility to students, which allows them to investigate new ideas and contexts (Pleasants et al., 2004). Consequently, a service learning program fits seamlessly within a well-designed student leadership curriculum. In particular, Pleasants et al. (2004) propose a framework for integrating service learning into the teaching of leadership theory. Their proposals call for a rigorous service learning experience that becomes the basis of classroom discussion and reflection. These carefully designed experiences challenge the student to "apply their newly acquired skills and knowledge "to real-world situations" (Pleasants et al., 2004, p. 21). In other words, a service learning program integrated within the larger leadership curricula motivates students to put that training to work in new and dynamic ways.

A more specific study investigates the kinds of skills service learning programs can foster for students in natural resource learning. Here again, the findings support the general claim that service learning plays an integral role in skill development. Students who have a service learning option are better equipped for the skill-based leadership roles that they are preparing for. Newman, Bruyere, and Beh (2007) investigated a service learning program in the protected-areas management class in Colorado State University. The authors noted that core leadership skills, including interdisciplinary focus, problem-solving, and adaptation, are widely regarded as central to the changing and complex shape of resource management. Drawing on Kolb's (1984) Experiential Learning Theory, the authors conducted a survey that helps assess the students' ability to work within groups, think outside of their traditional disciplinary boundaries, and engage in problem-solving practices, all skills that are essential to the practice of resource management (Newman et. al, 2007).

This survey was an action research approach that addressed a specific problem in a specific land-management context that included the participation of the entire class of twenty-six students. The survey found that students were able to recognize that good leadership requires a "hybrid of traits" (Newman et al., 2007, p. 65). The students found that leadership involves a number of personal characteristics, including trust between the leader and others and the capacity of the leader to empower others to perform required actions. The authors also found the service learning helped "bond" students to the land (i.e., the object of their leadership focus), which produced a deeper capacity to function effectively (Newman 2007, p. 67).

Alternative Spring Break Programs

Very little literature is found about alternative spring break (ASB) programs in the U.S., despite their increasing popularity on college campuses. According to McElhaney (1998), organized alternative spring breaks have their roots in the 1970s and 1980s, but it was in the early 1990s that organizations such as Break Away and others began to support alternative break programs nationally. This timeline coincides with the creation of other national-level community service programs. ASB programs fall on a spectrum of designs, but typically contain many of the same elements from program to program, including opportunities for direct, hands-on service as well as opportunities for reflection and discussion. According to Break Away, a national nonprofit started by two pioneers in the ASB movement, there are eight "quality components" to ASB programs:

- **Strong direct service:** Programs provide an opportunity for participants to engage in direct or "hands-on" projects and activities that address critical but unmet social needs, as determined by the community. Community interaction during service projects and throughout the week is highly encouraged during breaks.

- **Orientation:** Prior to departure, participants should be oriented to the mission and vision of their community partner or organization(s). Participants are encouraged to look at the context of the work of the organization within the broader community and to become allies to their mission and vision through direct service.

- **Education:** Programs include issue specific educational sessions which participants attend prior to and perhaps during their alternative break. These sessions provide participants with the historical, political, social, and cultural context of the social problems they will be working with during the break. Effective education provides faces and opinions from all perspectives on the issue, including ways that the participants' personal life choices are connected to them.

- **Training:** Participants are provided with adequate training in the skills necessary to carry out tasks and projects during the trip. Ideally, this training should take place prior to departure, although in some instances it may occur once participants have reached their site. Examples of training include teaching basic construction, learning how to read with children, or gaining first aid skills.

- **Reflection:** During the trip, participants reflect upon the experiences they are having—synthesizing the direct service, education, and community interaction components. Applying classroom learning and integrating many academic disciplines can occur. The site leaders should set aside time for reflection to take place, both individually and in a group setting.

- **Reorientation:** Upon return to campus, programs carry out reorientation activities for all participants where they can share their break experiences and translate them into a lifelong commitment to active citizenship. Through these activities, participants continue their volunteer efforts in their local area, learn about possible internships, engage politically in their community, obtain resources for continued education on social issues, and make life choices that benefit the entire community.

- **Diversity:** Strong alternative break programs include participants representing the range of students present in the campus community. Coordinators should recruit, design, implement and evaluate their program with this end in mind. Break programs should also plan to intentionally address the issue of diversity and social justice, or privilege and oppression, and how it relates to service work.

- **Alcohol and Other Drug Free:** Programs must be aware that issues of legality, liability, personal safety, and group cohesion are of concern when alcohol and other drugs are consumed on an alternative break. Programs provide education and training on alcohol and other drug-related issues as well as develop a policy on how these issues will be dealt with on an alternative break. (Break Away, n.d.)

There is no literature about why and when institutions that host ASB programs began using the "immersion" model of programming. However, a basic Google search of the phrase "spring break immersion trip" uncovers results from almost four dozen colleges and universities that use "immersion" language as part of their programming. Immersion-style trips are those that incorporate service experiences alongside education, formation, and exposure-type activities. Immersion programs have long been associated with foreign language study (Johnson & Swain, 1997). Mills, Bersamina, and Plante (2007) found that students who participated in spring break immersion programs coped with stress more effectively and had a better sense of vocation than those who did not. Plante, Lackey, and Hwong (2009) found that students who participated in immersion style ASB programs had greater measures of developed compassion than did students who did not participate in these programs. Maher (2003) reported that students who used specific reflection tools (indicative of immersion-style ASB trips) learned more about themselves and the service sites than students who did not use the reflective tools on other ASB trips. Noll (2012) found that students who participated in immersion-style ASB programs at one institution had increased measures in certain aspects of servant leadership.

While most of this literature deals primarily with secular alternative spring break programming, there has been a limited number of research reports regarding short-term missions (STM), or spring break trips, and college student development. Linhart (2005) examined one- to four-week trips but focused primarily on high school students. Burkholder examined the effect of a six-month training program on college students. In short, while STMs are increasingly studied (Howell, 2012), little research has been done on spring break trips and their impact on students.

The Belmont Context

As mentioned earlier, our decision to adopt new language in describing our spring break trips was rooted in the context of our trips. Belmont University is located in Nashville and is a private, Christian university with a total enrollment of 7,300 students. Approximately 5,000 of those are undergraduate students, and nearly 50 percent live on campus. Historically affiliated with the Tennessee Baptist Convention, Belmont severed ties with the convention in 2007 in an effort to diversify its Board of Trustees in recognition of the increasing diversity of its student body and other constituencies. Belmont has since then been intentional in both maintaining and enhancing its Christian identity. Faculty and staff are still required to profess a lived Christian faith, though there is considerable diversity as to what that means, with representation from the broad range of Christian traditions and denominations.

It is also important to note that Belmont does not require a faith commitment or statement on the part of its applicants and accepts students regardless of faith commitment. According to the most recent Common Data Set (a standard report of institutional facts and data), the overwhelming majority of incoming students identified themselves as Christians, with the largest groups being Roman Catholics and Baptists with nearly equal percentages. While those identifying as Christians are still in the majority, the past few years have seen a doubling of the number of students who choose "none" or "other" as their religious identity, and those two groups now constitute nearly 10 percent of the incoming student population. Muslims make up the majority in the "other" category.

Belmont students are required to take two religion classes as part of the core curriculum, and all students must gather sixty "convocation" credits in order to graduate. Students can gain these credits in a variety of categories but must accumulate ten credits in a category called "Christian faith development." Notably, the University included a 280-seat chapel as a centerpiece in its new $70 million Wedgewood Academic Center, which is the flagship building on campus.

Belmont maintains an Office of University Ministries, separate and distinct from the Division of Student Affairs. The staff of University Ministries answers directly to the vice president for spiritual development, who holds a position on the president's cabinet. University Ministries oversees a broad portfolio of spiritual formation, outreach, and chapel programming, and all of its professional staff hold adjunct teaching positions at the University.

Belmont is a member of New American Colleges & Universities (NAC&U) and in recent years has sought to raise its national profile. While still largely a regional university, the percentages of incoming students from outside of the Southeast have increased significantly in recent years. Belmont is nationally recognized for having one of the best music business programs in the country, and a significant number of students come to study music business, audio engineering technology, or commercial music performance.

Over the past decade, the University has seen significant growth in both enrollment and campus resources. In the early 2000s, the total enrollment was only 3,000 students; in the past ten years, the University has built seven new residence halls and will soon break ground on another. Additionally, the University has recently opened a graduate pharmacy program, a law school, and expanded its nursing programs significantly. Its business school is nationally recognized, and Belmont was one of the first schools to offer an undergraduate degree in social entrepreneurship. Thus, many Belmont students are attracted to Belmont because of its particular programs.

In mid-2009, the Office of University Ministries reorganized to bring local outreach and missions programming under the same director. At that time, missions programming was struggling to maintain viability both financially and in terms of student involvement, so the decision was made to "rebuild and rebrand" and place special emphasis on spring break trips. As mentioned above, the trips were renamed "immersion" trips and were redesigned to reflect certain realities at Belmont, especially the increasing diversity of Belmont's student body.

"Missions trip" language is fraught with an assortment of meanings, and my hunch was that many students found themselves to be in a place, religiously or spiritually, where they felt uninspired, uninterested, or uninvited to participate in such programs. The idea that "missions" or "mission" means different things to different people is not new—David Bosch's seminal work of missiology, *Transforming Mission* (1992), explores this at great length. Missions is typically something done by agents of the church, or more specifically, churches. And yet, churches often disagree as to what constitutes missions, or at least what the focus of missions should be. Without an ecclesial identity, it was hard to identify the framework by which Belmont could continue to do "missions." Confusion also exists because the University has its own mission statement, with which our programming is intended to align. As "*missions*" in the church are to be centered on the activity of God, the *mission* of Belmont University is explicit in its intention to put students at the center of our activity. Thus, if we asked the question, "Whose mission?," the denominational and religious plurality of our students makes it difficult to answer "God's." Plus, many students automatically associate missions language with the church and its activities.

Some recent work on missions also problematizes this language. Howell (2012) found the narratives that shape participation in short-term missions create a tension, for many participants, between learning and reflection on the one hand and humble but transformative service on the other. In comparing and contrasting short-term missions work with pilgrimage, Howell argued that

> Narratives of pilgrimage and tourism emphasize the individual and her or his experience of travel and transformation. Even where group dynamics are intrinsic to the experience of the journey, the narrative of personal transformation remains at the center of the tourist *cum* pilgrim narrative. For the STM traveler, personal transformation, adventure and spiritual growth can only ever be by-products of the trip. (p. 57)

At this point, I wish to bring the work of moral philosopher Alasdair MacIntyre into this discussion. Though MacIntyre's (2007) project is far too large to even summarize in a piece like this, suffice it say that his work critiques post-Enlightenment notions of morality as incoherent, in large part because the Enlightenment rendered meaningless any discussion of *telos*. For MacIntyre, the only way to overcome this is a reclamation of Aristotle's notion of *telos* and its necessary reliance on notions of virtue, practices, and the narrative unity of a life. For our purposes, we can stick with the idea of practice to get a sense of why missions language needs to be revised, at least in the context of Belmont and in light of Howell's work on STM.

MacIntyre (1984) defines a practice in the following way:

> By a "practice," I am going to mean any coherent and complex form of socially established cooperative human activity through which goods internal to that form of activity are realized in the course of trying to achieve those standards of excellence which are appropriate to, and partially definitive of, that form of activity, with the result that human powers to achieve excellence, and human conceptions of the ends and goods involved, are systematically extended. (p. 187)

For MacIntyre, practices are essential for the flourishing of the virtues, which themselves are essential for moral coherence. He continues,

> Tic-tac-toe is not an example of a practice in this sense, nor is throwing a football with skill; but the game of football is, and so is chess. Bricklaying is not a practice, but architecture is. Planting turnips is not a practice, but farming is. So are the enquiries of physics, chemistry and biology, and so is the work of the historian, and so are painting and music. (1984, p. 187)

Thus, in the particular context of Belmont and in light of Howell's work on STM, missions is not a practice in the MacIntyrean sense. Because the goods internal to missions are external—that is, the goods that those of us involved higher education seek to instill in our students—it becomes difficult to practice missions work with any coherence. This is why I stressed the context of Belmont so heavily. Because of the diversity of perspectives on religion, the gospel, and discipleship at Belmont, we can see most clearly that missions *as a practice* requires a far different context than the current one at Belmont.

This immersion language allows for understanding of the kinds of travel programs that students participate in through their colleges and universities. In no small part, this is because immersion language is open enough to allow for a kind of creativity. As I noted above in the literature review, a quick search revealed some forty schools or universities that use immersion language, which means it has meaning outside of any one institution. Yet because the language seems to be so specific to higher education, those of us who oversee and design such trips have the capacity to develop the standards of excellence that would continue to shape immersion trips in ways that extend them into greater coherence and distinction.

This prompts the question of what constitutes those standards, and here I want to draw on other practices, particularly practices of the church, that might inform how we understand immersion trips. Howell (2012) discussed one of them, that of pilgrimage. Much literature exists about pilgrimage, both theologically and anthropologically, and it is beyond this chapter to explore all of that. However, the pilgrimage language gives us a window into travel and trip experiences that place the spiritual formation of students at the center of what we hope to do. Like pilgrimages, immersions can make the formation of students a good that is internal rather than external to the practice. Immersion can situate travel experiences in a context of seeking God (rather than bringing God), and of finding God in both expected and unexpected places.

Our students are not merely pilgrims; they are also students. Because most immersion trips do not bear course credit of any kind, it might seem difficult to understand how to apply learning goals and outcomes to the work that happens. This is why I think that *catechesis* is a useful practice to consider. Historically, catechesis was the means by which converts—children and adults—were taught what John Paul II described as "the fullness of the Christian life" (John Paul II, *Redemptoris Missio*). While it would be incoherent to deploy a particular catechism in this case, the mode of catechesis can be useful. For example, Belmont's mission statement asserts that a Belmont education "equips men and women of diverse backgrounds to engage and transform the world with disciplined intelligence, courage, compassion and faith." Immersion trips allow a unique space in diverse locations to catechize students into a fuller understanding of the concepts of "disciplined intelligence, courage, compassion and faith." Recall MacIntyre's argument that the role of practices in the moral life is to cultivate the virtues; immersion as a practice allows us to cultivate the kinds of virtues—courage, compassion, faith—that our mission statement proclaims as central to life as a Belmont student.

Another church practice that informs our sense of immersion is that of liturgy. Liturgy comes from the Greek words meaning "the work of the people," and immersion trips are about the work of the people in many ways. However, the similarities to pilgrimage and catechesis demand a daily order that mirrors the regular gathered prayer and worship of God's people. In the Belmont context, this looks very much like liturgy; each immersion team takes with them the immersion prayer book, a book of prayer common to all immersion participants that invites reflection and action in each separate context. Last year, we extended this liturgy to the entire campus, sharing the immersion prayer book with faculty and staff so that they might also pray with our students all over the country.

Thus, immersion does something quite remarkable in my mind. It brings together practices of the church—pilgrimage, catechesis, liturgy—and contextualizes them in a higher education setting. Immersion sees the mission of the church and the mission of the university neither disjunctive nor synonymous. Rather, it takes the constitutive practices of the church and allows them to shape what might become a constitutive practice of the university in ways that are coherent in the context of increasingly pluralized settings. But it also does so in ways that speak to the long-term formation of students, hopefully, as servants of the church.

This brings us back to Eric. I need to offer another disclaimer: I recognize that lots of students go on mission trips, come home considering missions as full time vocation, and return to the locations where they felt recruited. I am not claiming something particularly special or unique about Eric's decision to move to Jackson. Nor am I oblivious to the fact that Eric in another sense is an outlier; plenty of folks go on immersion trips and experience what Robert Coles called "the epiphany of recruitment" (as cited in Mahan, 2002, p. 27). What I am trying to narrate is that Eric's decision makes a perfect kind of sense when considered in light of the case for immersion language argued in this chapter. Having made a pilgrimage shaped by a liturgy of prayer and reflection and having been catechized in a laboratory of virtues—particularly those of disciplined intelligence, courage, compassion, and faith—Eric acted virtuously. In a way, it was surprising even to me, the one who designed his experience. But in a way, it was entirely coherent to a life lived "in the fullness of the Christian faith."

References

Astin, A. W., & Sax, L. J. (1998). How undergraduates are affected by service participation. *Journal of College Student Development, 39*(3), 251–263.

Astin, A. W., Sax, L. J., & Avalos, J. (1999). Long term effects of volunteerism during the undergraduate years. *Review of Higher Education, 22*(2), 187–202.

Bosch, D. (1992). *Transforming mission: Paradigm shifts in the theology of mission.* Maryknoll, NY: Orbis Books.

Boss, J. A. (1994). The effect of community service on the moral development of college ethics students. *Journal of Moral Development, 23*(2), 183–198.

Break Away. (n.d.). Eight components of a quality alternative break. www.alternativebreak.com. Retrieved from http://www.alternativebreaks.org/wp-content/uploads/2014/06/8-Components-2014.pdf

Burkholder, J. B. (2003). An evaluation of Grace University's 1997, six-month, missions training program in Mali, West Africa. (Unpublished doctoral dissertation). Trinity International University, Deerfield, IL.

Dalton, J. C. & Petrie, A. M. (1997). The power of peer culture. *Educational Record, 78*(3-4), 18-24.

Eyler, J. S., Giles, D. E., Jr., & Braxton, J. (1997). The impact of service-learning on college students. *Michigan Journal of Community Service Learning, 4*, 5–15.

Eyler, J. S., & Giles, D. E., Jr. (1999). *Where's the learning in service-learning?* San Francisco, CA: Jossey-Bass, Inc.

Giles, D. E., & Eyler, J. S. (1994). The impact of a college community service laboratory on students' personal, social and cognitive outcomes. *Journal of Adolescence, 17*, 327–339.

Gray, M. J., Ondaatje, E. H., Fricker, R., Geschwind, S., Goldman, C. A., Kaganoff, T., . . . Klein, S. P. (1998). Coupling service and learning in higher education: The final report of the evaluation of the learn and serve America higher education program. The RAND Corporation.

Howell, B. (2012) *Short term mission: An ethnography of Christian travel narrative and experience.* Downer's Grove, IL: InterVarsity Press.

John Paul II. (1990). *Redemptoris missio*: Encyclical letter on the permanent validity of the church's missionary mandate. *Libreria Editrice Vaticana.* Retrieved from http://www.vatican.va/holy_father/john_paul_ii/encyclicals/documents/hf_jp-ii_enc_07121990_redemptoris-missio_en.html.

Johnson, R. K., & Swain, M. (Eds.). (1997). *Immersion education: International perspectives.* New York, NY: Cambridge University Press.

Keen, C., & Keen, J. (1998). Bonner student impact survey. Princeton, NJ: Bonner Foundation.

Kendrick, J. R. (1996). Outcomes of service-learning in an introduction to sociology course. *Michigan Journal of Community Service Learning, 2*, 72-81.

Knee, R. T. (1999). *Service-learning in social work education: Building democracy through informed citizenship.* (Unpublished doctoral dissertation). University of Denver, Denver, CO.

Kolb, D. A. (1984). *Experiential learning: Experience as the source of learning and development.* Englewood Cliffs, NJ: Prentice-Hall.

Linhart, T. (2005). Planting seeds: the curricular hope of short term mission experiences in youth ministry. *Christian Education Journal, 2*(2), 256-272

Mabry, J. B. (1998). Pedagogical variations in service-learning and student outcomes: How time, contact and reflection matter. *Michigan Journal of Community Service Learning, 5,* 32–47.

MacIntyre, A. (2007). *After virtue* (3rd ed.). South Bend, IN: University of Notre Dame Press.

Mahan, B. (2002). *Forgetting ourselves on purpose: Vocation and the ethics of ambition.* San Francisco, CA: Jossey-Bass.

Maher, M. J. (2003). Individual beliefs and cultural immersion in service-learning: Examination of a reflection process. *Journal of Experiential Education, 26*(2), 88–96.

Markus, G. B., Howard, J. P. F., & King, D. C. (1993). Integrating community service and classroom instruction enhances learning: Results from an experiment. *Educational Evaluation and Policy Analysis, 15*(4), 410–419.

McElhaney, K. A. (1998). *Student outcomes of community service learning: A comparative analysis of curriculum-based and non curriculum-based alternative spring break programs.* (Unpublished doctoral dissertation). University of Michigan, Ann Arbor, MI.

Mills, B. A., Bersamina, R. B., & Plante, T. G. (2007). The impact of college student immersion service learning trips on coping with stress and vocational identity. *Journal of Civic Engagement, 9,* 1–8.

Newman, P., Bruyere, B. L, & Beh, A. (2007). Service learning and natural resource leadership. *Journal of Experiential Education, 30*(1), 54–69.

Noll, C. A. (2012). *An alternative spring break of leadership and service: Interpreting the servant leadership, motivations, and service participation of millennials who participated in project LEAD between the years 2008—2010* (Doctoral dissertation). Retrieved from ProQuest Dissertations and Theses. (3499354)

Ostrow, J. M. (1995). Self-consciousness and social position: On college students changing their minds about the homeless. *Qualitative Sociology, 18*(3), 357–375.

Peterson, E. A. (1998). What can adults learn from community service? Lessons learned from AmeriCorps. *Community Education Journal, 25*(1–2), 45–46.

Plante, T. G., Lackey, K., & Hwang, J. (2009). The impact of immersion trips on development of compassion among college students. *Journal of Experiential Education, 32*(1), 28–43.

Pleasants, R., Stephens, K. R., Selph, H., & Pfeiffer, S. (2004). Incorporating service learning into leadership education: Duke TIP's leadership institute. *Gifted Child Today, 27*(1), 16-21.

Raskoff, S. (1997). Group dynamics in service-learning: Guiding student relations. *Michigan Journal of Community Service Learning, 4,* 109–115.

Rockquemore, K. A., & Schaffer, R. H. (2000). Toward a theory of engagement: A cognitive mapping of service-learning experiences. *Michigan Journal of Community Service Learning, 7,* 14–25.

Vogelgesang, L. J., & Astin, A. W. (2000). Comparing the effects of service-learning and community service. *Michigan Journal of Community Service Learning, 7,* 25–34.

Wade, R. C., & Yarborough, D. B. (1997). Community service-learning in Student teaching: Toward the development of an active citizenry. *Michigan Journal of Community Service Learning, 4,* 42-55.

Wielkiewicz, R. M. (2002). Validity of the leadership attitudes and beliefs scale: Relationships with personality, communal orientation and social desirability. *Journal of College Student Development, 43*(1),108–118.

Wielkiewicz, R. M. (2000). The leadership attitudes and beliefs scale: An instrument for evaluating college students' thinking about leadership and organizations. *Journal of College Student Development, 41*(3), 335–347.

Zawacki, K. G. (1997). *Personal and family factors related to service learning in an undergraduate course on diversity.* (Unpublished doctoral dissertation). Michigan State University, East Lansing, MI.

6

ON CREATING SPACE FOR MENTORS TO BECOME

GUY CHMIELESKI

Belmont University

Every spring, Belmont University hosts a baccalaureate service that features four to six student speakers who share how they encountered God and had a transformational experience during their time as a student. Without fail, they all mention a faculty or staff member who had a profound impact on them—someone who formally or informally played the role of mentor in their lives.

However, as I began to do some inquiring among faculty and staff around campus, I quickly learned that the vast majority of them felt overwhelmed by the possibility of serving as a "spiritual" mentor (beyond the scope of their work and/or discipline) and really had no idea where they would begin such a task.

The desire was there—it is why most of them chose to pursue working at a Christian institution—but they collectively believed that they lacked the tools in order to adequately live into this role.

This uncertainty among the institutional personnel prompted me to begin hosting spiritual mentoring reading groups for our faculty and staff as a way of creating conversation around the topic of mentoring. My intent with this group was to encourage, equip, and inspire all members of the professional campus community to better recognize existing opportunities around them. Ideally, the group would help them establish a common language of spiritual formation, equip them with ideas about how to initiate this kind of intentional relationship, and encourage them to prayerfully take their role on campus to a whole new level.

Why Is All This Necessary?

Because increasingly students are not making the most of their formative college years.

Yes, they are still getting their degree, but most are not growing and maturing in the ways the college years ideally facilitate. Thus, instead of graduating and feeling confident in their ability to go out and make a difference in the world, more and more students opt to return home after they graduate while they figure out what comes next (Elmore, 2010).

I do not think we should view this result as a successful matriculation. Our students should not be looking to move back home as a part of "Plan A" for their life upon graduating from our institutions.

So what am I suggesting as a counter to this unfolding predicament?

The Return of the Mentor

That's right. We need to return to an educational pedagogy that makes intentional mentoring—spiritual mentoring—core to our work with students.

So before we get to reading groups that will unleash waves of mentors throughout our campus, let us start by exploring some of the reservations and challenges that most potential mentors face when considering the task of serving in this pivotal role.

Common Reservations

As I have met with different faculty and staff, inquiring about their roles and relationships with students, I regularly hear my colleagues rave about how gifted and inspiring our students are. Yet, when I begin to talk about the role they play in the lives of students—specifically the role of mentor—they often shrink back. Whether it is a true (or false) sense of humility, many of these talented and faithful individuals are downplaying—if not flat out denying—the role they play in the lives of their students outside the normal scope of their work. As I have pressed them on this hesitancy, I have run into a few common themes that seem to hold back these critical members of our educational system.

Common Reservation #1: A Sense of Being Ill Equipped

The first and most consistent message I get from different faculty and staff is that they do not feel prepared or equipped to serve in the capacity of spiritual mentor. Certainly, when it comes to talking about business, nursing, music, leadership, or whatever their particular area of expertise is, they are confident to speak into the hearts and minds of their students. However, when it comes to speaking about their faith, encouraging students in their faith formation, or even weaving themes of faith into their teaching or instruction, many of them feel overwhelmed by the task. They do not believe they have much of anything to offer in this arena, even though they have a very deep and vibrant faith.

Also, for those who do recognize that they have something of value to offer as it relates to the theme of faith, they struggle to know how, or when, or where to start. Again, it is clear that the desire is there, but they remain unsure of how to get the ball rolling, how to discern if the ball is rolling in the right direction, and how to know if they are actually doing it "right." Worse than not knowing where to start is the unsettling thought that, as mentors, they could unknowingly lead a student astray by their words or example.

Common Reservation #2: The Belief that Students Are Too Busy

There is another common reservation that I have heard numerous faculty and staff express: students today are simply too busy. Even if the faculty or staff member wanted to initiate a more intentional mentoring relationship, most students do not seem to live with any sort of time margin for such a thing. They appear overwhelmed by their workloads, relationships, and basic life management that make up their everyday existence. The last thing these would-be mentors want to do is further overload and overwhelm their students by giving them one more weekly appointment to commit to.

"Besides," many rationalize, "if students really wanted something like this [a mentoring relationship], they know they could just come and ask me about it. If they did that, then I'd know for certain that they were interested in taking our relationship to a different level."

What most of these individuals do not realize is that most students who are interested in this kind of relationship too often observe the faculty and staff in their day-to-day life and think the exact same thing: "They look so busy. And even if they had a spare moment, why on earth would they want to take the time to invest in me?"

Common Reservation #3: The Cultural Call for "Tolerance"

A third roadblock is the overwhelming call for "tolerance" in our North American culture today. This crushing mandate for people to keep their beliefs to themselves is what many feel the world-at-large is requesting. If we want to play in the sandbox of campus and society, we are going to have to play by the rules of the day: everyone gets their own space in which they are free to think, believe, and do as they want, as long as their thoughts, beliefs, and actions do not infringe upon the rights of anyone else to think, believe, or do as they want.

Now, one might think that faculty and staff on a Christian campus would recognize that they are afforded certain privileges and opportunities that their counterparts at non-Christian institutions are not. Instead, most faculty and staff whom I have encountered often feel compelled to abide by the cultural call to "tolerate" and not intrude upon the personal beliefs of others. This claim is especially true with the understanding that there are a percentage of non-Christians on campus, and potentially even in their classroom, whom they would never want to offend.

Unknown Challenges

If these challenges and reservations indicated by many faculty and staff are not enough of a deterrent, a number of lesser-known challenges will likely send potential mentors running for the hills. I hesitate to share them, yet I believe that all potential mentors need to understand the full reality of what we are up against. We have some control over many of the things mentioned in the previous section. They are impediments that we have either put in our own way or allowed others to place in front of us.

However, some of the unknown challenges are bigger than we are. They are outside of our control. Yet their existence does not let us off the hook. We are still called to serve in the role of mentor for our students. Thus, before we embark into this calling, we must make known what is unknown.

Unknown Challenge #1: The Postmodern Tenets of (1) a Lack of Trust in Authority and (2) Students' Desires to Make their Own Way

With all of the baggage associated with the term "postmodernism," a couple of shifts have taken place within our culture that seem to come into direct tension with the practice of mentoring. The first is an inherent lack of trust for authority and people in positions of authority. This is true in the case of most young people as they think about and relate to older individuals and institutions that hold any kind of power or authority, but it is especially true of religious leaders and institutions. We have all seen the disgraceful stories of religious leaders misusing and abusing their power and trust by committing egregious acts. Our media outlets have made these falls from grace trending topics, cover stories, and headline news.

Our young people have grown up in a world where they have been told to make good choices and think of others first, only to see time and time again people in positions of power seemingly disregard the well-being of others for the sake of their own needs. This double standard, especially as it relates to faith and authority, does not set us up well. Given the nature of our roles, we are seen as people of authority working within institutions of power—and Christian institutions at that.

When we couple this inherent lack of trust in authority with a second postmodern tenet—that of desiring to blaze one's own trail—we can begin to see how the context for creating mentoring relationships is neither fertile nor friendly.

Generally speaking, students today are much less interested in hearing what we have to say about how they should spend this formative season of life. They do not want to be told where to go, how to go, when to go, why to go, or what to avoid as they go. They want to explore things for themselves. They want to find their own way—even if this means making some mistakes along the way. Many students want us to stay out of their way, while simultaneously staying just close enough that, if they should need us for some reason, we are ready.

Unknown Challenge #2: Post-Christian America?

The second relatively unknown challenge faced by potential mentors, especially Christians, is that the U.S. is apparently becoming a post-Christian country. Now, a lot will still need to play out in the years to come to see if the U.S. does actually become like many of the "godless" countries of Europe. However, we can identify several unfolding factors within our own borders that do seem to speak to a growing challenge as it relates to the acceptance and influence of the Christian faith.

One of the more obvious factors is what we know about the shifts of religious interest and engagement across the land. Geographically speaking, the South is the last region holding on to an overall cultural acceptance of Christianity. In most other regions of the United States, we have seen Christianity struggle to retain any sort of general or positive influence. The Northeast, Northwest, and far West were among the first to "give up" on the Christian faith, with the Midwest and central regions of the country now showing signs of following suit. Yes, most of us work on Christian campuses with many students consciously deciding to attend a school where matters of faith will be central to their learning experience. However, most of these same schools admit a percentage of non-Christian students, many of whom are gaining confidence in standing in direct opposition to the faithful influence of their institution. Likewise, all campuses will probably enroll a percentage of students from regions of the country where they have likely grown up experiencing mixed, if not hostile, feelings toward the Christian faith in America.

One can see how this shifting landscape naturally flows into another major factor that speaks of our nation's cultural change: the biblical illiteracy of today's young people. A lethal combination exists of youth programs overly focused on entertaining students, as well as families struggling to incorporate spiritual conversations and practices into their home life. As a result, many of today's students come to campus with minimal exposure to what the Bible says or its intended role in shaping their life.

The natural outcome of these first two factors is what social analysts refer to as the "Rise of the Nones" (Pew Research Center, 2012). If your admissions office keeps track of how enrolling students identify themselves spiritually, they would likely be able to attest to the growing number of students who are checking the "none" box under the question asking about religious affiliation. With a rising cultural acceptance for non-Christians above Christians, plus a lack of faithful foundation from their growing-up years, many of today's students feel the freedom not to pretend to be something they are not—namely, a Christian.

One final point to mention is the trend away from wayward college students returning to the church (and their faith) once they get married and/or begin to have a family. If you have worked on a college or university campus for very long, you have likely encountered Christian individuals who have major concerns about the ways that the university all too often destroys the faith of young students. While much could be said about this point, I only bring it up to say that the trend has long been that those students who do walk away from their faith during the college years eventually make their way back to the church. Whether it was marriage or the start of a family, a major life event not long after college graduation would serve as a re-entry point into the local church and Christian faith.

This same prodigal return is becoming less and less the norm for today's young adults and adolescents who opt out of church life. When and if they make the decision to leave, it is far less likely that they will ever return. This is a group that Barna Group President David Kinnamann has dubbed the "prodigal" (Barna Group, 2013).

Unknown Challenge #3: An Unhelpful Season of Life: Emerging Adulthood
You may have heard about this season of life. It is a relatively new developmental period that has cropped up over the last forty to fifty years between the major life stages of adolescence and adulthood. According to Dr. Jeffrey

Arnett, who first identified and named this new developmental stage, this season of life starts at age eighteen and runs through age twenty-nine (Arnett, 2006). It is a period of life that is most simply defined by a desire to explore and experience newfound freedoms while doing everything possible to avoid the corresponding responsibilities.

Many of the students on our campuses naturally fall into this category—wanting to be given all of the rights and privileges that come with being an adult, while retaining the status of "adolescent" when it comes to expectations and accountability. While the college experience invites some intentional steps toward maturation and adulthood, much of our culture encourages students in this formative season to enjoy "the good life" in every way—and put off any urge to grow up too soon.

Unknown Challenge #4: Unlimited Access to Information—a False Sense of "Knowing"

One final "unknown challenge" worth noting is the shift that has come with regard to information. It used to be that information (related to faith or anything else) was "held" by those in the know. If you wanted "access" to the information, you sought out the company and wisdom of the experts. This information "gap" made mentoring of every kind much more prevalent, primarily because it was necessary for gaining knowledge.

However, with the rise of the Internet and major search engines like Google, mentors are no longer the gatekeepers to information. Today's student has nearly limitless access to information. In mere seconds, they can look up almost anything they want to know. Wherever they are able to pick up a signal or tap into Wi-Fi, they can pursue answers to every question they conjure. This unlimited access to information has created in many students a false sense of knowing. They come to believe that, if they can find the answer on Google in less than sixty seconds, they have all they need.

Although they now have unfettered access to information, my concern is who is helping them understand the information they take in? Who is helping them to discern the good information from the bad?

Are all of these challenges and reservations legitimate? To some degree, yes. However, we must consider what may transpire if we do not act now.

What's at Stake?

In light of these reservations and challenges, we see the future at stake.

Most students are not growing and developing in all the ways they should during their formative college years. They are taking four to six or seven years to have fun, experience the world, figure out life—oh, and amass a lot of debt. Many will then spend as many years of their 20s trying to figure out what they want to do with their life. Once they figure that out, they will get a master's degree if their undergraduate degree has not sufficiently qualified them to do what they now know they want to do.

This prolonged lack of direction is where I believe faith is supposed to make a difference.

Students who do not make faith central to their college years will struggle to understand their education as preparation for a vocation, their relationships as an opportunity to be good stewards of their own heart and the hearts of others, or their decisions as having implications that reach beyond themselves and ultimately implicate them in the in-breaking kingdom of God.

If our students are coming to campus with a faith that lacks foundation and true ownership, one without congruence between belief and lifestyle, we have a short window of time in which to help them consider some of the most profound and life-altering questions (and truths) in the world. This has to happen before they decide to walk away, potentially for good.

Ultimately, it is the future of these students—not to mention our country and our world—that is at stake if we do not do something.

A Call to Action

Mentors, consider the following points as a call to action!

We need to take the initiative. Given everything you have just read, we cannot sit back and wait for students to seek us out. The majority will not come. Instead, we need to go to them.

We need to be people that tend to our own spiritual growth and development. Students need to see Jesus in us, but this will not happen if we are not actively pursuing him in consistent and engaging ways.

We need to model a better way of life. We need to mirror the priorities of God in the ways in which we lead, teach, relate and live. Students should be able to observe our lives and see a noticeable difference from most others in our world—not because we are something special, but because we are living life with God.

As we make our faith in Christ a priority, we will become more aware of the Holy Spirit's moving in our midst, more in tune with how the Spirit is leading us and more sensitive to those with whom the Spirit might want us to connect.

As this happens, our response needs to be willing obedience. We need to take steps of faith as we sense God leading and give him every opportunity to work in others as he works through us.

So where can we start? This is the big question . . .

How Reading Groups Have Worked at Belmont University

While there might be several different ways to initiate or enhance mentoring relationships on your campus, reading groups have proven to be a very easy and effective way to start the conversation with the faculty and staff at Belmont, activate their imaginations, and encourage them to move in this direction.

Extend an Invitation

This is where it begins. It seems altogether too simple, yet it has been working on our campus. As I have extended multiple invitations for interested faculty and staff to come together each semester over the past few years, I have found that each semester draws out individuals who earnestly desire to impact the spiritual lives of their students. An invitation, as opposed to a requirement gives potential mentors the opportunity to join in the conversation on their terms—when it best suits their schedule.

Give Them a Common Text to Think Through and Discuss

I have found that a reading group provides a few significant things: (1) a shared resource for the group to work through; (2) a reference to be revisited in the future; and (3) a clearer understanding of the required time commitment. Our students are not alone in their fear of time commitments. I have found that offering a three- or four-week reading group is much more likely to gain me a healthy number of interested and engaged faculty and staff than will a six- or eight-week study. A shorter time frame not only feels more doable in the midst of a busy academic semester, but it also allows the group to get into the book before deciding together whether a slower pace and a few more gatherings are needed.

In addition, I have found that using a shared text serves to communicate an expectation that each person will read in preparation for each gathering and that members will come ready to both share and learn from others about what they are reading.

Develop a Common Language for Talking about Mentoring and Spiritual Formation on Campus

As these groups continue to come together and work through the text in relation to their specific campus context, they can collaboratively create a common language for describing and understanding their evolving work and role with students. The language serves as a reinforcement of what they are learning, how they are living, and even how they can encourage one another around campus.

An Important Reminder: Students Have Chosen to Attend a Christian Institution

Just as significant as the learning that takes place in these times of shared space and conversation is the collective reminder that we work at a Christian university—serving students who have chosen to attend a Christian university. In many respects, this means that we are given the green light to weave the theme of faith into our conversations in the classroom, office, cafeteria, and other environments.

We do our best to create a space for people to believe what they believe—maintaining a posture of openness and humility—while still sharing what we believe to be the only hope for a lost and hurting world: the Good News of Jesus Christ. I am consistently amazed by the different faculty and staff who thank me for this simple reminder, and our reading groups have proven to provide an excellent space for faculty and staff to explore this reminder together.

Conclusion

The mentoring relationship has long served as a significant vehicle for encouraging growth and maturation in many areas of life whenever individuals have chosen to intentionally give of their time to impart wisdom and understanding to others. These kinds of relationships have become much less common on many college and university campuses in more recent years—in part because of some of the common reservations and lesser-known challenges identified above.

But even considering all of the reservations and challenges, the mentoring relationship is one that we cannot allow to fade into the twilight of history. Instead, we need to be among those who step up and step out in faith—believing that God wants to use us in the lives of those we teach and lead. While this kind of investment should take on a number of different forms, I believe the mentoring relationship must become much more central to our how we approach our role and work with students. I do not want to overstate the role or capacity of potential mentors on campus, but I do not want to understate it either. This is a model of education—discipleship, really—that must be re-introduced to this generation of students!

References

Arnett, J. J. (2006). *Emerging adulthood: Books and articles.* Retrieved from
    http://jeffreyarnett.com/articles.htm
Barna Group. (2013). *Three spiritual journeys of millenni-*
    als. Retrieved from https://www.barna.org/barna-update/
    teens-nextgen/612-three-spiritual-journeys-of-millennials
Elmore, T. (2010). Seven reasons boys struggle: Part Two.
    Growing Leaders. Retrieved from http://growingleaders.com/
    blog/7-reasons-boys-struggle-part-2/
Pew Research Center. (2012). "Nones" on the rise. *Religion and Public*
    Life Project. Retrieved from http://www.pewforum.org/2012/10/09/
    nones-on-the-rise/.

7

CULTIVATING FAITH

Toward a Phenomenological Model
of Spiritual Formation

BILL KUHN

Crown College

Students may describe experiences of spiritual formation as "God rocking my world," or as a "mountaintop experience with God," or sometimes simply, "God met me last night in prayer." Personal and spiritual experiences are complex phenomena that stretch the bounds of ordinary language (James, 2004/1902). Expression of such experiences often revolves around nuanced and metaphorical descriptions.

Still, what life change is occurring in such experiences? What precipitates these experiences, if anything? What exactly does a "spiritually high moment" entail? How does one interpret the ideas of spiritual growth for today's emerging adults? As scholars often remark, the field of spiritual formation lacks a cohesive vocabulary, making investigation of the dynamics of spiritual formation difficult (Estep & Kim, 2010; Thayer, 2004; Tisdell, 1999; Willard, 2002).

Context of the Research

One life stage of particular interest in the study of spiritual formation has recently been labeled as emerging adulthood. The emerging adult years present a unique transition in life from adolescence to adulthood (Arnett, 2006; Robbins & Wilner, 2001; Smith & Snell, 2009). The years from ages eighteen to twenty-nine are mired with identity crisis (Love & Talbot, 1999), searching (Fowler, 1987), career decisions and relationships (Chambers & Parks, 2002). Parks (Chambers & Parks, 2002) stated that she is increasingly concerned for twentysomethings who feel the tension between the expectation to "produce" and the desire for exploration, or to "self-author" their emerging adulthood (p. 21).

The quarter-life crisis (Robbins & Wilner, 2001) that results creates a hunger for transcendence and purpose often framed in the language of "spiritual formation." But, the nature of these formative spiritual experiences is elusive (Milacci, 2006). The nebulous and vague nature of spirituality in the lives of emerging adults can make its assessment indefinite, misleading, or even meaningless. Thus, continued research on the formation of the inner, spiritual lives of emerging adults can help to elucidate the unique elements of this season of life.

This study occurred at a private Midwestern Christian college with a traditional undergraduate population of approximately 600 students. The college is a member of the Council of Christian Colleges and Universities (CCCU), and its mission, values, and strategic initiatives articulate a consistent desire to develop students holistically, including Christian spiritual formation. The mission and vision of this institution include an emphasis on integrating spiritually formative experiences into the academic setting.

The following questions guided this research: How do traditional undergraduate college students at a Midwest Christian college experience Christian spiritual formation?

Rationale for the Study

Much of the spiritual formation research tends to define spirituality according to established constructs then measure the degrees in which such constructs are present in the research subjects (Hall, 2004; Hall, Brokaw,

Edwards, & Pike, 2000; Hall & Edwards, 2002; Hall, Reise, & Haviland, 2007; Thayer, 2004). The result is insufficient narrative and limited exploration of the phenomenon of spiritual formation. More descriptive and narrative investigation may provide a more nuanced understanding of a phenomenon as complex as spiritual development. The use of an interpretive phenomenology of spiritual formation will provide support to higher education professionals seeking to more fully understand the process of spiritual growth.

Definition of Key Terms

Spiritual/Spirituality
"Spiritual" is a notoriously elusive term (Thayer, 2004; Tisdell, 1999; Willard, 2002). The word "spiritual" refers to that which affects the spirit, or the immaterial part of a person (*Merriam-Webster's Collegiate Dictionary*, 11th ed., 2003). For the purposes of this study, spirituality will be understood as a general sense of encounter with something sacred or transcendent (McMinn & Hall, 2000; Otto, 1958), which then influences the person's inner life and shapes the person's core values, beliefs, and behaviors (Tisdell, 1999; Willard, 2002). This definition is narrow enough to exclude some experiences. For example, if the experience leaves no impact on the person's inner life, it can be discarded. Yet, the definition is broad enough to allow a range of experiences from the vantage point of the subjects.

Formation
Formation is the process of growth and development. It assumes movement or change. In spiritual formation literature, this is sometimes referred to as a spiritual journey (Estep & Kim, 2010). Mulholland (1993) famously defines Christian spiritual formation as the process of being conformed into the image of Christ. Willard (2002) indicates that spiritual formation for the Christian is growth caused by the Holy Spirit, which has the effect of transforming the spirit of the person. In phenomenological research, a more open-ended definition is preferred, one that allows a broad enough articulation to incorporate the subject's experiences without definitional

dismissal. As a result, for this study, spiritual "formation" is a growing inner impact or conviction due to encounters with the sacred, which subsequently transforms a person's core values, beliefs, and behaviors (Hill et al., 2000; Otto, 1958). This approach aligns with constructivist phenomenological research methods, which seek to rely "as much as possible on the participants' view of the situation" (Creswell, 2007, p. 20).

Literature Perspectives

Table 1 provides an abbreviated summary of several theories of spiritual formation. To pursue a complete understanding of Christian formation, it is useful to recognize the varied approaches to spiritual formation represented by different academic traditions. As might be expected, differing disciplinary perspectives influence the understandings of spiritual formation. In an effort to avoid potential biases and incomplete evaluations regarding spiritually formative experiences, a composite view that incorporates multiple perspectives offers the richest understanding of the nature of Christian spiritual formation. For the purpose of brevity, this review summarizes and differentiates the literature according to broad categories; however, it should be understood that many scholars do make efforts to represent multiple disciplinary perspectives with their work.

The approaches to spiritual formation summarized here are psychological, educational, theological, and neurological. Table 1 reflects these approaches, provides a sampling of the contributors to the field, and notes some core contributions each offers to the study of spiritual formation.

Table 1

Spiritual Formation: Approaches and Contributions

Spiritual Formation Approach	Contributors	Contributions to Spiritual Formation
Psychological	Edgell (2007) Hall (2004) James (2004/1902) Loder (1989) VanderCreek et al. (2006)	• Relationships • Experiential nature of spiritual formation • Crisis—confronts belief systems

Educational	Astin, Astin, & Lindholm (2011) Fowler (1987) Love & Talbot (1999) Parks (1999) Tisdell (1999, 2006, 2008)	• Spiritual growth as process • Developmental theories • Culturally responsive epistemologies which inform spirituality • Interweaving—rituals, symbols, values • Role of doubt and questioning • Spiral learning—cyclical lessons
Theological	Bowe (2003) Foster (1998) Mulholland (1993) Ortberg (1997) Sittser (2007) Willard (2000)	• Appeal to external authority • Personal growth as active, not passive process • Purgation, illumination, and union • Apophatic vs. kataphatic theologies • Practice of spiritual disciplines
Neurological	Newberg & Waldman (2009) Vaillant (2008)	• Relationship of physical to spiritual condition • Activities that support healthy brain—meditation, exercise, diet, yawning

A holistic or integrative view of spiritual formation, informed by these academic approaches, guided this research project. The contributions offered by these four approaches provided a meaningful foundation for exploring the spiritual formation. Research interview questions incorporated the four approaches in an effort to discover links between the academic fields and foster more nuanced, cross-disciplinary understanding.

The qualitative approach used in this study offered the potential to distill the spiritual "manifestations" that mold one's perspective of spiritual growth. As Tisdell (2008) discusses, there is a need for understanding spiritual formation through different socio-cultural lenses. In keeping with this need, this qualitative analysis of spiritually formative experiences is intended to be a key to advancing a "multilingual" approach to spiritual formation that transcends current categories.

Research Methodology

In phenomenological studies, the researcher "is concerned with the nature, explanation and understanding of phenomena" (Ryan, Coughlan, & Cronin, 2009, p. 309). In such studies, the focus of the research is to glean "in-depth meaning and processes" of a designated phenomenon (Ryan et al., 2009, p. 309); thus, it is important that each research participant purports to having experienced the phenomenon under investigation.

The population for this study consisted of traditional, undergraduate students at the participating college. Most of the approximately 600 students (80.3 percent) hail from the Upper Midwest. Participants were selected based on recommendations from student development professionals at the college. The researcher conducted an orientation interview with the candidates to survey their interest in and availability for the study. The researcher then secured twelve participants divided according to a maximum variation sampling strategy. This resulted in an equal mix of male and female participants, a favorable distribution across class rank (two freshmen, three sophomores, four juniors, three seniors), and students representing six different majors.

Data for this research were generated using semi-structured individual interviews with the participants. The researcher designed an interview protocol that was subsequently validated by content experts. Data gathering included an iterative process of interview and analysis (Ryan et al., 2009). Member checks and validation of themes by multiple coders minimized bias and enhanced the likelihood of obtaining consistently reliable data (DiCicco-Bloom & Crabtree 2006). Member checks were conducted by sending transcripts of interviews to each participant to secure that the transcript accurately represented what they intended to say.

Consent forms for each participant were completed after careful explanation of the purpose and procedures. Semi-structured interviews were conducted with each participant in a private setting allowing maximum freedom for each participant to recall his or her spiritual formation experience.

Data Coding and Analysis

Auerbach and Silverstein's (2003) five-step process for manuscript analysis guided the method of analysis for this research. This process includes: reducing text to only that which is relevant; cataloguing repeating ideas; grouping themes into clusters and constructs; linking constructs to literature data; and organizing constructs into a theoretical narrative. The data were collected and analyzed concurrently in an iterative process enabling the researcher to adjust or augment the interview questions, if necessary.

This also allowed the researcher to determine when data saturation was achieved. Member-checked transcripts were analyzed with the help of *QSR NVivo* software to tag and manage data points. Theme clusters were identified with the assistance of two trained coders (Creswell, 2007).

Research Findings

Analysis of the interview data revealed six core themes. Themes were confirmed and defined in consultation with two external coders. Table 2 displays the six major themes, provides descriptive definitions of these themes, and presents related literature.

Table 2

Major Themes in Phenomenology of Spiritual Formation

Theme	Definition	Related Literature
1. Spiritual dissonance	The conscious inadequacy of the familiar in the life of the student. A memorable spiritual experience in which spiritual discord occurs from life circumstances. These situations cause internal disequilibrium that seeks stasis.	Astin et al. (2011) Edgell (2007) Loder (1989) Love & Talbot (1999) Sandage & Shults (2007) Sittser (2007) Tisdell (2008) VandeCreek et al. (1995)
2. Spiritual disciplines	Exercises performed by students in a search for the sacred and in order to grow spiritually. These consist of such practices as reading of the Scriptures, prayer, solitude, and silence.	Foster (1998) Kauffman (2005) Moreland (2007) Nouwen (1981) Ortberg (1997) Piper (1997) Willard (2000)
3. Kinship systems	Personal relationships in the lives of students that provide interpretation to spiritual experiences and resiliency in life.	Bednarowski (2006) Boers (2005) Chambers & Parks (2002) Gangel (1999) Greer (2007) Kauffman (2005) Ma (2003) Reisz (2003)
4. Humble submission	Experience whereby students consciously "surrender" in humility before God. This is an acknowledgment of the student's finiteness and God's sovereignty.	Astin et al. (2011) James (2004/1902) Sandage & Shults (2007) Sittser (2007)

5. Affective transformation	Renewed affective dimensions in the lives of students as a result of spiritually significant experiences. Consists of heightened joy, hope, and gratitude.	Astin et al. (2011) Lewis (1955) Vaillant (2008)
6. Reconceptualization of God	A student's view of God is challenged during seasons of spiritual dissonance and is resolved to a new concept of God.	Boers (2005) Fee & Ingram (2004) Ma (2003)

Theme One: Spiritual Dissonance

The most consistent and pervasive reality of the students' spiritual formation was the experience of spiritual dissonance. While the source of the dissonance was unique for each student, the presence of a transforming trial in each student's life was not. One quiet, reflective, and articulate student summarized the outcome of these disorienting moments as producing an inner "look" upward, as he stated:

> I would loosely define almost any spiritually formative experience or time in my life as a time of stress at its best, or at its worst, desperation or frustration. Whenever somebody hits the wall, I think, in terms of their own abilities or their own aspirations or plans and everything kind of falls apart; I think in those moments people, including myself, begin to—instead of looking forward or around—we start to look upward.

Spiritual dissonance seems to surface in doubt and questioning for students. Doubting appears frequently during the participant's disorienting moments. Elena, who experienced uncertainty in her life during her episode with cancer, spoke of the ongoing reality of doubt in her spiritual growth:

> Doubts on "God are you going to provide a job for me? Should I really have been doing this field?" All of these different questions and doubts. And I think that they've made me explore what it really means to truly trust in God.

Cloe, a sophomore Christian ministries major, remarked,

> I don't love the [spiritually] dry times when I'm in them, but I love them when I'm out of them because I can look back and see everything

that [God] did do in that. That's where I can see that most of the lessons I've learned have been in those times.

Fowler (1987) wrote that revealed inconsistencies in beliefs and practices are
necessary to force critical reflection on a person's life during the emerging
adult years. Such reflection develops an individual's personal responsibility
and ownership of their faith. Hall (2010) noted in his research with college
students that suffering is a catalyst for spiritual growth. Hall (2010) proposed that trials "shake up our expectations of God," which prompt new
discovery of one's faith (p. 16). Love and Talbot (1999) added that spiritual
formation is a process that is "punctuated by crises" (p. 370).

Theme Two: Spiritual Disciplines

The phenomenon of spiritual growth for students often involved reaching
out to God via spiritual disciplines. Students referenced a number of spiritual exercises, including prayer, Scripture reading, journaling, solitude,
fasting, and silence. For example, when Elena encountered unexpected
health issues, she turned to journaling:

> I literally got out a notebook and wrote "vertical ventilations" on it and
> started just throughout that year and the rest of the process, writing
> out whenever I was frustrated with God and kind of learning to bring
> that to him realizing how little control I had.

She also turned to the Bible, saying trials "cause me to spend more time
in [God's] word and be looking for his truth and his affirmation especially
on days where I'm feeling like just a lot of doubts."

Grace, a student leader on campus, turned to disciplines in her time
of distress.

> My understanding of what God was telling me didn't happen until I
> took a time of solitude, just to pray and work through stuff. I guess
> just being able to have alone time with God without the potential to be
> interrupted and having silence, less distraction, being able to just pro-
> cess things and talk to God about them for a longer period of time.

These students describe spiritual disciplines as a foundational contributor to spiritual growth. Foster (1998) contends that spiritual exercises

introduce people to God's resources for life, thus providing a means for inner-life growth.

Theme Three: Kinship System

Drawing from Stack's ethnographic study in the mid-1970's called "All My Kin," Greer (2007) asserted that poor families survive due to a "richly complex system of kinship" (p. 12). This system provides a sense of identity and belonging that results in resiliency in its members. Hall's (2010) research with college students found that relationships were the highest-ranking contributor to a student's spiritual formation. These student interviews revealed similar findings.

Cloe stated,

> There's something about someone who is older than you and that they can have coming in from the outside. And how over a year how close you can become to someone and how especially now during this time [at college] we need the advice from someone older than us.

It appears that students view the work of God in other people's lives as a possible template for God's work in their own lives. Jad experienced his own season of doubt; when asked what encouraged him through the season, he remarked, "Seeing God's hand in other people's lives . . . just over and over seeing God provide for friends who couldn't financially make it to [the college], including myself." Jad concluded, "It's just easy for us to lose track of even our own experiences. So it was nice to have guys like [the professor] to be able to go to."

Theme Four: Humble Submission

The interview data revealed a pattern of humble submission on the part of the participants, which they describe as integral to their spiritually formative experiences. As articulated by students, this humble submission involves a conscious moment of surrender to God. Word frequency analysis revealed that students used the words *submit* or *surrender* and their conjugates eighty-seven times in the twelve interviews.

Jon spoke of struggling with identity issues then declared,

That's a wall experience where I hit a wall and I'm frustrated and then
I finally surrender and then I get to go over the wall and there's a peace
of knowing that I don't need to know everything and I don't need to be
able to do everything.

Grace, speaking about the escalating responsibilities of college life and the
accompanying dissonance, shared this comment:

When things didn't go the way I was planning, I knew it was because
I was trying to do things my own way. And when I was completely
drained and exhausted . . . in those times when I was legitimately
without strength, I just was totally confident that God would bring me
through. And I was totally even more surrendered to that fact that it
wasn't going to be because of me and my great strength and abilities.

James (2004/1902) postulated that religion "consists of the belief that
there is an unseen order, and that our supreme good lies in harmoniously
adjusting ourselves thereto. This belief and this adjustment are the religious
attitude in the soul" (p. 57). What James considered "adjustment" might be
similar to what is here called "humble submission."

Theme Five: Affective Transformation

The affective domain consists of a person's attitudes, dispositions, and
emotions. C. S. Lewis (1955), writing in his autobiography *Surprised by Joy,*
described the experience of joy as a signpost of genuine spiritual experiences. Data from this research confirmed this sentiment. Research participants referred to a life of joy, hope, peace, and thankfulness. All twelve
students spoke of these features in their faith narrative.

Liam told of the time when he felt called into ministry after a mission
trip. It was a time of awe and wonder:

I played guitar and bass at the worship team at my church that
night—it was the day after I got back from my missions trip to Costa
Rica—and all the equipment just stopped working—all the amps, the
sound system, and everything. So we were just like "all right, well we
will just sit in a circle and practice acoustic." And the sun was shining
in just the right way. And that's just the kind of stuff I remember. And
I just felt God's presence so strong there. And that was the first time I

had really felt his presence. I just had this awesome feeling that is completely indescribable.

Asked to explain the "awesome feeling" of the presence of God, Liam remarked, "I would associate hope with it. And I feel a lot of it comes with that joy, so I'm optimistic and I'm just really sensitive to spiritual things."

When asked to summarize what was described as a night of wrestling with God, Cloe remarked, "I remember thinking that I just had a peace that I hadn't had in a really long time. I felt God's presence for the first time in a really long time." Asked to elaborate, Cloe added, "Just my peace that I had that morning was so—peace almost filled with joy."

Willard (2002) refers to "love, joy, and peace" as the "three fundamental dimensions" that are common to Christian maturity and gives specific instructions for cultivating them into one's life (p. 128). Such declarations indicate the blossoming fruit of the Spirit in the lives of students (Gal. 5:22–23).

Theme Six: Reconceptualization of God

Analysis of the interview transcripts revealed that a student's spiritual experience represents a challenge to the student's concept of God, resolving to a new perspective of God. The phenomenon of spiritual formation causes students to amend their understanding and vision of God.

Centurion relayed a moment in his life of kneeling under the stars in an act of surrender. When asked about the difference that experience had on his spiritual life, he revealed,

> So it is with God with spiritual formation, and these spiritual experiences so to speak, that as God takes me through some of these things, sometimes I'm wrong about Him, but more often than not, it's understanding Him more. Something I hadn't understood before and now I see at a deeper level.

Note the discovery expressed by Elena, "I think [God] humbles us sometimes, and we realize how big and powerful God is when he pulls us out of a pit that we've gotten ourselves into." She continued:

> Experiences that God has taught me something through have an effect on how I would describe God. Sometimes he is healer to me,

sometimes he is friend, and sometimes he is Father, just based on what
he has been teaching me. Sometimes I need to remember he is a for-
giver. So I think those moments that I have had spiritual growth have
been moments where I have had a clearer understanding of God.

As voiced by students, spiritually formative experiences include a spiritual
dissonance that challenged their spiritual equilibrium. Inconsistencies and
contradictions in a student's spiritual assumptions gave rise to internal
conflict. Given this inward dissonance, students sought solace and understanding via spiritual disciplines and kinship networks. Students seem to
be scanning for interpretive clues to release the tension of the dissonance.
Eventually, these experiences led to critical moments of humble surrender.
The enduring impact of these experiences resulted in transformed affective
dimensions in the lives of students—renewed peace, hope, and gratitude.
The overarching impact of the spiritual formation process was an altered
concept of God whereby the student's vision of God was enlarged and
embraced, providing a greater sense of spiritual equilibrium.

Toward a Phenomenological Model of Spiritual Formation
The preceding description of spiritually formative experiences in the lives
of college students reflects the interconnectedness of the six themes, thus,
raising the question, "Do the data themes expose a discernible pattern
of spiritual formational experiences?" Models must be offered cautiously
because they may reduce attention to the phenomenon being studied.
Further, models of human experiences should be proposed with an understanding that such models are imperfect in their capacity to capture a
dynamic reality and present it in ways discernible to others and useful for
future research. Keeping this in mind, the data does seem to indicate relationships among the themes. Figure 1 represents the observed relationship
among the data themes.

Figure 1 depicts a linear correspondence of the themes of spiritual formation. The problem is that it seems to decouple the salient components of
what students describe as a fluid, almost ineffable experiential reality. The
arrows indicate the general sequence of experience for students. The dotted
line connecting spiritual disciplines with kinship systems and affective

transformation with reconceptualization of God reveals a concurrent experience that often interrelates.

Figure 1

Relationship of Spiritual Formation Themes

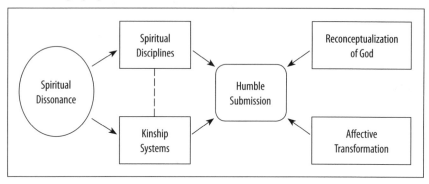

Table 3 reveals four phases to the spiritual formation phenomenon derived from the emerging themes. It suggests that the themes exist in a linear relationship. While signifying the relationship of the noted themes, the model appears static and lacks the fluidity and dynamic of human experiences.

Table 3

Model Titles and Themes

MODEL TITLE	Disorientation	Exploration (spiritual inputs)	Capitulation	Reorientation (spiritual outcomes)
THEME	• Spiritual dissonance	• Spiritual disciplines • Kinship systems	• Humble submission	• Affective transformation • Reconceptualization of God

The emerging model captures the six themes into four movements of the spiritual experience. In order to portray the model as more dynamic and fluid, which conforms better to the reality of human experience, Figure 2 depicts the model as a cycle.

The dynamic of this model reveals that the entire phenomenon of spiritual formation is asynchronous, fluid, overlapping, and cyclical.

Figure 2

Model of the Phenomenon of Spiritual Formation

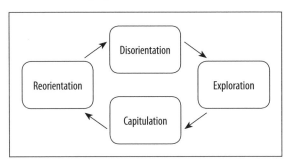

Brief Comparison with Other Theories

This model of spiritual formation intersects with other theories in the field of human development, particularly the concept of disorientation moving toward reorientation. For example, Piaget's (1977) theory of cognitive development is built upon the concept that cognitive disequilibrium stimulates or motivates growth that subsequently allows equilibrium to be restored. This pattern is very similar to the experience of the students in this study whose sense of disorientation moved them to take action that would reestablish their sense of stability or equilibrium.

Clinton's (1988) theory of leadership development includes periods of testing and experiences of isolation and struggle during a phase Clinton refers to as the "Inner Growth Phase" that corresponds to the disorientation found in the experiences of students. Following this, Clinton notes that "leaders reach out to other leaders," not unlike the search for solace in kinship networks during the exploration phase in the proposed model (p. 45). Clinton also refers to the need for submission to authority and concludes his model with a "convergence" phase in which the leader integrates life's experience into fulfilling and effective leadership practices.

Fowler (1987) identified a critical phase of development in the emerging adult years, which he titled the Individuative-Reflective stage. In this stage of development, students reconsider and even reject prior beliefs. Contradictions in life and faith emerge that cause students to probe and form new commitments in an effort to individualize their spirituality. Parks (1999) found that during the emerging adult years the need for self-selected mentors is vital for processing one's faith and finding meaning in the midst of contradiction and reassessment of childhood beliefs. The treatment of spiritual formation offered by Fowler and Parks corroborates certain elements of the proposed model and lends credibility to the findings.

Discussion

One fascinating consideration is the relative lack of themes commonly associated with religious life. Multiple explanations for the absence of these topics in the student testimonies can be made, many of which are self-evident. However, it is worth noting as we seek to discern the meaning of spiritual formation in the lives of emerging adults.

Spiritual Formation and Organized Religion

It is curious that students describing their spiritual formation experiences rarely conversed about their church experience. This is not to say that church experience was insignificant; it simply did not get much mention. A few students spoke of childhood or adolescent experiences at church, and these comments were favorable. Researchers consistently discuss the relationship and differences between spirituality and organized religion, with religion designated as the formalized practices of spirituality and faith (Hill et. al., 2000; McMinn & Hall, 2000; Tisdell, 2008). The participants' lack of comments regarding formal religion and church when discussing significant spiritual experiences may reinforce that dichotomy. However, since the focus of the research and the interview questions was on the exploration of personal spiritual experiences, deductions about relationships between spiritual formation and organized religion should be made cautiously.

How should one interpret the absence of church references in students' narratives? One might question, should college personnel reinforce the role of the church in life of the Christian? Or, is this perhaps a result of the American evangelical emphasis on "discovering one's personal relationship with Jesus"? These questions are worthy of further exploration by future researchers and professionals in higher education. And such explorations will be needed if we are to form reliable conclusions regarding these issues.

Spiritual Formation and Social Behavior

A second fascinating omission from the data regards issues of personal moral or social behavior and its relationship to student growth. To be certain, mention of spiritual disciplines represents behaviors such as prayer and journaling. However, absent from the discussion are matters commonly associated with fundamentalism and personal piety. Students did not talk about spiritual growth in terms of what media to avoid or what social practices to dodge. For example, no one mentioned sobriety as a contributor to his or her spiritual development, neither as a means to spiritual formation or as evidence of it. This is interesting in so far as such behaviors have often been associated with organized religion and have been a source of assessment of genuine spirituality. Students were more interested in exploring the inner stirrings of the soul, spiritual dispositions, and affective realities of their faith than considering the importance of adherence to prescribed behaviors.

Although omissions from the data are of interest and worthy of discussion, they do not allow the formation of conclusions. While such ancillary findings may be revealing and represent interesting avenues for further research, arguments from silence may reflect more on the research methodology and context than credible data findings. Therefore, while fascinating to consider and worthy of discussion, omissions in phenomenological data warrant a measured response.

Implications for Student Development Professionals

The proposed model for spiritual formation elucidates potential fields whereby higher education professionals can influence students' spiritual lives. While higher education professionals cannot manipulate the outcomes of affective transformation or reconceptualizing of God, other elements of the proposed model do present opportunities for critical reflection on practices that prompt spiritual formation. The following suggestions are offered to stimulate thoughtful campus practices that will best promote spiritual formation.

Spiritual Dissonance

Students consistently revealed a pattern of experiencing spiritual dissonance on the pathway to development. Higher education professionals should seek to create a culture that fosters authenticity, even in—or especially during—life's difficult times. Parks (1999) speaks of the gift of a mentoring culture that allows college students freedom to ask penetrating questions and find solace alongside experienced mentors.

Students need safe places in which they can explore and receive support as they seek to interpret their disorienting experiences. Campus resources such as convocations, school newspapers, dorm meetings, and other similar venues can be meaningful forums for discussion of the realities and responses to life's hardships. If the elements of this model are shown to be common experiences in the journey toward spiritual maturity, students may more quickly embrace and explore them in their own lives. With honest and vulnerable leadership, a campus atmosphere hospitable to hurting students can emerge. Such a community will greatly aid the spiritual development of students.

Kinship Systems

The data revealed that students seek kinship systems in times of spiritual turbulence. College professionals would be wise to provide opportunities and network systems to foster nurturing relationships. For kinship support, colleges may provide mentoring programs, life coaching, discipleship opportunities, and small discussion groups. Training mentors in the realities of spiritual formation, how to ask probing questions, the role of dissonance in the spiritual life, and other relevant topics could promote more meaningful mentoring interactions. Mentors and life coaches need to be encouraged to express vulnerability and authenticity in an effort to create rapport with students. Such rapport will encourage a culture of spiritual authenticity and provide support and validation for students living with the tension of spiritual dissonance.

Spiritual Disciplines

College leaders should reinforce and promote engagement in spiritual disciplines consistent with the exploration of students during the disorientation period. Spiritual disciplines could be explored via prayer groups, Scripture lessons, silent retreats, and times of solitude. Promoting such activities in small initiatives, such as dorm floor events, or in large group gatherings, such as campus-wide invitations to prayer, will offer students both a model and an opportunity to personally explore these potentially unfamiliar exercises. Colleges and universities could establish spaces on campus for students to find solitude and silence. Prayer rooms, for example, could be set aside for students to retreat for prayer and meditation. Such spaces not only create a location for retreat but also symbolically affirm the need for spiritual exercises in people's lives.

Further, institutions could appoint or recruit a team of students to sponsor creative programming for spiritual disciplines. This team would have oversight of events and be responsible for providing literature that would aid others in their development of personal spiritual disciplines. Newspaper articles, brochures, blog sites, and Facebook pages could be developed to inspire students to deepen their engagement in spiritual disciplines. Familiarity with these practices before entering a season of spiritual dissonance will help to anchor a student when such dissonance arrives.

Conclusion

This study represents an exploration of the question, "What is the experience of spiritual formation in the lives of traditional, undergraduate college students at a Midwest, Christian college?" Given the limited presence of qualitative research in the field of spiritual formation, a phenomenological and narrative model of research was utilized to discover themes of spiritual formation. As a result, a four-movement model of spiritual formation experiences was presented along with implications for practice.

Spiritual formation epitomizes humanity's attempt to honor their sense of the transcendent and to discover a sacred purpose for life. The complexities of one's inner life and the noble search for significance deserve utmost attention from those who aspire to nurture students. This research represents a modest effort to honor that life and that search.

References

Arnett, J. (2006). *Emerging adulthood: The winding roads from the late teens through the twenties.* New York, NY: Oxford Press.

Astin, A., Astin, D., & Lindholm, J. (2011). *Cultivating the spirit: How college can enhance students' inner lives.* San Francisco, CA: Jossey-Bass.

Auerbach, C. F., & Silverstein, L. B. (2003). *Qualitative data: An introduction to coding and analysis.* New York, NY: NYU Press.

Bednarowski, M. (2006). Minding the spirit: The study of Christian spirituality. *Church History, 75*(2), 479–481.

Boers, A. (2005). So much more: An invitation to Christian spirituality. *Christian Century, 122*(8), 39–40.

Bowe, B. (2003). *Biblical foundations of spirituality: Touching a finger to the flame.* Lanham, MD: Rowman & Littlefield.

Chambers, T., & Parks, S. (2002, November-December). Helping students find their place and purpose. *About Campus,* 20–24.

Clinton, R. (1988). *The making of a leader.* Colorado Springs, CO: NavPress.

Creswell, J. (2007). *Qualitative inquiry and research design* (2nd ed.). Thousand Oaks, CA: Sage.

DiCicco-Bloom, B., & Crabtree, B. (2006). The qualitative research interview. *Medical Education, 40,* 314–321.

Edgell, M. (2007). Afrocentric Christian worldview and student spiritual development: Tapping a global stream of knowledge. *Journal of Education and Christian Belief, 11*(1), 49–62.

Estep, J., & Kim, J. (2010). *Christian formation: Integrating theology & human development.* Nashville, TN: B&H Publishing Group.

Fee, J., & Ingram, J. (2004). Correlation of the Holy Spirit questionnaire with the spiritual well-being scale and the spiritual assessment inventory. *Journal of Psychology and Theology, 32*(2), 104–114.

Fowler, J. (1987). *Faith development and pastoral care.* Minneapolis, MN: Fortress Press.

Foster, R. (1998). *Celebration of discipline: The path to spiritual growth.* San Francisco, CA: Harper.

Gangel, J. (1999). *Facilitating spiritual formation at Toccoa Falls College.* (Unpublished doctoral dissertation). Dallas Theological Seminary, Dallas, TX.

Greer, E. (2007). Single mothers' transition to self-sufficiency. *Occupational Therapy in Mental Health, 23*(3/4), 7–23. doi:10.1300/J004v23n03_02

Hall, T. (2004). Christian spirituality and mental health: A relational spirituality paradigm for empirical research. *Journal of Psychology and Christianity, 23*(1), 66–81.

Hall, T. (Fall 2010). Christianity at a Crossroads. *Biola Magazine,* 16–19.

Hall, T., Brokaw, B., Edwards, K., & Pike, P. (2000). An empirical exploration of psychoanalysis and religion: Spiritual maturity and object relations development. *Journal for the Scientific Study of Religion, 41*(2) 303–313.

Hall, T., & Edwards, K. (2002). The spiritual assessment inventory: A theistic model and measure for assessing spiritual development. *Journal for the Scientific Study of Religion, 41*(2), 341–357.

Hall, T., Reise, S., & Haviland, M. (2007). An item response theory analysis of the spiritual assessment inventory. *The International Journal for the Psychology of Religion, 17*(2), 157–178.

Hill, P., Pargament, K., Hood, R., Jr., McCullough, M., Swyers, J., Larson, D., & Zinnbauer, B. (2000). Conceptualizing religion and spirituality: Points of commonality, points of departure. *Journal for the Theory of Social Behavior, 30*, 51–77.

James, W. (2004). *The varieties of religious experience.* New York, NY: Barnes and Noble Books. (Original work published 1902).

Kauffman, R. (2005). Anxious souls will ask . . . : The Christ-centered spirituality of Dietrich Bonhoeffer. *Christian Century, 122*(7), 30–30.

Lewis, C. S. (1955). *Surprised by joy.* Orlando, FL: Harcourt Brace & Company.

Loder, J. (1989). *The transforming moment* (2nd ed.). Colorado Springs, CO: Helmers & Howard Publishers.

Love, P., & Talbot, D. (1999). Defining spiritual development: A missing consideration for student affairs. *NASPA Journal, 37*(1), 361–375.

Ma, S. (2003). The Christian college experience and the development of spirituality among students. *Christian Higher Education, 2*, 321–339.

Milacci, F. (2006). Moving towards faith: An inquiry into spirituality in adult education. *Christian Higher Education,* 211–233.

McMinn, M., & Hall, T. (2000). Christian spirituality in a postmodern era. *Journal of Psychology and Theology, 28*(4), 251–253.

Moreland, J. (2007). *Kingdom triangle: Recover the Christian mind, renovate the soul, restore the spirit's power.* Grand Rapids, MI: Zondervan.

Mulholland Jr., M. (1993). *Invitation to a journey.* Downers Grove, IL: InterVarsity Press.

Newberg, A., & Waldman, M. (2009). *How God changes your brain.* New York, NY: Ballantine Books.

Nouwen, H. (1981). *The way of the heart.* New York, NY: HarperCollins.

Otto, R. (1958). *The idea of the holy.* London, UK: Oxford University Press.

Ortberg, J. (1997). *The life you always wanted.* Grand Rapids, MI: Zondervan.

Parks, Sharon. (1999). *The critical years.* San Francisco, CA: Jossey-Bass.

Piaget, J. (1977). *The development of thought: Equilibrium in cognitive structures.* New York, NY: Viking Press.

Piper, J. (1997). *A hunger for God.* Wheaton, IL: CrossWay Books.

Reisz, H. (2003). Assessing spiritual formation in Christian seminary communities. *Theological Education, 39*(2), 29–40.

Robbins, A., & Wilner, A. (2001). *Quarterlife crisis.* New York, NY: Penquin Putnam.

Ryan, F., Coughlan, M., & Cronin, P. (2009). Interviewing in qualitative research: The one-to-one interview. *International Journal of Therapy and Rehabilitation, 16*(6), 309–314.

Sandage, S., & Shults, F. (2007). Relational spirituality and transformation: A relational integration model. *Journal of Psychology and Christianity, 26*(3), 261–269.

Sittser, G. (2007). *Water from a deep well: Christian spirituality from early martyrs to modern missionaries.* Downers Grove, IL: InterVarsity Press.

Smith, C. & Snell, P. (2009). *Souls in Transition: The religious and spiritual lives of emerging adults.* New York, NY: Oxford University Press.

Thayer, J. (2004). Constructing a spirituality measure based on learning theory: The Christian spiritual participation profile. *Journal of Psychology and Theology, 23*(3), 195–207.

Tisdell, E. (1999, Winter). The spiritual dimension of adult development. *New Directions for Adult and Continuing Education, 84,* 87–95.

Tisdell, E. (2006). Spirituality, cultural identity, and epistemology in culturally responsive teaching in higher education. *Multicultural Perspectives, 3,* 19–25.

Tisdell, E. (2008, Fall). Spirituality and adult learning. *New Directions for Adult and Continuing Education,* 27–36.

Vaillant, G. (2008). *Spiritual evolution.* New York, NY: Broadway Books.

Willard, D. (2000). Spiritual formation in Christ: A perspective on what it is and how it might be done. *Journal of Psychology & Theology, 28*(4), 254–258.

Willard, D. (2002). *Renovation of the heart.* Colorado Springs, CO: NavPress.

8

WHAT'S WRONG WITH "MEANING MAKING" TO DESCRIBE FAITH?

The Problem with Sharon Daloz Parks's Kantian Assumptions for Student Development

STEPHEN W. RANKIN

Southern Methodist University

Sharon Daloz Parks has been a leading theorist on young adult faith development for a generation. She is referenced, for example, in *How College Affects Students* (Pascarella & Terenzini, 2005), a compilation of research often used as a standard textbook in student development courses. Sean J. Gehrke's (2013) essay on race and pro-social involvement credits Parks with significantly helping to prompt his research interest as a scholar. Jenny L. Small's (2011) examination of methodological weakness in understanding the diversity of student spirituality also indicates the ongoing relevance of Parks's work. Though Small's project offers a critique and states her concern for Parks's overdependence on Christian ideas, it still acknowledges her influence.

Parks's well-known book, *Big Questions Worthy Dreams: Mentoring Emerging Adults in Their Search for Meaning, Purpose, and Faith* (hereafter referred to as *Big Questions*) was originally published in 2000. It has been revised and was rereleased in a tenth anniversary edition in 2011, giving it another round of exposure to scholars and practitioners. This work has been especially influential among chaplains, campus ministers, and other student affairs professionals who work in so-called mainline Protestant colleges and universities because it provides an expansive and dynamic concept of faith. Furthermore, the concept of faith as presented by Parks seems to make sense of and provide meaningful guidance for interacting with students in a nonsectarian environment. In *Big Questions,* the central concept is that faith is "meaning making." In thinking of faith in this way, Parks accepts Immanuel Kant's epistemological boundary between knowable objects of experience (*phenomena*) and their true nature ("things in themselves" or *noumena*), which are not humanly knowable. This starting point provides grounds for Parks to downplay dogma as of secondary importance and to suggest that it easily becomes counterproductive in the faith development of college students.

Parks's (2011) view of faith poses a largely unrecognized dilemma for schools affiliated with Protestant denominations known (anachronistically) as "mainline" and "nonsectarian."[1] How do such schools, as a matter of integrity, authentically represent the church affiliation and contribute to the church's mission? On the other hand, how do the schools avoid what may appear to many in the academy as arbitrary and artificial constraints and thereby uphold and protect academic freedom? Furthermore, college and university communities are made up of people with a wide range of beliefs and faith traditions. This diversity seems to call for any downplaying religious particularity of the school in order to provide an inclusive and effective educational environment. This in turn creates a dilemma for institutions as they seek to determine how much of the church identity should "show" and by what means they should balance that identity with their commitment to academic values.

---

[1] Though "nonsectarian" can cover a range of descriptions, it usually means that schools do not require any religion-related activities such as compulsory chapel attendance or mandatory doctrine-specific academic courses.

In this context, Parks's (2011) approach to faith development seems eminently reasonable and a good fit for these types of schools. It offers what is taken to be an intellectually sound way of supporting faith development, which purportedly helps to maintain the church affiliation, yet steers clear of allowing control by the sponsoring church's dogmatic beliefs. It fits well with the growing literature on spirituality in higher education, especially the writings that resolutely distinguish spirituality from religious faith.

This chapter aims to criticize that view. I will argue that Parks's (2011) definition of faith as meaning making, governed as it is by a Kantian epistemology, unwarrantedly mixes a descriptive account of the dynamic psychological processes in faith development with a normative stance regarding religious dogma. She thus has supplanted one set of (religious) dogmatic assumptions with what has become—in many quarters since Kant—another (philosophical) dogmatic assumption about religious knowledge or theological claims. Although many Christians who hold to clear, orthodox boundaries could readily decry an attitude that rigidly forecloses on belief exploration, Parks's use of "dogma" does not keep this distinction clear. As her argument unfolds, it consistently holds this term in a negative light without qualifying how we are to understand her usage in those places. An uncritical acceptance of this approach, therefore, may cause student development professionals to misread the quality of students' faith development and more generally create undue suspicion of institutional promotion of a sponsoring church's theological claims.

This chapter will first summarize Parks's (2011) definition of "faith" and related concepts, followed by an analysis of her use of the term "dogma." To support the separation of faith and dogma, she leans especially on the historical spadework of Wilfred Cantwell Smith. The chapter will then turn to an analysis of the relevant aspects of Immanuel Kant's thought and, using work by Nicholas Wolterstorff (1998), will show the appropriateness of questioning a central feature of that thought, which opens an avenue for criticizing Parks's characterization of dogma. Once we see that Parks's starting point is assailable, her conclusions about dogma can also be challenged. This challenge contains important implications for student faith development and provides a means for religiously affiliated schools to reconsider their relationship with the sponsoring church.

"Faith" as "Meaning Making"

As noted above, the basic term for "faith" in *Big Questions* is "meaning making." Parks (2011) describes meaning making in the following manner:

> The activity of composing a sense of the connections among things: a sense of pattern, order, form, and significance. To be human is to seek coherence and correspondence. To be human is to want to be oriented to one's surroundings. To be human is to desire relationship among the disparate elements of existence. (p. 27)

From this dense description come several tantalizing questions. First, we note the ambiguous phrase "composing a sense of connections among things." How does one "compose" a "sense"? The gerund suggests conscious, reflective action, analogous to constructing. The meaning for "sense" is harder to discern. If we take "sense" as akin to the phrase "making sense of," it stands consistent with the activity of composing and directs one's attention to the formal, psychological process of meaning composition. However, Parks builds this exposition on Wilfred Cantwell Smith's etymological distinction between "faith" and "belief." Faith is experiential, emanating in certain dispositions like loyalty, trust, and commitment. It precedes belief experientially and logically. "Belief," on the other hand, fixes on the cognitive, on intellectual assent with certain ideas that help one understand the experience of faith (Parks, 2011). Faith is primary. Belief is secondary. "Composing a sense of connections" allows Parks to lean more heavily on the "faith" part of Smith's distinction and prepares the ground for Parks's subsequent hesitance about dogma (pp. 24–26).

Another step in Parks's (2011) argument (following Smith's lead) is to note the universality or commonality of the experience (or psychological activity) of faith, whereas people differ dramatically regarding belief. By this reasoning, we should see dogma, then, as of secondary importance in faith development. In this way, she can find common ground—even common experiences—recognizable by people of differing belief systems, therefore opening up the possibility of more peaceful relations in a world riven by ideological and religious conflicts. This approach seems to fit very well on college campuses that have no faith-based requirements and that aim to avoid the privileging of any particular approach to faith.

Meaning making is such a critical feature of young adult development that Parks (2011) says, with a good deal of urgency, "We human beings are unable to survive, and certainly cannot thrive, unless we can make meaning" (p. 9). Parks sees this aspect of young adult development as of such importance that she uses forceful terms: "[The] central work of young, emerging adulthood . . . [lies] in the experience of the birth of critical awareness and consequently in the *dissolution and recomposition* of the meaning of self, other, world, and 'God'" (p. 8).

Again, questions arise. What does she mean by "dissolution and recomposition"? Clearly, these words imply Parks's (2011) dynamic view of faith, but even if one accepts this dynamism, does it require thinking of the process as dissolution and recomposition? Taking note of Parks's reference to the "birth of critical awareness," the phrase calls to mind how she positions her contribution to emerging adult faith development relative to the 1981 work of her mentor and doctoral advisor, James Fowler. In his *Stages of Faith* he wrote that, during the early to mid-twenties, young people are challenged to make the transition from stage three faith (synthetic-conventional) to stage four (individuative-reflective) (Fowler, 1981). This movement takes the young person from being "authority bound" to being aware of competing truth claims (various forms of relativism) to having convictional commitment or convictional knowledge (Parks, 2011). We can anticipate Parks's concern about dogma in this description of the psychological process of dynamic faith. From her viewpoint, dogma tends to leave young people "stuck" in stage three, in unthinking acceptance of traditional teachings without gaining appropriate self-awareness and grappling with life's complexities.

Given that faith seeks to make meaning of life and that spirituality and religion lie at the heart of such efforts, we sense the inevitable pull toward theological questions. Parks (2011) wants to hold them at bay. Every time she makes reference to "God," she puts the word within quotation marks as a way of signaling the "fraughtness" of the word, how it means different things to different faiths and peoples. To anticipate briefly what the next section of this chapter explores, we thus encounter a fundamental problem that Parks thinks the philosophy of Immanuel Kant helps us solve. In making this move, however, it becomes logically impossible even for Parks to refrain from some concept of "God," and this impossibility calls into question the advisability of following her lead, especially for those working in nonsectarian schools and seeking to deal properly with the religious pluralism of their students.

Before turning to the philosophical question raised by Parks's (2011) arguments for faith as meaning making, we need to add one more question to our study. If faith is about making meaning, then what does "meaning" mean? She defines it thus:

> Broadly speaking, the awareness of connectedness, importance, and felt significance among perceived objects both external and internal; narrowly speaking, it is the attribution of positive value to a particular configuration of attitudes, ideals, and connections that stand close to the center of one's identity and are the key to judging importance in relation to time, person, events, and the natural world. (p. 290)

Parks explains "meaning" by the signal words "awareness" and "attribution." In relation to the first description of faith as meaning making, "awareness" mirrors "sense" while "attribution" parallels "compose." As with the other key terms, she offers a formal description consonant with her observation of the psychological dynamics of faith development. This work is based on years of conversations, interviews, and data collecting, and we can be grateful for Parks's nuanced and sensitive awareness of young people's faith experience. Using this formal terminology permits a person of faith to coordinate awareness of the psychological movements with the particular beliefs of a faith tradition, which is obviously a necessary part of faith development.

This is also precisely the point at which we begin to run into problems with Parks's (2011) work. Whenever "dogma" appears in *Big Questions,* Parks consistently associates it with negative outcomes, thus as a roadblock to mature faith. The next step in our study is to examine how she characterizes "dogma." To undertake this task, we will walk step-by-step through the five separate references that Parks makes and see along the way that her dependence on Immanuel Kant's epistemology dramatically impacts how she thinks.

Faith and Dogma

In the first reference, Parks (2011) opposes static dogma to the dynamism of faith. Immediately, we see her concern that dogma unhelpfully limits faith development: "When faith is linked with religious dogma, the word is not generally used to connote something dynamic that undergoes change, transformation, and development over time" (p. 22). The "general use" of dogma, in Parks's view, stands in virtual opposition to the dynamics of faith development, and it therefore puts the brakes on faith's growth. This starting point prompts two questions: Has Parks accurately described how dogma functions? Is it actually static, or has she confused the foreclosing narrowness of a dogmatic attitude with dogma itself?

Dogma next appears in a discussion of the role of imagination in faith. Imagination connects vision and affect, an important feature of faith that points beyond the merely cognitive. To illustrate, Parks (2011) recounts an emerging adult's experience of "a feeling of enlargement and a new quality of relationship between self and world" (p. 156). We notice again the dynamic motion of faith that envisions an improved relationship between self and world. Then Parks makes the turn toward dogma: "Thus faith as the activity [of] meaning-making and realization is indeed something quite other than wishful thinking or mere assent to irrelevant dogma of whatever kind" (p. 156). What makes the dogma irrelevant to this experience of enlargement? Parks does not say, but clearly she sees dogma as a hindrance.

With Parks's (2011) focus on individual faith development, the role of dogma for communal identity understandably gets little attention; however, she does acknowledge the power of religious communities in faith formation. We might expect the teachings of a community to stand out in more positive light here. Nonetheless, she minimizes dogma's positive role and instead turns to "images, stories, symbols and songs" (Parks, 2011, p. 276) as superior to dogma:

> At its best, religion is a distillation of shared and worthy images power-
> ful enough to shape into one the chaos of our existence. Neither mere

dogma nor simply an optional thread in the composing of a lifestyle, religion functions religiously when it serves as a shared means of inter-preting the whole of life—continually tested and revised in the ongoing lived experience of individuals and their communities. (p. 268)

Parks thus valorizes a stock of resources (stories, images, and symbols) over "mere" dogma. Her preferred sources seem more malleable—and therefore more useful—than dogma. Stories and symbols allow for "play," for shaping according to the contemporary needs of the community. While this attitude seems the most flexible and open, one also must ask: Who remains in control of the process of engaging those resources? Who helps a young person decide what is an appropriate use of the images and stories? We come close to the role of dogma in a community here even while Parks seeks to create distance.

Her final reference to dogma draws from another well-known scholar of religion and works in concert with her earlier reference to Wilfred Cantwell Smith: "If Harvey Cox has it right . . . the deep currents beneath the religious divides worldwide are transforming religious cultures and we are moving from an Age of Belief and institutionalized dogma to an Age of Spirit and revitalized imaginations of faith" (Parks, 2011, pp. 273–274). While Smith helps to define important terms like "faith" and "belief" (which extends to "dogma"), Cox offers a large-scale view of envisioned historic changes in attitude toward religion.

In view of the foregoing summary, we can see how Parks's (2011) the-oretical work in psychology coordinates with scholars of religion and the-ology (Smith and Cox). To round out this study, we add one more source, Immanuel Kant, to the authorities that Parks identifies in *Big Questions*. It is important to keep in mind that Parks moves from a descriptive mode to a prescriptive one—from describing the psychological dynamics of faith as making meaning to a normative stance in epistemology, especially regard-ing the limits of what we can know. In watching her make this move, we can infer what amounts, ironically, to Parks's own dogmatic assumptions that she then maps onto her theory of faith development. This final step makes clear why people working with students in nonsectarian, faith-based col-leges and universities have reason to take Parks's jaundiced view of dogma with a grain of salt and why they may—like other Christian schools—consider the role of the sponsoring church's doctrine in a more positive light.

Parks's Kantian Background Belief

Immanuel Kant (1724–1804) continues to wield broad influence in the American academy, even if his name is not mentioned. In fact, in addition to Kant's influence on mainline theologians, his work has also held sway in psychology and student development: James Fowler and Lawrence Kohlberg both identify as Kantians. Likewise, in political theory, the work of John Rawls, also a self-identified Kantian, has contributed to the shaping of dimensions of college life. Putting religion in the domain of "private," while knowledge falls within "public," is but one major example.

In terms of epistemology as it applies to an understanding of God, religion, and faith development, Kant argued that substantive claims about God are at best metaphorical, imagistic, and suggestive because we have no direct knowledge of the transcendent (*noumenal*) dimension; that is, we cannot know God as God exists in his own nature. In Kant's view, then, every claim about God (that God *is* this or that or that God *does* this or that) turns out to be little more than a description of how people understand the experience or feeling that they take to be God's action. Parks (2011) takes this conclusion as her starting point:

> At least since Immanuel Kant, we have been aware that all of our learning and knowing is a composing activity. The human mind does not receive the world-as-it-is in itself. Rather, we act on the world to compose reality. (p. 137)

In Parks's usage of this philosophy, we see why she thinks dogma is a problem. It seems appropriate, then, to ask if this view hangs together and is as compelling as Parks suggests. The philosopher Nicholas Wolterstorff (1998) will provide guidance for engaging this question.

According to Kant, when we reflect on the phenomena of our experiences, we see that reality presents itself to us as appearances or representations. An object's appearing is an "episode of intuition, of awareness of *Anschauung*" (Wolterstorff, 1998, p. 8). Intuitions alone, however, do not produce knowledge. Concepts are necessary to render the intuitions understandable and useful. In other words, an object must *appear as* a something. As Wolterstorff (1998) says, every intuitional experience comes "*already* conceptualized, always *already* conceptually interpreted. I don't just hear something, I hear it as middle C; I don't just see something, I see it as a dog" (p. 9). The concepts provide the means to make sense of the intuition presented by the object.

While Wolterstorff readily agrees with Kant that experience comes conceptualized, he does not accept a central feature of Kant's formulation: the metaphor of "boundary" that Kant used to distinguish things-as-experienced from things-in-themselves. This boundary ostensibly lies "between" the object and our concept of that object, which suggests that the boundary, as it were, stands in the way of access to the object itself. Wolterstorff demonstrates convincingly that "boundary" unnecessarily inserts a barrier into the process of knowing and that it does not square with our actual phenomenal experience. It is both an unnecessarily restrictive and logically self-defeating description of the knowing process. In other words—and this is a critical point—*any* talk of God, whether on Kantian terms or otherwise, assumes some ability to grasp something of God in order to be able to say anything at all about God. If such a boundary exists, no talk of God per se is possible, only references to experiences we take as coming from God. Yet, Kant himself spoke of God quite easily. As Wolterstorff observes, Kant thought he had God well enough in mind to say what he said about God. "Boundary," therefore, seems to speak against the very assumption that Kant held:

> A condition . . . of being able to form convictions concerning God, is that, on the one hand, we can somehow get God in mind well enough for our convictions to be convictions *about* God rather than about something else or nothing at all, and, on the other hand, that *what* we believe *about* God, once we have God in mind, is something which, so far as we know, might well be true of God. (Wolterstorff, 1998, p. 12)

Here, Wolterstorff raises the topic of reference. The problematic train of thought goes like this: if when I speak of God, I am actually speaking of "what I take to be" God, then I am not speaking of God at all but of my conceptualized experience of God. I have replaced reference to God with reference to my construal. This is what Kant's boundary metaphor does, says Wolterstorff, and, if it is true, it defeats all that Kant said about God. It separates the object of experience from the concept of that object.

Wolterstorff (1998) argues constructively that, working from the same phenomenal experience that Kant had in mind, it makes as much sense to think of objects of perception as "of" the objects:

> If we understand perception of an object as awareness of the object—rather than as awareness of a mental representation caused by the object—then it will not make sense to follow Kant in the further step he takes of thinking of concepts as rules for structuring the objects of our awareness. (p. 17)

As Wolterstorff says, "To perceive an eagle under the concept of eagle is to perceive it to be what it is" (p. 18). This is how reference works; and it reflects, in fact, how we experience the world. With concepts referring to objects, not to mental representations, those concepts serve as links, not boundaries or barriers.

Conclusion

Besides arguing that Kant's boundary concept is self-defeating, Wolterstorff (1998) also speaks of the chilling effect Kant's work has had on theology. We can see the chill in this study of *Big Questions, Worthy Dreams*. Parks (2011) takes a restricted view of dogma's value, and she searches for generic terms like "Spirit" and "Mystery" to refer to the experience of transcendence. She also consistently encloses "God" in quotation marks as a way of signaling her cautious and open use of the term. In nonsectarian schools, Parks's approach is quite common, which brings us full circle to the dilemma mentioned at the beginning of this chapter: how a religiously affiliated college or university committed to academic excellence can also be called upon to participate in the sponsoring church's mission, at least at some level.

Kant's work seems to require this approach, but Wolterstorff's (2011) analysis calls that conclusion into question. At some point, when speaking of faith, we have to give a name (or names) to the object(s) of faith. We have to refer to something or someone that transcends our particular experience. Paradoxically, the act of making reference to that object requires that something about our reference actually makes contact with the reference point. To repeat and paraphrase Wolterstorff: to say anything about God, we must believe that we have God well enough in mind to say anything at all about God. The hard boundary between "faith" and "knowledge" posed by Kant—and deployed by Parks—therefore has been breached.

This conclusion calls for rethinking the practice of downplaying or even ignoring altogether the doctrinal stance of the nonsectarian college's or university's sponsoring church. Whereas many people working in these schools assume that this practice is necessary, it not only is not necessary, it likely militates against the goal of faith development. It will take significant institutional courage for a school to re-engage the theological foundations of the sponsoring church in imagining its academic mission.

We can also work more effectively in a nonsectarian environment if we lean on the descriptive part of Parks's (2011) work in terms of the psychological dynamics of young adult development but leave aside her prescriptive or normative view of the sources that contribute to this development. If we do not recognize this flawed aspect of Parks's work, we will unwittingly impose some dogmatic viewpoint on students and likely one that stands in opposition to the sponsoring church's teachings. It is much better to make all our beliefs explicit, while at the same time leaving the door wide open for students to explore, criticize, discuss, and experiment. A nonsectarian school that actively embraces its Christian foundations will thereby offer students of all faiths—and no particular faith—a rich educational experience.

References

Fowler, J. W. (1981). *Stages of faith: The psychology of human development and the quest for meaning.* San Francisco, CA: HarperOne.

Gehrke, S. J. (2013). Race and pro-social involvement: Toward a more complex understanding of spiritual development in college. In A. B. Rockenbach and M. H. Mayhew (Eds.), *Spirituality in college students' lives: Translating research into practice* (pp. 35-48). New York, NY: Routledge.

Parks, S. D. (2011). *Big questions, worthy dreams: Mentoring young adults in their search for meaning, purpose, and faith* San Francisco, CA: Jossey-Bass.

Pascarella, E. T., & Terenzini, P. T. (2005). *How college affects students: Volume 2, a third decade of research.* San Francisco, CA: Jossey-Bass.

Small, J. L. (2011). *Understanding college students' spiritual identities: Different faiths, varied worldviews.* Discourses and Processes Series. New York, NY: Hampton Press.

Wolterstorff, N. (1998). Is it possible and desirable for theologians to recover from Kant? *Modern Theology, 14*(1), 1–18.

9

ADMINISTRATIVE PERSPECTIVES ON CHURCH-AFFILIATION QUALITY WITHIN THE CAMPUS MINISTER ROLE

AARON MORRISON

Nebraska Wesleyan University

American higher education began as a religious endeavor with the Puritan founding of Harvard College in 1636 (Marsden, 1994). Along with the Puritans, other Christian denominations established institutions designed not only to create clergy (Rudolph, 2011) but also to produce laypeople who could instill Christian ethics and ideals into society (Chickering, Dalton, & Auerbach, 2006; Thelin, 2003).

Over the next three centuries, the influence of religion within American higher education declined. Secularization cast doubt on the value of religion to direct the ends of higher education, leaving only a small number of institutions that remained committed to their religious identity (Burtchaell, 1998; Marsden, 1994; Ringenberg, 2006).

Burtchaell's *The Dying of the Light* (1998) and Marsden's *The Soul of the American University* (1994) cite institutional attitudes toward campus chapel services as indicative of a college or university's religiosity. In particular,

Burtchaell's narrative correlates the policy change that reduced chapel services from mandatory to voluntary with institutional decline in religious commitment (Burtchaell, 1998).

Both Burtchaell and Marsden connect an institution's religiosity to its attitude toward chapel exercises. These researchers also have said the significance of a campus minister role indicates institutional religiosity as well. While the full-time campus minister role did not exist until the rise of student affairs in the late nineteenth century (Nuss, 2003), institutions hired clergy to preside over chapel exercises from the beginning of American higher education (Marsden, 1994). Church tradition tied chapel and the campus minister together, and secularization of the academy affected the influence of both (Marsden, 1994).

Despite the impact of secularization, students still value the exploration of spirituality in their lives. Data from the Higher Education Research Institute (HERI) at UCLA suggests college students maintain high levels of interest in spirituality, and many partake in active religious engagement (Astin, Astin, Lindholm, & Bryant, 2005). HERI defines spirituality as a "multifaceted quality" marked by a "spiritual quest, an ecumenical worldview, an ethic of caring alongside charitable involvement, and equanimity," while "religious engagement" is defined as "attending religious services, praying, and reading sacred texts" (Astin et al., 2005, pp. 6–8). In light of this data and in line with an over-arching institutional desire to develop students holistically, many colleges and universities still provide a variety of opportunities for students to explore their spirituality (Fidler, Poster, & Strickland, 1999; Nuss, 2003).

Of all colleges and universities in America, nearly nine hundred identify as "religiously-affiliated" (Andringa, 2005). Their provision for the spiritual development of students typically includes an institutionally demarcated campus minister(s) who presides over chapel exercises (Davis, 2004). While the existence of the campus minister role commonly marks these institutions, the nature of their church affiliation varies greatly depending upon institutional ethos and culture.

Burtchaell (1998) identified a number of church-affliated colleges and universities whose founding denominational or theological tradition diminished in influence, while Benne (2001) identified six colleges and universities—including Notre Dame, Wheaton, Calvin, Baylor, Valparaiso, and St. Olaf—who remained faithful to their denominational or theological tradition in the midst of secularization.

Cherry, DeBerg, and Porterfield (2003) in their journalistic work, *Religion On Campus,* explored the extent to which secularization removed religion from higher education. They interviewed faculty, students, and administrators at four different schools and found a varied religious vitality at each school. Their account noted that faculty and administrators at these schools expressed concern about offending students by supporting distinctly religious rules and regulations or by teaching Christian doctrine. These researchers advocated for a less distinctive spirituality that emphasized "togetherness" and commonality, implying that religious vitality excludes intellectually serious and morally authoritative activity (Cherry et al., 2003).

This chapter reflects the author's current study of how administrative perspectives on the campus minister role indicate church-affiliation quality and builds on these previous studies. While one study exists that provides campus ministers' perceptions of their roles (Davis, 2004), there is no research on *administrative* perceptions of the campus minister role, especially as indicative of church-affilation quality. If as Burtchaell (1998) and Marsden (1994) propose, an institution's value of its chapel exercises is an indicator of religious commitment, then how an insitution perceives the campus minister role might be as well. However, due to the limited scope of this study, the research design will focus on the perspectives of only one population within an institution; future, more exhaustive institutional studies are anticipated.

Using a sociological understanding of religiosity, this chapter considers the words, phrases, and images used by administrators to describe the presence of church affiliation within the campus minister role. This study also provides a picture of how administrative perceptions of the role of the campus minister are evolving. Finally, this study illuminates the perceived relevance the campus minister role plays in meeting the criteria of church affiliation. The research question that guided this investigation is "How do administrators at a small, United Methodist Church-affiliated, liberal arts institution in the Midwest perceive the quality of church affiliation within the role of the campus minister?"

Literature Review

Religiosity as a sociological term encompasses the entirety of religious expression. Cornwall, Albrecht, Cunningham, and Pitcher (1986) divided religiosity into multiple conceptual dimensions. This study will focus on the "institutional" mode, which is one mode within the definitional framework of religiosity. Dittes (1971) identified and differentiated institutional mode as a sub-mode under religion as "objective" position (public, social, institutionalized, and formalized) as opposed to religion as a more "subjective" approach (deeply held personal attitudes, values, loyalties, and commitments). The institutional mode comprises:

> the religious beliefs, feelings, or behaviors related to formalized and institutionalized religion. Institutional mode includes acceptance of religious beliefs which are unique to a sect or denomination, personal feelings and attachments to a particular church or congregation, and participation in religious ritual and worship services. (Cornwall et al., 1986, para. 13)

By this description, the institutional mission statements and descriptions of the campus minister role reflect the institutional mode of religiosity as well. References to a denomination or theological tradition within a mission statement or in perceptions of the campus minister role also reflect religiosity.

Perspectives on Church Affiliation

Church-affiliated colleges and universities make up a significant percentage of American higher education quantitatively (Andringa, 2005). However, it is less clear whether American higher education is *qualitatively* influenced by these church-affiliated colleges and universities. Burtchaell (1998) offered a somewhat pessimistic narrative of colleges and universities disengaging from their religious foundations. Marsden (1994) agreed, characterizing institutions as moving from a perspective of "Protestant establishment" to one of "established non-belief."

However, not everyone agrees with the pessimistic characterization of secularization's impact on church and university relations. Merrimon Cuninggim, a Methodist minister and Vanderbilt University administrator, took a more optimistic tone. He thought the onset of secularization in the church-university relationship reflected necessary changes for their mutual benefit and described the current state of church and university relations as a time of church officials and college leaders adjusting the quality of the relationship in light of trends in churches, in colleges, and in broader culture (Cuninggim, 1995). His concern focused more on the threat to academic freedom through privileging only one kind of denominational ideology and less on the threat posed by secularization.

Cuninggim identified three phases of the relationship between the college and the church traditions that founded them: (1) church as senior partner; college as junior partner, recognizing the college's need for the church's direct support; (2) a time of equality, when neither college nor church has an upper hand in normal situations; and (3) the college as senior partner, more in control of its own destiny. Cuninggim observed most institutions currently fall into the final category and no longer depend on the church for financial resources and leadership.

Cuninggim also believed in order to understand the church and university relationship, their common and yet distinctive missions must be recognized, although both share a similar aim regarding mission and service. Cuninggim saw the church's primary responsibility as addressing spiritual and communal needs and responsibilities. He described the college's primary responsibility as providing quality education in principle with the sponsoring religious organization's values, but not necessarily ontologically the same. For an effective, healthy relationship, churches and their colleges must respect and appreciate the distinctive mission of each partner (Cuninggim, 1995).

Contemporary Debates on Church-University Relationship

Since a conservative shift in the late 1970s, the Southern Baptist Convention and their colleges, universities, and seminaries have often engaged in controversy regarding church authority (Nelson, 2012). As a result of the controversy, multiple traditionally Baptist institutions discontinued their formal relationships with the Southern Baptist Convention in order to reduce denominational control of the institutions. Others, such as Cedarville University, strengthened their bonds (Bailey, 2013).

During the latter half of the twentieth century, Catholic colleges and universities also engaged in discussions regarding the authority of their local diocese. In 1967, a group of administrators from Catholic colleges and universities (including the University of Notre Dame, Boston College, and St. Louis University) signed the *Land O'Lakes Statement* (International Federation of Catholic Universities, 1967). This statement sought to define the relationship between the Church and Catholic higher education and, in effect, functioned as a the universities' way of declaring independence from Catholic hierarchy in the name of academic freedom (Gleason, 1995).

The *Land O'Lakes Statement* launched many debates about the nature of Catholic church-university relationships, leading to the formal response from the Vatican in Pope John Paul II's *Ex Corde Ecclesiae* (Gleason, 1995). *Ex Corde* strongly asserted Church authority in relation to Catholic colleges and universities. New institutions claiming Catholic church affiliation needed approval from "the Holy See, by an Episcopal Conference . . . or by a diocesan bishop" (Paul II, 1990, para. 52). Current Catholic institutions were required to maintain their Catholic identity through norms established by local bishops and to gain the approval of the local bishop for any theology faculty appointments (John Paul II, 1990).

Brief History of the Campus Minister

The campus minister's historic significance helps to illuminate the significance of church affiliation. Although early Protestant, colonial colleges of New England did not hire full-time ministers, the role became more common in higher education later in the nineteenth century, paralleling the emergence of student affairs (Nuss, 2003). As the need for student affairs positions arose, the campus minister role emerged when presidents and faculty could not effectively meet the spiritual and moral needs of students by themselves (Shockley, 1989).

One particular primary document touches on the perception of the campus minister role within the twentieth century. In the summer of 1966, the University of Georgia and the National Campus Ministry Association hosted the National Campus Ministry Convocation. The theme of the conference focused on "Personal Wholeness and Professional Identity in the Campus Ministry." One of the topics at this conference examined the question "Why Do We Have a Campus Minister?" In his answer to this question, Hofmann (1966) described the times in which they operated as an antireligious era, where the world held "the Church . . . the religious people" in suspicion and "nobody dares" to claim them. Because of this suspicion toward religious people, he thought the campus minister needed to exist as someone who stood as a bridge or liaison between two worlds, "the world of the Heavenly City" and "the world of the earthly relativists, which is Academia" (p. 3). In order to be a bridge, Hofmann (1966) strongly advocated for the campus minister to maintain a "keen and imaginative mind, together with a stubborn and courageous stand" (p. 3).

Recent Developments

While the primary responsibility of early chaplains was to coordinate mandatory chapel exercises, (Marsden, 1994), today the role often includes additional responsibilities. In response to the rise of those who claim no religious identification and the increasing emphasis on helping students find a sense of purpose (Smith & Snell, 2009), some colleges are considering using a campus minister as more of a spiritual advisor or counselor rather than an officiant over chapel services. Some research supports how the campus minister's role today can correspond to that of typical college mental health counselors (Aten, 2004). Augustana College has responded to this development by moving one of their campus ministers into their career and counseling department:

> Over the three years that Kristen Glass Perez has been one of two
> campus chaplains at Augustana College, there's been a notable dip

> in the number of students walking through the doors of the college's Ascension Chapel. It's been going that way for a while now, the college said, as students at the Lutheran institution have become less interested in organized religion. Just 13 percent of this year's freshman class are Lutheran and many don't worry about attending. (New, 2014, para. 1)

Despite the lack of chapel attendance, students were still looking for spiritual guidance, particularly in discerning their sense of purpose in life. In acknowledgement of this need, Augustana College moved Perez's office out of the chapel and into the college's "Career, Opportunities, Research, and Exploration Center" and added "director of vocational exploration" to her title (New, 2014, para. 3). The article speculated the move was "a sign of the times," marking the "increasing pressure" institutions feel in proving the educational experience worthwhile to student investment (New, 2014).

Similar Studies

Davis's (2004) work on campus ministers' perceptions of their roles and purpose at large public and small private insitutions in the southeastern United States provided a helpful framework for creating the research design for this study. In particular, the questions for the semi-structured interviews of administrators made a good comparative model.

Summary

Through the institutional mode of religiosity, researchers can examine the quality of church affiliation. Church affiliation evolved over time, with differing perspectives on whether secularization diminished its quality. Within the past century, different parts of the church have debated the future of the church-university relationship, as some institutions lessened church control and others increased it. The role of the campus minister represents one symbolic area within the university that manifests church affiliation. This study examines the quality of church affiliation by observing how administrators at a small, Midwestern institution affiliated with the United Methodist Church see church affiliation manifested in the campus minister role.

Methodology

The researcher chose a case study methodology because it offers the best explanation of the perceptions given in light of a particular institutional context. Through this method, the quality of perceptions is considered. Instead of imposing concrete criteria upon a subjective construct, a case study method looks at the depth and extent of perceptions. According to Flyvbjerg (2006), the case study approach produces knowledge that is context-dependent and, in the study of human affairs, also rules out the possibility of epistemic theoretical construction. Flyvbjerg (2006) also identifies how the closeness of the case study approach to real-life situations can provide a wealth of details helpful to our understanding of knowledge, particularly in developing a nuanced view of reality.

This study examines the perceptions of mid-level and president's cabinet-level administrators regarding the presence of church affiliation within the campus minister role at a small, Midwestern, liberal arts institution affiliated with United Methodist Church. Because case studies by definition seek holistic description (Creswell, 2007), administrators who operated from different offices on campus were selected because they presented the opportunity to form a holistic picture of the campus minister's role.

Data Analysis

The researcher recorded interviews digitally, transcribed them, and then analyzed each individual interview independently for significant statements (Creswell, 2007). After the significant statements in each interview were identified, the findings were compared to discern major theme clusters (Creswell, 2007). Similar ideas were brought together and condensed, revealing the major themes. These themes were then described in the most concise yet broadly recognized form.

With regard to Wolcott's model (1994), the researcher placed the themes within the literature while comparing and contrasting with previous studies. Names and titles of participants were altered to ensure confidentiality. Three administrative departments were represented: student life, alumni relations, and academic affairs. Seven individuals, including four women and three men, were interviewed. Five respondents were mid-level administrators who reported to president's cabinet-level administrators, while two were president's cabinet-level administrators.

Findings

Three main themes emerged from the respondents' descriptions of their perspective on the nature of church affiliation within the role of the campus minister: (1) church affiliation in spiritual or vocational counseling responsibilities; (2) the campus minister as positional marker of church affiliation; and (3) a nonsectarian approach as indicative of church affiliation.

Church Affiliation in Spiritual or Vocational Counseling Responsibilities

Several respondents marked the presence of church affiliation within the campus minister role by emphasizing spiritual or vocational counseling responsibilities. Respondents described the campus minister's role as someone who helps with students' "personal growth" or meets "one-on-one" with them to help process questions of faith and purpose in life.

For example, one respondent thought the campus minister's role connected with the church-related nature of the institution through helping students in their "personal growth" or by "helping students to find their place in the world." The idea of reflecting the church-related mission of the institution meant that the campus minister aided students in processing their philosophical questions of life through a spiritual lens.

Another respondent referenced counseling as a marker of church affiliation in the campus minister's role: "I don't think there isn't a student on campus that at some point in their career won't be looking at the bigger questions and searching." By this notion, he argued the campus minister needed to exist in order to support students "in their personal development." The campus minister helped students process these questions through "chapel services, Bible studies, introducing other denominations to the campus community, and [giving their own] understanding of the world."

A third respondent connected church affiliation in the campus minister role to spiritual or vocational counseling. He emphasized the campus minister as a resource for students to "put into focus" how they experience the institutional mission in relation to the students' own values or to "fit into the bigger picture . . . what [they are] learning as a student." He also noted his appreciation of the opportunity for students "[to] access [the counseling] if they want, but they . . . are left to decide how much of their college experience it is."

A fourth respondent characterized the qualities of church affiliation within the campus minister role to spiritual or vocational counseling responsibilities. While she acknowledged the responsibilities of presiding over chapel exercises, she primarily thought of the role as someone who met one-on-one with students:

> I see him as not only having chapel, but also as a counselor and an advisor—a one-on-one resource person for students. I know he does chapel, but I think of him as working more one-on-one, as general meeting with students.

Campus Minister As Positional Marker of Church Affiliation

Another theme emerged from respondents' comments. Because of the distinctly religious responsibilities attached to the role, the campus minister's mere existence met at least part of the criteria for church affiliation. Whether the respondents made these comments assuming the absence of religious elements in other administrator positions is unclear. However, this assumption might be suggested in some of the respondents' comments.

For example, one participant described the necessity of the campus minister to "help create dialogue for things that [students] don't get in the classroom." He thought conversations with a campus minister were something students "[might] want as part of their college experience." The campus minister "needs to be there, so [students] can think about . . . what makes them a part of a bigger community or as a global citizen . . . outside of a business class." While perhaps the respondent did not mean students could not talk about these things with a faculty member or administrator, he thought of the campus minister as the person students should meet with to hold such conversations and viewed the campus minster as "vital to the success of the university."

In the words of another administrator, just "as a university has to have a president, faculty, and a provost, you need to have a campus minister to serve the needs of students." She emphasized how the campus minister role needed to be a "different outlet" for students in comparison to other administrative roles. She also regarded the role as "important a role as" faculty have. Perhaps most notable, she believed the campus minister role was so vital to the church-related nature of the university that the institution "could not exist without the position."

Another participant acknowledged the variety of "resource places for students," but regarded it necessary for the university to have "somebody with a specifically religious perspective to meet the university mission." The campus minister "is a part of our institutional identity."

Lastly, one respondent approached his answer to the question by describing the founding denomination of the institution as "the foundation." Because of this foundation, he believed "no matter what anybody thinks or feels, it's appropriate to have someone on staff in that position." He then went on to talk about how "it's necessary to have a go-to person for all spiritual needs," as though the campus minister represents the resident expert on spirituality.

Nonsectarian Approach As Indicative of Church Affiliation

A third theme that emerged from the data was the belief that the nonsectarian approach taken by the campus minister indicated the presence of church affiliation within his role. By "nonsectarian" approach, the respondents meant that the campus minister's role should not function solely within the limits of teaching Methodist doctrine. For example, a respondent, who spoke as a member of the United Methodist Church, felt the campus minister represented the UMC in his role by being "open to all students . . . teaching them about different religions, other religious practices." She pointed toward the campus minister bringing in "people from different religions" and holding "interfaith dialogue" as being representative of church affiliation in his role. She viewed the campus minister as a "bridge builder" between different religions because "[he is] just naturally open to all kinds of people and [helps] sometimes [with bridging] the gap in our diverse ideas or ethnicity or religiosity." She also argued that he "bring[s] all the groups together" as a part of his "community building" and that his approach was "very open, very supportive—not quizzing, not judging."

Another respondent thought the nonsectarian approach taken by the campus minister in inviting speakers from the United Methodist Church and "other faiths" indicated church affiliation. Such an approach meant the campus minister believed it "[important] on our college campus, to learn about the faiths of other people." The respondent thought this posture sent "a particularly powerful message coming from the campus minister, more than even if it came from the provost."

Discussion

The results revealed three major themes representing administrators' perceptions of church affiliation present within the campus minister role. These themes included: (1) church affiliation in spiritual or vocational counseling responsibilities; (2) the campus minister as a positional marker of church affiliation; and (3) a nonsectarian approach as indicative of church affiliation.

When integrated with the literature on religiosity, the nature of church affiliation, and the history of the campus minister's role, the data becomes more relevant. The findings and available literature help to illuminate how administrators understand church affiliation as manifest through the campus minister's responsibilities.

Church Affiliation in Spiritual or Vocational Counseling Responsibilities

Administrators described the campus minister's role of spiritual or vocational counseling as a marker of church affiliation; this idea is consistent with the literature regarding the history of campus ministers. At least since the emergence of student affairs roles in the late nineteenth century, campus ministers' responsibilities have included counseling elements (Aten, 2004; Craft, Moran, & Menke, 2009).

However, a shift might be occurring in the primary responsibilities of the campus minister. Several studies suggest changing emphasis in the understanding of faith in Millennial college students, as they hold more of an aversion to religious practice and a greater attraction to faith as a "spiritual journey" (Astin et al., 2005; Smith & Snell, 2009). These changes factored into Augustana College's decision to adjust their campus minister's responsibilities away from officiating chapel exercises and toward counseling students in their spirituality and sense of vocation (New, 2014). It is unclear if other institutions will make similar changes in the future.

The Campus Minister As Positional Marker of Church Affiliation

In the second theme, administrators described the necessity of the campus minister role both to signify the legitimacy of the institution's church affiliation and to serve as the expert or "go-to" person on matters of spirituality and religion. Some of these comments might even suggest an assumption that other administrators' roles did not have religious elements.

These results connect with Cuninggim's work on church-university relations. Cuninggim expressed concern over the level of control which the founding denominational/theological tradition maintained over colleges and universities. He believed secularization represented a necessary development in the church-affiliation relationship. To him, less centralized control from the founding denominational/theological tradition allowed for more academic freedom.

When a university or college achieved a stage of independence from its founding denominational/theological tradition, Cuninggim identified this stage as "the college as senior partner." Within their comments, some respodents expressed an expectation that the campus minister's responsibilities would include distinctively religious elements. Because of this expectation, perhaps the respondents percieved the *practice* of distinctively Methodist values as irrelevant to their own responsibilities and wholly the domain of the campus minister. If true, Cunninggim might say these respondents understood their insitution as largely independent from the founding theological/denominational tradition, at least in the execution of their respective roles on campus.

Nonsectarian Approach as Indicative of Church Affiliation

In the third theme, some respondents thought the nonsectarian approach taken by the campus minister in his responsibilities indicated church affiliation. Cuninggim, as a Methodist minister, might be helpful in explaining this phenomenon at an institution affiliated with the United Methodist Church. Perhaps several of the administrators could relate to Cuninggim's concern that one denomination maintaining too much control could impinge on academic freedom. Yet they connected the institutional identity as a United Methodist Church with an openness to other faiths, which appears quite paradoxical. For them, to be United Methodist meant the campus minister would not teach only Methodist doctrine but also create opportunities for other faiths to have an audience.

Limitations

The researcher sought to account for limitations in the semi-structured interviews. However, some limitations to this study's findings and applicability exist. For example, selection bias might mark the findings. This study also reflects only a small segment of perceptions administrators have toward the role of the campus minister because these respondents chose to take part in this study.

Another limitation of this study is sample size. Several participants shared extended comments and arguments, while others only shared their most basic opinion on the campus minister role. Because of this, the sample size reached a less than desirable saturation point, meaning the themes are not a completely accurate representation of reality.

The participant population was drawn from a small, United Methodist Church-affiliated university in the Midwest, and thus, the applicability of this study to other institutions is limited (Creswell, 2007). Radically different cultural norms occur at other institutions, and thus their administrators may have different experiences than those included in this study (Wolcott, 1994).

Researcher bias may also be a potential limitation of this effort. The case study methodology attempted to maintain objectivity in this qualitative study, especially in terms of minimizing the researcher's preconceptions and prejudices. However, a researcher cannot separate from the topic or people he or she is studying. Rather, the value of the research lies in the interaction between the researcher and the research itself. The open-ended nature of the interview questions sought to avoid steering participants to a particular response. In this manner, compelling results emerged that are less tainted by research bias.

Finally, some of the interviews took place very soon after a student death. Because of this circumstance, some respondents may have had the campus minister's counseling responsibilities more in mind than would be typical.

Suggestions for Further Research

Given the potential impact of church-university relationships, the opportunity for further research is significant. Due to the lack of similar empirical research, this qualitative case study on administrative perspectives of church affiliation within the campus minister role was ultimately a necessary starting point for future research. The researcher believed a particular richness and breadth of data lay in administrative descriptions of the campus minister role, which could aid scholars in how they consider the quality of church affiliation.

Several respondents suggested the campus minister's role should have specifically religious elements while the roles of other administrators or faculty do not. A study regarding the ways in which employees at church-affiliated colleges and universities perceive the relevance of church values within their job responsibilities would contribute to the existing research. A quantitative survey to assess various characteristics unique to the founding denomination or theological tradition would also be beneficial to this research.

Conclusion

This chapter focused on a study that sought to determine how administrators perceived the presence of church affiliation within the role of the campus minister at a small, United Methodist Church institution in the Midwest. Utilizing a case study methodology, the researcher interviewed mid-level to president's cabinet-level administrators who represented different departments. By doing so, the study explored how administrators perceived the presence of church affiliation within the campus minister role.

While this study represents only one population within a single institution, it illustrates an extent to which a college or university describes church affiliation, at least within the context of the campus minister. Some prominent scholars have offered a pessimistic narrative of church affiliation diminishing in light of secularization (Burtchaell, 1998; Marsden, 1994), while others have told of church affiliation maintained faithfully in spite of secularization (Benne, 2001). Scholars have even described the diminishing of church affiliation in optimistic terms (Cuninggim, 1995). Church affiliation within higher education remains a topic worthy of additional research, and this study attempts to bring more understanding of that topic in higher education.

Despite the influence of secularization, the desire for spiritual exploration remains strong among students (Astin, Astin, & Lindholm, 2011; Smith & Snell, 2009). Church-affiliated colleges and universities continue to seek to foster the spiritual development of their students as a part of overall holistic development. To meet the needs of spiritual development, the campus minister role remains relevant to students by providing counsel, teaching doctrine, and practicing social justice.

Additionally, for church-affliated colleges and universities to maintain their church-affliated identity, these insitutions require the campus minister's presence. As history shows, this identity will evolve in light of changing culture (Burtchaell, 1998; Marsden, 1994). It is less clear what exactly will change or stay the same within the church-affliated identity of these colleges and universities as they evolve within a more secularized culture. Secularization presents a strong opposition to the relevance of Christianity in the world. Future discussions on the nature of church affliation in higher education will include not only how faculty and staff practice Christian faith in their roles every day, but also how Christianity as a way of life responds to the philisophical challenges of secularization.

References

Andringa, B. (2005, April 1). 900 Religiously affiliated and accredited institutions of postsecondary education in the USA. *Council for Christian Colleges and Universities.* Retrieved from https://www.cccu.org/filefolder/900_Religious_Colleges.pdf

Astin, A. W., Astin, A. W., Lindholm, J. A., & Bryant, A. N. (2005). *The spiritual life of college students: A national study of college students' search for meaning and purpose.* Los Angeles, CA: Higher Education Research Institute, UCLA.

Astin, A. W., Astin, H. S., & Lindholm, J. A. (2011). Assessing students' spiritual and religious qualities. *Journal of College Student Development, 52*(1), 39-61.

Aten, J. D. (2004). Improving understanding and collaboration between campus ministers and college counseling center personnel. *Journal of College Counseling, 7*(1), 90-96.

Bailey, S. P. (2013, December 22). Cedarville University "faculty shakeup" appears to indicate conservative Southern Baptist future. *Huffington Post.* Retrieved from: http://www.huffingtonpost.com/2013/12/22/cedarville-university-faculty_n_4469241.html

Benne, R. (2001). *Quality with soul: How six premier colleges and universities kept faith with their religious traditions.* Grand Rapids, MI: Wm. B. Eerdmans.

Burtchaell, J. T. (1998). *The dying of the light.* Grand Rapids, MI: Wm. B. Eerdmans.

Cherry, C., DeBerg, B. A., & Porterfield, A. (2003). *Religion on campus.* Chapel Hill, NC: University of North Carolina Press.

Chickering, A. W., Dalton, J. C., & Auerbach, L. S. (2006). *Encouraging authenticity and spirituality in higher education.* San Francisco, CA: Jossey-Bass.

Cornwall, M., Albrecht, S. L., Cunningham, P. H., & Pitcher, B. L. (1986). The dimensions of religiousity: A conceptual model with an empirical test. *Review of Religious Research, 27*(3), 226-244.

Craft, C. D., Moran, W. W., & Menke, D. J. (2009). Campus ministers in public higher education: Facilitators of student development. *College Student Affairs Journal, 28*(1) 61-80.

Creswell, J. W. (2007). *Qualitative inquiry and research design: Choosing among five traditions* (2nd ed). Thousand Oaks, CA: Sage Publications.

Cuninggim, M. (1995). *Uneasy partners: The college and the church.* Nashville, TN: Abingdon Press.

Davis, J. S. (2004). In their own words: Campus ministers' perceptions of their work and their worlds. *College Student Affairs Journal, 23*(2) 173-184.

DiCicco-Bloom, B., & Crabtree, B. (2006). The qualitative research interview. *Medical Education, 40*(4), 314-321.

Dittes, J. E. (1971). Two issues in measuring religion. In M. P. Strommen (Ed.), *Research on religious development* (pp. 79-106). New York, NY: Hawthorne.

Fidler, P. P., Poster, J., & Strickland, M. G. (1999). Extra hands for tough times: Utilizing campus ministers for student development in public institutions. *College Student Affairs Journal, 18*(2), 16.

Flyvbjerg, B. (2006). Five misunderstandings about case-study research. *Qualitative Inquiry, 12*(2) 219-245.

General Board of Higher Education and Ministry. (2014, November 6). University Senate. *Higher Education and Ministry—United Methodist Church.* Retrieved from http://www.gbhem.org/education/university-senate

Gleason, P. (1995). *Contending with modernity.* Oxford, UK: Oxford University Press.

Hofmann, H. (1966). Why do we have a campus minister? In *Symposium on personal wholeness and professional identity in the campus ministry* (pp. 3-10). Athens, GA: University of Georgia Libraries.

International Federation of Catholic Universities. (1967). *The idea of a Catholic university: The Land O'Lakes statement.* Land O'Lakes, WI: International Federation of Catholic Universities.

John Paul II, Pope. (1990, August 14). Apostolic constitution of the supreme pontiff, John Paul II. *Libreria Editrice Vaticana.* Retrieved from http://www.vatican.va/holy_father/john_paul_ii/apost_constitutions/documents/hf_jp-ii_apc_15081990_ex-corde-ecclesiae_en.html

Marsden, G. (1994). *The soul of the American university: From Protestant establishment to established nonbelief.* Oxford, UK: Oxford University Press.

Nelson, L. A. (2012, November 14). Shorter's exodus, a year later. *Inside Higher Ed.* Retrieved from https://www.insidehighered.com/news/2012/11/14/cultural-change-tears-georgia-baptist-college-apart

New, J. (2014, October 6). Finding a student's calling. *Inside Higher Ed.* Retrieved from https://www.insidehighered.com/news/2014/10/06/college-moves-campus-pastor-out-chapel-and-career-counseling

Nuss, E. M. (2003). The development of student affairs. In S. R. Komives & D. B. Woodard Jr. (Eds.), *Student services: A handbook for the profession* (pp. 65-68). San Francisco, CA: Jossey-Bass.

Ringenberg, W. C. (2006). *The Christian college: A history of Protestant higher education in America.* Grand Rapids, MI: Baker Academic.

Rudolph, F. (2011). *The American college and university: A history.* Athens, GA: University of Georgia Press.

Shockley, D. G. (1989). *Campus ministry: The church beyond itself.* Louisville, KY: Westminster/John Knox Press.

Smith, C., & Snell, P. (2009). *Souls in transition: The religious and spiritual lives of emerging adults.* Oxford, UK: Oxford University Press.

Thelin, J. R. (2003). Historical overview of American higher education. In S. R. Komives & D. B. Woodard Jr. (Eds.), *Student services: A handbook for the profession* (pp. 3-22). San Francisco, CA: Jossey-Bass.

Wolcott, H. F. (1994). *Transforming qualitative data: Description, analysis, and interpretation.* Thousand Oaks, CA: Sage Publications.

10

NURTURING HOLY GRIT

Hope College's Emmaus Scholars Program

MARK HUSBANDS

Hope College

Adulthood promises emerging adults considerable freedom. This freedom, however, comes with considerable challenges. Lacking moral and spiritual formation, we should not be surprised to learn that the majority of emerging adults will *not* likely become thoughtful, committed, and purposeful Christian adults. Emerging adults have been socialized to adopt high expectations for personal fulfillment without the burden of self-sacrifice. This makes it all the more unlikely for them to consider forming bonds with either God or the church. Accordingly, Christian Smith et al. (2011) reckons that the majority of emerging adults (between the ages of nineteen and twenty-three) are "morally at sea in boats that leak water badly." Central to this analysis is the belief that "if these emerging adults are lost, it is because the larger culture and society into which they are being inducted is also lost" (pp. 60–61). According to Smith, the adult world of American society has failed emerging adults by "sending many, and probably most, of them out into the world without the basic intellectual tools and basic personal formation needed to think and express even the most elementary of reasonably defensible moral thoughts and claims" (p. 61).

For those whose professional responsibilities demand a clear-eyed focus upon the well-being of the church and Christian formation, the consequence of these broader sociological forces is significant. What will become of Christianity and its witness to the Gospel in a culture ill-disposed to value vital faith, purpose, and the abiding love of God? Even if the goal of directing emerging adults toward finding meaning and purpose was adopted by institutions of higher education, there is no guarantee that widely held instruments of evaluation (such as the *U.S. News & World Report* college rankings) would reward such pursuits.

Given the importance of helping emerging adults to become individuals who can make a lasting difference in the world, institutions of higher education would do well to rediscover the importance of calling. When the Puritans asked Rev. John Harvard ("a godly gentleman and a lover of learning") to give one half of his estate to found Harvard College, they had specific goals in mind. One such guiding principle of this new college was to

> let every student be plainly instructed, and earnestly pressed to consider well [that] the main end of his life and studies is, to know God and Jesus Christ which is eternal life, John 17:3 and therefore to lay Christ at the bottom, as the only foundation of all sound knowledge and learning. (Sabin, 1865, p. 26)

Evidently, the task of helping young adults to become agents of renewal and hope in the areas of scholarship, the work of reconciliation and mission is worthy of great sacrifice (one half Rev. Harvard's estate). What would this task look like today?

At a bare minimum, one would need an academic and residential program that recognizes the need to mine the riches of the Christian tradition and to teach this material in a way that helps emerging adults to flourish in spite of the manifest cultural impediments to spiritual formation. Accordingly, this chapter considers the sociology of religion offered by a number of the discipline's leading figures and then presents a brief account of the strategic importance of Hope College's Emmaus Scholars Program (hereafter called Emmaus). As we shall see, this program's commitment to nurturing students and encouraging them to think critically, love deeply, and do justice constitutes spiritual and moral formation necessary in a post-Christian age. Moreover, this experience in integral mission represents an innovative strategy to form emerging adults in ways that enable them to re-enact the loving obedience of Christ and thus serve as a sign of God's redemptive purposes for the world.

Christian Smith: *Lost in Transition*

Christian Smith's 2011 work, *Lost in Transition: The Dark Side of Emerging Adulthood,* is a perceptive analysis of the cultural priorities and practices of emerging adults (nineteen- to twenty-three-year-olds) in the United States. One of the distinguishing features of this research is its fitting deployment of a "sociological imagination" (pp. 8–9). In so doing, this work moves considerably beyond mere description to a more substantive mode of providing a moral evaluation of the priorities and practices of emerging adults. This study sets the experiences of individuals in relation to the broader social and cultural forces at work in shaping the very persons themselves.

At a crucial point in the analysis, Smith writes, "We think it is good for people to be able to think coherently about moral beliefs and problems, and to explain why they believe whatever they do believe" (p. 8). To which he adds, "We think it is good for people to develop and enjoy loving relationships in community, to pursue spiritual truths and values as best as they can understand them, to learn contentment and generosity, to spend themselves in service of the well-being of other people" (p. 9). Even though positive life outcomes flow from participating in loving and supportive community, seeking spiritual truths, and learning to follow them, many emerging adults fail to give themselves over to such positive human goods. Instead, Smith writes, they tend to focus "almost exclusively on materialistic consumption and financial security as the guiding stars of their lives. We think that too is a problem" (p. 9).

If institutions of higher learning hope to redress the substantial deficits in the moral and spiritual imagination of emerging adults, they will first need to come to terms with how this tragic deficit arose in the first place. Looking closely at the lives of emerging adults, one soon realizes that broader cultural mores and commitments bear the weight of responsibility for the narrow field of vision among emerging adults. As Smith (2011) writes: "One way or another, adults and the adult world are almost always complicit in the troubles, suffering, and misguided living of youth, if not the direct source of them" (p. 11). Consider the following rather alarming observation in *Lost in Transition:* "Fully one in three (34 percent) of the emerging adults we interviewed said that they simply did not know what makes anything morally right or wrong" (Smith, 2011, p. 36). When you add the number of emerging adults who could not remember ever facing a moral dilemma to those who were either utterly confused about what constitutes a moral dilemma or who refused to answer the question, you arrive at a staggering 66 percent of emerging adults. In short, a total of two-thirds of emerging adults are dramatically unprepared to either understand or reflect upon the moral dimension of their lives (Smith, 2011).

Committed to both individualism and a soft version of moral relativism, emerging adults struggle to make moral decisions without the guidance of religious traditions or authorities. We should not be surprised by the consequence of all of this: when faced with an actual moral dilemma, the majority of emerging adults default to "what would personally make them happy or would help them to get ahead in life" (Smith, 2011, p. 60). Unprepared to objectively distinguish real moral truths and facts from mere perceptions of reality, the majority of emerging adults are simply lost. What is more, many end up making decisions that risk forever damaging the possibility that they can make their way safely back to shore. The hidden truth, however, is that the adult world is principally at fault for the pain, confusion, and nihilism manifest in the lives of emerging adults. Smith writes:

> Colleges and universities appear to be playing a part in this failure as well. There are many explanations for this situation that deserve to be better understood. But for the moment our point is simply this: the adult world of American culture and society are failing very many of its youth when it comes to moral matters. We are letting them down, sending many, and probably most, of them out into the world without the basic intellectual tools and basic personal formation needed to think and express even the most elementary of reasonably defensible moral thoughts and claims. And that itself, we think, is morally wrong. (p. 61)

Smith's words point to a critical observation: no serious attempt to help emerging adults safely navigate adulthood should be undertaken without seeking to address the looming moral and spiritual deficits. Moreover, institutions of higher learning—particularly church-related institutions with a distinct Christian mission—would do well to determine more effective ways of forming the intellectual, moral, and spiritual lives of emerging adults and devote significant financial resources. To resist doing so is to risk consigning generations of emerging adults to lives of moral confusion, purposelessness, and spiritual barrenness.

With tragic spiritual, intellectual, and moral condition of emerging adulthood in view, let us turn our attention to the work of Tim Clydesdale. Like Smith, Clydesdale is a sociologist of religion whose work underscores the importance of nurturing holy grit.

"Holy Grit" and Lives of Purpose, Resilience, and Meaning

Tim Clydesdale, professor of sociology at the College of New Jersey and author of *The First Year Out: Understanding American Teens after High School* (2007), is responsible for the turn of the phrase "holy grit." Holy grit plays a leading role in his *The Purposeful Graduate: Why Colleges Must Talk to Students about Vocation* (Clydesdale, 2015).

The genesis of Clydesdale's interest in the formation of "grit" began with an invitation from the Lilly Foundation to evaluate its $225 million investment in eighty-eight religious colleges throughout the United States. This Lilly Endowment initiative, called the "Program for the Theological Exploration of Vocation" (PTEV), was established to encourage college students to engage in extended theological reflection on their religious ethics, practices, sense of purpose, and vocation (Clydesdale, 2007). This important program funded a variety of different approaches to this goal. Seeking to determine its return on investment, Lilly invited Clydesdale to conduct a broad study. Clydesdale undertook an evaluation of twenty-six campus programs devoted to the theological exploration of vocation. His study included interviews with 284 students and alumni and 274 faculty and staff and the analysis of 2,111 responses. He also conducted panel interviews of sixty students in their senior year and re-interviewed these students one year later. A comparison sample involved interviews with sixty-five students from nine campuses that did not have a PTEV program.

Clydesdale's training as a sociologist of religion predisposed him to believe that these PTEV programs would make things worse—not better— by fostering maladaptive idealism that would set up idealistic young adults for future disappointment. In fact, however, Clydesdale was surprised to find that these programs successfully encouraged a form of "grounded idealism." When he speaks of "holy grit," it is precisely this "grounded idealism" that he has in view. Why is his study significant? Clydesdale's work provides substantial evidence to support the mandate for church related institutions to invest considerable time and energy helping emerging adults to explore questions of purpose, calling, and meaning (Clydesdale, 2014). However, let us not run too far ahead of the argument.

When you ask emerging adults "Do you hope to make a difference in the world?" they invariably answer "Yes." Tragically, though, the vast majority of emerging adults lack any clear sense of how to begin working toward achieving this otherwise salutary goal. Seldom do their answers deviate from the cultural script of finding a high-paying job, pursuing fun, and finding someone to meet their emotional need for intimacy. This rather limited cultural toolkit is well documented by sociologist Mary Grigsby in her work, *College Life through the Eyes of Students* (2009).

Seeking to understand how emerging adults attempt to navigate life, Grigsby's research identifies three distinct paths. Each of these three approaches serves as an ideal of one kind or another and can easily be placed along a continuum of options; however, emerging adults tend to find themselves on one of the three trajectories. This way of characterizing the "live options" available to emerging adults is so helpful that Clydesdale simply adopts Grigsby's pattern, allowing her three paths to become an interpretive lens through which he examines the research that emerged from his analysis of the Lilly PTEV initiative. Given this, it would be best to learn something about the dominant characteristics of each path.

The dominant path followed by over 50 percent of emerging adults is called an "independent individualist blueprint" (Grigsby, 2009, p. 144). The principal characteristic of this "individualist trajectory" is its view of the self as an autonomous agent. One of the many downsides of this approach is how it necessitates reducing external institutions and persons to mere adjuncts. The vision of the "good life" for someone following this path extends no further than having a physically attractive partner to meet one's needs for personal intimacy and acquiring enough money to purchase as many consumer goods as one desires.

Slightly less than 40 percent of emerging adults decide not to follow the "independent trajectory" and instead choose a "traditional individualist" trajectory. This dominant strategy takes the shape of seeking to occupy traditional roles of responsibility in the once stable social institutions of family, marriage, work, church, and community. While identity and meaning are still very much individual constructions, one seeks to make progress in these areas by leveraging participation in traditional roles of responsibility.

Not all emerging adults, however, choose to follow an "independent" trajectory of one kind or another. The remaining 10 percent of emerging adults elect to follow what is called an "interdependent trajectory." This approach to the notion of the "good life" is characterized by purposeful, productive living and global citizenship. Key to this approach is the fact that it is decidedly *not* an individualist approach to life. Here, emerging adults seek to discover meaning, purpose, and identity in a *community*. Although participation in communities is still voluntaristic, those who follow this trajectory choose to do so in spite of the inevitable flaws and shortcomings to be found in any given community. Furthermore, interdependent participants tend to demonstrate a greater awareness of the structural inequalities that make it all the more difficult for the most vulnerable in society. Crucially, those who follow this trajectory intentionally blur the lines between self-interest and the common good, private and public. In short, emerging adults who follow this path realize that the foundation of identity, meaning, and purpose lies beyond self-interest (Grigsby, 2009).

Returning to Clydesdale's analysis, we learn that telling problems exist with the first two trajectories. The independent individualist eventually finds that it is often quite difficult to cultivate an intimate relationship while sacrificing considerable time and energy in pursuit of professional advancement. High-paying employment can be hard to find in one's twenties, and paying off the accumulated debt of college or university bills can be a significant challenge. These impediments frustrate the pursuit of autonomy and intimacy.

Likewise, heretofore stable institutions such as family, marriage, employment, and church have been rendered fragile by the economic, social, and cultural condition of late modernity. The decline of these institutions makes it harder to inhabit the "traditional individualist" trajectory. The effort to live out this script is further compromised, Clydesdale adds, by the highly voluntarist nature of such communities. The capacity for communities to function as stable and enduring centers of support is dramatically undermined when participation in a given community follows from the exercise of autonomous will or preference. When a community fails to meet someone's needs, that person simply walks away. Even more problematic is that—in such a highly individualist culture like ours—we no longer have a shared vocabulary with which to settle upon the nature and purpose of community.

What should we take away from the work of Clydesdale, Grigsby, and Smith? If nearly 90 percent of emerging adults have adopted an untenable strategy for development and growth, leaders of institutions should think long and hard about what can be done to foster greater participation along the interdependent trajectory. One of the best places to start is to look more closely at a number of the identifiable characteristics found among those emerging adults who are attracted to the interdependent trajectory. It turns out that one of the leading characteristics of this cohort is something called "grit."

For the past eleven years, Angela Lee Duckworth of the University of Pennsylvania has undertaken groundbreaking research on the subject of grit. Duckworth defines grit as "perseverance and passion for long-term goals" requiring work "toward challenges, maintaining both effort and interest over years and years—despite failure, adversity, and even just stalls in progress" (Duckworth, n.d.). She adds, "Whereas disappointment or boredom signals to others that it is time to change trajectory and cut losses, the gritty individual stays the course." Put simply, grit is sticking with your plans for the future and not getting thrown off course. By way of illustration,

Duckworth adds, "There are many talented individuals who simply do not follow through on their commitments. In fact, in our data, grit is usually unrelated or even inversely related to measures of talent" (Duckworth, 2013). There are many fascinating elements to Duckworth's study, two of which deserve considerable attention. First, unlike intelligence, talent, height, or good looks, grit can be nurtured. Second, possessing a high degree of grit appears to be a better indicator of future success than how much raw intelligence or talent a person possesses (Duckworth, n.d.). Duckworth's research raises an important question: what should we make of the fact that grit is neutral? In other words, possessing a high "grit value" fails to tell you which goals are worth pursuing.

Entirely germane to our analysis is the correlation Clydesdale draws between possessing grit and being committed to an interdependent path. It is here where we begin to see how deep commitment to the Christian faith can make a difference in being able to identify long-term goals that will lead to purposeful and productive lives of significance. Importantly, Clydesdale (2014) found that emerging adults who thrived in the PTEV programs on vocation were exactly the same individuals who possessed what he calls "holy grit."

Grit is neutral. Holy grit is not. As Clydesdale notes, holy grit is focused upon specific goals tied to the love of God and neighbor. Accordingly, emerging adults who possess holy grit choose to participate in PTEV-funded programs for a number of compelling reasons. These programs provided an outlet for their desire to grow in community and live in ways that have genuine social impact. In contrast to many of their peers, those who possess a high degree of holy grit embody a grounded, rather than maladaptive, idealism. It is instructive to see that those who demonstrate a commitment to this kind of idealism also possess an honest self-knowledge. These emerging adults have a keen sense of their skills, passions, strengths, and weaknesses. At the same time, they demonstrate a significant commitment to self-transcendence. They realize the importance of being involved in and committed to the lives of others, and they believe that life is not simply about "me." Consequently, they are committed to sacrificing for the benefit of broken individuals and flawed institutions.

What should we take away from all of this? We should not miss the fact that programs explicitly encouraging students to thoughtfully and actively explore questions of purpose and meaning attract the ones who already have these values as part of their core identity. Furthermore, academic programs that provide a clear path to intentional communities aimed at living out the consequences of Christian moral teaching actually succeed in nurturing the kind of moral and spiritual development necessary to make lasting social and spiritual impact in the world. Institutions whose mission corresponds to this kind of moral commitment and action would do well to learn from the correlation between holy grit and participation in supportive, intentional, Christian communities of faith and witness.

We began our discussion by observing that the vast majority of emerging adults are ill-equipped to safely navigate many of the cultural and moral challenges in their way. We subsequently noted that this makes it all the more difficult to nurture lives of vital faith, purpose, and the love of God and neighbor. However, encouragement may be found in recognizing that the minority of emerging adults who possess a high degree of holy grit also demonstrate a capacity for honest self-knowledge and self-sacrifice. In short, these emerging adults are the kind who can flourish in intentional Christian community. Evidently, nurturing holy grit in the context of intentional community holds remarkable promise.

With these key elements of the sociology of religion vis-à-vis emerging adulthood, and with brief introduction to Duckworth's research on grit in place, let us turn our attention to a new and innovative program at Hope College. This year-long program in lived theology seeks to help students to discover purpose and calling in the context of seeking to obey the prophet Jeremiah's exhortation to "seek the welfare of the city" (Jer 29:7). In short, Emmaus is dedicated to helping a cohort of emerging adults to re-enact the loving obedience of Christ and thus serve as a sign of God's redemptive purpose for the world.

The Emmaus Scholars Program: Lived Theology

Christian institutions of higher education carry significant responsibility for the spiritual and moral formation of emerging adults. If the goal of higher education concerns helping emerging adults to recover enduring meaning and purpose for their lives, there is simply no better place to turn than the living witness of God manifest in testimony of the prophets and apostles. Here we encounter God's true purpose for life and calling: to learn and live in the light of the risen Lord. Barth (1962) expresses this point well:

> as the individual himself does not come to Jesus Christ and thus become a Christian under the impulsion and in the power of his religious and moral disposition, but only in virtue of the fact that Jesus Christ calls him and thus unites him with Himself, so it is Jesus Christ Himself . . . [that] calls these individuals. (p. 682)

It follows that "calling" cannot be an individual project. Again, Barth sees this issue with telling clarity, maintaining that there is simply no "*vocatio* (calling), and therefore no *unio cum Christo* (union with Christ), which does not as such lead directly into the communion of saints, i.e., the *communio vocatorum* (communion of saints)" (p. 682). At the founding of Harvard College, there may well have been no pressing need to draw the connection between Jesus Christ as the "only foundation of all sound knowledge and learning" and the mission and witness of the *community* of faith—no pressing need, that is, beyond one of making plain the foundation of light and life. In our day, however, every facet of this christological foundation is contested, rendering the task of cultivating spiritual, intellectual, and moral formation all the more difficult.

Realizing that Christ is present as he speaks, we cheerfully confess that Holy Scripture is the locus of the Word's authoritative and creative direction, and that there is no better place to turn when helping young adults investigate their calling. In view of this, the strategic importance of Emmaus becomes all the more clear as it aims to provide an innovative example of lived theology. Key to this program is its commitment to foster lives of faithful obedience capable of carrying out the work of justice. Stated in the most concise way possible, the Emmaus Scholars Program embodies a commitment to integral mission.

Believing that human identity and purpose (calling) is grounded in the person and work of Jesus Christ (cf. Col. 1:15–20), Emmaus was developed in the knowledge that the Spirit is the active presence of the Word in gathering, nurturing, and sending out a community of Christians capable of being agents of renewal and witness in the world (Barth, 1956). The following description of the program explains how Emmaus fosters the spiritual and moral transformation of emerging adults by helping them to see specific ways in which they are gathered into Christ, nurtured in the Spirit, and sent out in integral mission.

Christian Freedom, Joy in Learning

First, coming to realize that they have been gathered and claimed by God, Emmaus Scholars find Christian freedom and joy in learning. So, how does this come about?

One of the primary discoveries must be an understanding of the relationship between responsible moral action and divine grace. This is beautifully expressed by Barth, who, in the midst of offering a Bible study on Romans 12 to the Christian Student's Association in Münster, provided the following exposition of what it means to offer our bodies to God as a "living sacrifice":

> There are no areas of which we can say: God has nothing to do here or this is none of God's business. It is not true that there is a religious sphere in which we are willing to listen and, at the same time, another sphere where life has its own laws, where we may not allow the light of God to enter in. But just as the whole is met by mercy, in the same way the whole is also put under the discipline of grace. God wants and needs nothing less than everything! (Barth, as cited in Jehle, 2002, p. 34)

We would be hard-pressed indeed to find a more startling and profound exposition of the scope of divine mercy, love, and care. In short, emerging adult life is to take shape under the discipline of grace.

Barth's teaching bears directly upon the Christian formation of emerging adults. When set against the contemporary vision of the moral life as a near-endless buffet of options, Barth's grasp of the fundamental unity of creaturely life under the discipline of grace appears all the more attractive. Reflecting the essential thrust of classical Christianity, Barth commends a vision of a fully integrated life: one in which divine mercy, rule, and action constitute the ground of meaning, reconciliation, and purpose. How we understand and live out this unified vision of life under the discipline of grace is an important question with abiding consequences for the church's witness in the post-Christian West.

A number of common objections surface at this point. How, for instance, does divine action elicit lives of faithful correspondence? What should we make of Barth's claim that God desires to bring every facet of our lives into conformity with divine rule? Is it any less worrying to hear him speak of divine rule while employing the terms "light," "grace," and "mercy"? Put differently, should we be worried that the lordship of Christ over all (Col. 1:15–23) means our essential destruction?

We would do well to listen to Barth's (2004) account of the way in which Jesus's humanity graciously determines the way forward for all others: "The mystery and miracle of the event of which we speak consists in the fact that man himself is the free subject of this event on the basis of a possibility which is present only with God" (p. 5). The "possibility" of which Barth speaks—namely, to live a life reconciled to God—depends entirely upon the faithfulness and work of Christ. Jesus's fulfillment of the covenant sets us on an entirely new foundation so that the discipline of grace and divine mercy constitutes the basis of our humanity and fellowship with God. Set on a new footing, the miracle of new life in Christ takes shape in our living faith and obedience. Accordingly, we begin to see the fundamental importance of the discipline of grace. Granting God's redemptive action its proper place, we are delivered from the fundamental falsehood of our present age: the deadly pursuit of self-sufficiency. As objects of God's undeserved mercy and grace, we belong to God's covenant. Having been set free from the sinful pretense of creaturely autonomy, we begin to find our way with purpose and peace. The living voice of the Good Shepherd intrudes upon the wasteland of our creaturely rebellion and calls us to life and freedom in Christ. As Barth reminds us, this call to fellowship represents the basis of enduring obedience and partnership:

> The only possibility is to be faithful to God. This is our liberation
> through the divine change effected in the history of Jesus Christ
> . . . The divine change in whose accomplishment a man becomes a

Christian is an event of true intercourse between God and man. If it undoubtedly has its origin in God's initiative, no less indisputably man is not ignored or passed over in it. He is taken seriously as an independent creature of God. He is not run down and overpowered, but set on his own feet. He is not put under tutelage, but addressed and treated as an adult. (p. 22)

Given our interest in seeking constructive ways to foster Christian formation among emerging adults, Barth's exposition of the sovereign mercy, love, and grace of God is an invaluable account of the truth of the Gospel. In short, Barth's account of the constitutive reality of the history of Jesus succeeds at the point where so many colleges and universities fail emerging adults. Barth does this by underscoring the way in which divine reconciliation (2 Cor. 5:17–21) sets us free *for* corresponding lives of moral responsibility. Emerging adults desperately need to hear that, in Christ, God is *pro nobis* (for us). Far from putting them in the docks, God comes to set them on their own feet in the life-giving setting of the discipline of grace.

Barth (2004) further explains how the history of Jesus elicits corresponding lives of faithfulness:

The history of Jesus Christ, then, does not destroy a man's own history. In virtue of it this history becomes a new history, but it is still his own new history. The faithfulness to God to which he is summoned is not, then, an emanation of God's faithfulness. It is truly his own faithfulness, decision and act. He could not achieve it if he were not liberated thereto. But being thus liberated, he does it as his own act, as his answer to the Word of God spoken to him in the history of Jesus Christ. (p. 22–23)

In effect, human identity and calling are fundamentally created realities brought into existence by the transformative person and work of Jesus.

This brief account of the "history of Jesus" as the constitutive ground of forgiveness and renewal provides a better vantage point from which to see the connection between holy grit and integral mission. Before we document Emmaus's theological and biblical foundation for mission, let us briefly consider the role of the Spirit in nurturing Christian community.

An Intentional, Learning Community, Nurtured in Christ

Second, from its inception, Emmaus has been understood to be an intentional, Christian learning community gathered and *nurtured* in Christ. Dietrich Bonhoeffer's reflections on the formation of Finkenwalde, an underground seminary, had a formative influence upon the development of Emmaus. Bonhoeffer wrote to Barth about the seminary on September 19, 1936. Painfully aware of the surrounding post-Christian world, Bonhoeffer expressed his desire to provide a "completely different kind of training" for students than that being provided by the university. This letter documents his growing conviction that the cultural moment demanded spiritual formation "in a life governed by gathering around the Word morning and evening and by fixed times of prayer". To which Bonhoeffer added,

> If we cannot help them in this, we do not help them at all.... It is clear to me that all these things have a place only when really accurate theological, exegetical, and doctrinal work is done together with, and at the very same time as, these spiritual exercises. Otherwise, all these questions are given a false emphasis. (Bonhoeffer, 1996, pp. 121-122)

When leading figures in the German educational system were insisting that seminary education should do no more than prepare ministers to preach and teach the catechism, Bonhoeffer discerned the need to cast a broader vision. Emmaus was conceived as a contemporary representation of Bonhoeffer's approach to theological education: integrating theological, exegetical, and doctrinal work with spiritual practices of morning and evening prayer, concrete moral action, and reflection.

In the same way that Finkenwalde represented a decidedly non-ascetic community, Emmaus embodies a spirituality best characterized as prayer and action on behalf of the broken. Just as Bonhoeffer (1996) claimed that "only those who cry out for the Jews may also sing Gregorian chants" (cf. Editor's Afterword, p. 124), Emmaus locates academic study within the context of moral and spiritual formation as citizens of the kingdom of God. Two distinct expressions of the nurture offered by Emmaus command our attention: intellectual and spiritual.

Intellectually, the program requires Emmaus Scholars to participate in a research seminar, "Reconciliation and Integral Mission"; a leadership course, "Team Building, Servant Leadership, Christian Perspective"; and an experiential learning course, "Integral Mission and Community." Together, these courses provide a total of ten credit hours of academic work focused upon the biblical mandate to care for the cultural, social, economic, and political well-being of the city (cf. Jer. 29:7). As a catalyst for deep friendship, understanding, reconciliation, and community, Emmaus nurtures emerging adults in the discovery of a public voice for their scholarship and research. To this end, the program uses traditional venues for scholarly publication, including Hope College's Celebration of Undergraduate Research and the National Conference on Undergraduate Research (NCUR). Employing some of the techniques found within the field of the digital humanities, Emmaus Scholars also publish online their reflections on course readings, research, and experiential/service/learning events. For instance, Brandon Bowser and Nathan Longfield published online a fine introduction to the biblical and theological foundation for Christian political action (Bowser & Longfield, 2014). Similarly, the scope and nature of student research is well-represented by the scholarship of Jacob Boersma, Lauren Gentry, and Erick Skaff in their work, "Just Care: Healthcare on the Margins" (Boersma, Gentry, & Skaff, 2014). In addition, David Green and Abbie Larink developed an illuminating study of the problem of economic disparity and positive steps undertaken by the Church in community development, "Steeple2Sidewalk" (Green & Larink, 2014).

Spiritually, Emmaus is distinguished by a common worship-life that includes morning and evening prayer, regular involvement in churches throughout the community, and participation in Hope College's vibrant Campus Ministry programs, including weekday chapels and "The Gathering" Sunday evening service. In an increasingly post-Christian setting, expressions of genuine Christian community take on even more importance. Prayer and worship play a constitutive role in the integration of theological reflection, worship, leadership, and care for the poor. Together this forms a seamless pattern of discipleship. Two features of life together illustrate the approach to spiritual life and nurture within Emmaus.

First, in an increasingly post-Christian setting, expressions of genuine Christian community take on even more importance. In living fellowship with Christ, Emmaus Scholars learn that the "new history" to which they are summoned is a life of self-offering to one another in community and faith. New life in Christ constitutes the basis of the corresponding life and calling to embody gospel virtues of faith, hope, and love in mutual care, compassion, and prayer. At the beginning of their time together, Emmaus Scholars encounter Psalm 133:1, "How very good and pleasant it is when kindred live together in unity" (NRSV). Importantly, they are invited to consider Bonhoeffer's (1996) claim:

> The physical presence of other Christians is a source of incomparable joy and strength to the believer . . . But if there is so much happiness and joy even in a single encounter of one Christian with another, what inexhaustible riches must invariably open up for those who by God's will are privileged to live in daily community life with other Christians! Of course, what is an inexpressible blessing from God for the lonely individual is easily disregarded and trampled under foot by those who receive the gift every day. It is easily forgotten that the community of Christians is a gift of grace from the kingdom of God, a gift that can be taken from us any day—that the time still separating us from the most profound loneliness may be brief indeed. Therefore, let those who until now have had the privilege of living a Christian life together with other Christians praise God's grace from the bottom of their hearts. Let them thank God on their knees and realize: it is grace, nothing but grace, that we are still permitted to live in the community of Christians today. (p. 29)

Crucial to their formation as Christians is the recognition that the body of Christ is not a voluntary community. Knowing that human identity and calling are found in Christ, Emmaus Scholars experience the spiritual freedom found in following the Good Shepherd. Christ intrudes upon the wasteland of our autonomy and calls us into a living fellowship with other brothers and sisters. Given the powerful forces pressing in upon emerging adults that lead them to adopt high expectations for personal fulfillment without the burden of self-sacrifice, the experience of intentional Christian community represents a profoundly disturbing blessing.

Again, Bonhoeffer's (1996) theological reflections upon community frame our experience with Emmaus. He sees with acute clarity that the question of whether or not someone is my brother or sister has little to do with his or her expressed interest in being my friend. Bonhoeffer writes:

> My brother or sister is instead that other person who has been redeemed by Christ, absolved from sin, and called to faith and eternal life. What persons are in themselves as Christians, in their inwardness and piety, cannot constitute the basis of our community, which is determined by what those persons are in terms of Christ. (p. 34)

He then adds the profound claim: "We have one another only through Christ, but through Christ we really do have one another" (p. 34). Because of the constitutive work of Christ in our midst, Emmaus Scholars learn how to view each person in light of their true image in Christ. All of this makes, in turn, the practice of prayer and sharing in the Word a necessary part of mutual support. Accordingly, prayer frames daily life together in Emmaus.

Similarly, learning how to dwell in Scripture—to follow the drama of God's covenantal faithfulness with Israel and the early church—and to bring the concrete needs of the community and surrounding world before God in prayer is a transformative experience in Christian community. By sharing in the daily liturgy of prayer and Scripture reading, Emmaus students experience the blessing of being rooted in a community that brings its members into the presence of God through intercessory prayer. Together, they learn to find comfort, strength, and love in the presence and mercy of God. Daily common prayer and listening to God's Word is itself a profound experience and witness to the fact that, in Christ, we may truly care for one another.

The Integral Mission of a Sent Community

Third, Emmaus is not only an intentional Christian learning community gathered and nurtured in Christ, but it is also a sent (extrinsically oriented) community. Providing its Scholars with a transformative experience in lived theology, Emmaus endeavors to provide formative experiences that foster a grounded rather than maladaptive idealism. This is accomplished by introducing Emmaus Scholars to the practice of integral mission. The expression "integral mission" (misión integral) came into currency among the Latin American Theological Fraternity under the direction of C. René Padilla and is manifest in the critically important document "Theology and Implications of Radical Discipleship" (Douglas, 1975, pp. 1294–1296). Since then, integral mission has played an increasingly prominent role in a number of the leading Christian relief and development organizations around the world, including the Micah Network, Tearfund International, World Relief, and International Justice Mission.

Greater understanding of "integral mission" is gained by looking at the work of the Latin American Theological Fellowship, led by C. René Padilla and Samuel Escobar. These Global South theologians promoted a holistic vision of the church's mission and played a leading role in the development and articulation of *misión integral*—a movement committed to seeking the integration of the proclamation of the gospel and social-political involvement and advocacy on behalf of the poor and the oppressed. At the first International Congress on World Evangelization in Lausanne, Switzerland, held July 16–25, 1974 (with nearly 2,500 participants, 1,000 observers from 150 countries and 125 Protestant denominations represented), Escobar presented a paper entitled, "Evangelization and Man's Search for Freedom, Justice and Fulfillment." Standing in the tradition of eighteenth century evangelicals like John Wesley and William Wilberforce, Escobar challenged his audience to deepen their commitment to the "clear teaching of the Bible in relation to human needs and total liberation that the Gospel brings" (Escobar, 1975, p. 319). Refusing to accept the "otherworldly" emphasis of North American evangelicals—who, all too-often, reduced the Gospel to a verbal proclamation of a spiritual message of heavenly rewards divorced from the concrete realities of political, social, or economic injustice and oppression—Escobar asserted that "a spirituality without discipleship in the daily social, economic, and political aspects of life is religiosity and not Christianity" (1975, p. 310).

Only with considerable pressure from Global South theologians did the framers of Lausanne begin to see the connection between the character of God as Creator and God's work of reconciliation. This dawning realization led to the dramatic expression (in Article 5 of the proceedings, a statement on 'Christian Social Responsibility') of heartfelt penitence for having neglected social justice as an integral expression of the Gospel:

We affirm that evangelism and socio-political involvement are both part of our Christian duty. . . . The message of salvation implies also a message of judgment upon every form of alienation, oppression and discrimination, and we should not be afraid to denounce evil and injustice wherever they exist. When people receive Christ they are born again into his kingdom and must seek not only to exhibit but also to spread its righteousness in the midst of an unrighteous world. The salvation we claim should be transforming us in the totality of our personal and social responsibilities. Faith without works is dead. (Stott, 1997, p. 24)

Notwithstanding the importance of Article 5 of Lausanne, it is very difficult to imagine that North American and European evangelicals would have so readily adopted a transformed vision of the whole Gospel were it not for the pioneering work of Latin American theologians such as Padilla, Escobar, Emilio Antonio Nuñez, Orlando Costas, and Rolando Gutierrez-Cortéz. In short, Emmaus owes a considerable debt to the Latin American Theological Fellowship's development and formulation of *mision integral*.

Reflecting the biblical mandate of Micah 6:8, those who practice integral mission embody the conviction that the proclamation of the love of Christ cannot be separated from the work of justice. At the same time, it is crucial to see that integral mission says as much about the integrity of those involved in ministry and witness as it does about what they do. This point is particularly well made by the Sri Lankan theologian, Vinoth Ramachandra (n.d.), who asks:

When, for instance, Jesus voluntarily engaged a social outcast like the Samaritan woman (John 4) in face-to-face conversation, was he doing "evangelism" or was he performing a "political action" in challenging the political taboos of his society? When the early Church rescued infants left to die on the rubbish heaps outside cities in the Roman empire, or visited and fed enemy prisoners, or refused to join in the sacrificial cult of the emperor, were they political subversives or were they simply living out the Gospel in their world? (para. 5)

This principled commitment to the inseparability of the compassion of Christ and the work of justice constitutes the essential backdrop against which the entire Emmaus Scholars Program is lived out. Accordingly, the connection drawn between moral obedience and the worship life of the community of faith highlights the importance of *integrity*, *belonging* to, and *becoming* the people of God. As such, it is crucial to identify specific ways in which this commitment takes specific form.

The ninth chapter of Jeremiah's prophesy lies at the core of the way that Emmaus sees the connection between worship, the knowledge of God, and corresponding participation in the *missio Dei*. The Old Testament scholar and theologian Walter Brueggemann (1978) rightly insists that one of the central features of a prophet's ministry in ancient Israel was to "nurture, nourish, and evoke a consciousness and perception alternative to the consciousness and perception of the dominant culture around us" (p. 60). Jeremiah's ministry covered the most critical period of Judah's life as a kingdom. Serving under the rule of the last five kings of Judah, Jeremiah was called to pronounce God's judgment upon Judah's indifference, pride, idolatry, and syncretism. In the midst of God's indictment of Judah, we find the following exposition of the character and compassion of God:

> Thus says the Lord: Do not let the wise boast in their wisdom, do not let the mighty boast in their might, do not let the wealthy boast in their wealth; but let those who boast boast in this, that they understand and know me, that I am the Lord; I act with steadfast love, justice, and righteousness in the earth, for in these things I delight, says the Lord. (Jer. 9:23–24)

This exhortation to seek meaning and purpose by aligning oneself with the very things that characterize God's redemptive action and care for Judah is fundamentally important for those who seek to carry out integral mission.

Of course, the content of Jeremiah's pronouncement is as countercultural today as it was in the sixth-century B.C. True worship and understanding of God demand a form of ascetic separation from standard, but fundamentally misguided, strategies to secure wisdom and security. According to Jeremiah, these are only granted in covenantal fellowship with God. The disarming beauty and riches of the covenant here lie in the holiness and character of God. Yahweh is the One whose rule is concretely manifest in the exercise of *hesed* (translated here as steadfast love, often linked to God's enduring commitment to sustain salvation by upholding the covenant); *tsedeqa* (doing judgment and justice); and *mishpat* (the bringing of salvation/justice to the most vulnerable, those on the margins). Jeremiah lays bare the essential features of the kindly rule of God, effectively proclaiming that these things are closest to God's heart. Why then should emerging adults seek to do integral mission? Because doing so affords them the opportunity to align their lives with what matters most to God: steadfast love, justice, and mercy. In effect, the practice of integral mission focuses resilience toward the pursuit of *shalom*—the renewal and flourishing of God's creation. Given the formative significance of integral mission, where do Emmaus Scholars put their faith into practice?

The Emmaus Program has developed a strategic partnership with a local Christian Development Organization called 3Sixty (www.3-sixty.org). This relationship allows Emmaus Scholars to put community development theory and theology into practice while learning "best practices" from development leaders who have nurtured relationships of trust among the poor and marginalized. 3Sixty's practice of living out faith in sacrificial ways mirrors what James Davidson Hunter (2010) so ably defends in his work, *To Change the World*.

The conditions of late modernity commend different modes of Christian witness. In this pluralist setting, Hunter reminds us, "The presumption of God and of his active presence in the world cannot be easily sustained because the most important symbols of social, economic, political and aesthetic life no longer point to him" (p. 203). Christianity has lost its once-dominant position of cultural prominence. Accompanying this loss is the demise of the very plausibility structures that made belief a reasonable possibility for many. The absence of these symbols makes Christian self-understanding and witness all the more difficult. In this cultural moment, concrete love of neighbor and a commitment to building relationships of trust constitute a crucial witness of "faithful presence." Moreover, "faithful presence" is a necessary expression of care and love for those who face hardship, pain, loneliness, poverty, or hunger.

Of course, we all need effective models of integral mission. To this end, Emmaus travels to Washington, D.C., each spring to worship with other Christians, learn from their stories of how they live out their faith in the city, serve and share breakfast with homeless men and women, and hear from representatives of prominent nongovernmental organizations such as Bread for the World and the United States Conference on Catholic Bishops (UCSSB) Justice, Peace & Human Development office. Doing so affords Emmaus Scholars an invaluable opportunity to deepen their understanding of the biblical and theological mandates for advocacy while gaining an invaluable exposure to exemplary organizations committed to the work of the kingdom of God. In addition, they gain perspective on the distribution of domestic and international food aid in order to visit Capitol Hill and lobby their congressional representative on issues of hunger and food aid policy. Visiting International Justice Mission (IJM) and sharing in their daily staff worship afford Emmaus Scholars a unique vantage from which to appreciate a remarkably professional and faithful organization committed to freeing slaves (victims of sex trafficking and bonded child laborers). That IJM would set aside time each day for prayer and corporate worship in the face of such pressing demands illustrates the need for a fully integrated spiritual life and witness. We also visit Christ House, a truly astonishing example of what it means to be a faithful presence in the lives of homeless men and women. This intentional Christian community of healthcare workers, chaplains, and staff provides compassionate health care for some of the most vulnerable in the District of Columbia.

Finally, time spent volunteering at DC Central Kitchen exposes Emmaus Scholars to the work of the nation's first community kitchen. This "kitchen" is a leading advocate for repurposing surplus and donated food. At the same time, DC Central Kitchen seeks to break the cycle of poverty by training and employing previously unemployed adults, paying them a starting wage of $13.60 per hour with full health benefits and a 50 percent retirement match. Each day, the kitchen prepares just under 12,000 meals, including more than 6,000 meals for low-income D.C. schoolchildren with another 5,000+ for D.C.'s homeless shelters and direct service nonprofits (Cooper & Hienz, 2014). In seeking to free slaves, bind up the wounds of the broken, feed the hungry, and advocate for most vulnerable and oppressed, each of these organizations provides Emmaus Scholars with compelling models of integral mission.

Conclusion

As the post-Christian age dawns in the West, an important challenge falls to Christian churches, colleges, and universities. In the midst of a culture that has consigned a generation of emerging adults to moral confusion and spiritual barrenness, institutions of higher learning—particularly church-related institutions with a distinct Christian mission—need to devote considerable energy, commitment, and resources to form the intellectual, moral, and spiritual lives of emerging adults. Accordingly, Hope College's Emmaus Scholars Program represents a strategic commitment to educate students to think critically, love deeply, and do justice.

In spite of substantial cultural forces at work among emerging adults, a portion of young adults are attracted to programs that explicitly encourage thoughtful and active engagement with questions of purpose and meaning. Emmaus, for example, provides a clear path to substantial growth by nurturing the kind of moral and spiritual development necessary to make lasting social and spiritual impact in the world

With Christ as the constitutive ground of forgiveness and renewal, Emmaus Scholars come to view holy grit as a necessary gift of God. Caught up in the transformative work of the Spirit, Emmaus Scholars learn to employ their holy grit in ways that allow them to become a faithful presence of the love and mercy of God.

The Emmaus Scholars Program succeeds in forming a countercultural community of emerging adults by providing a cohort of Hope College students the opportunity to share in a vital community of worship, prayer, learning, and integral mission. Together, they learn how to seek the welfare of the city (Jer. 29:7). Finally, responding to the work of the Spirit in their lives, they become emerging adults capable of living lives of purpose, meaning, and resilience by pursuing the reconciliation and renewal of all things in Christ.

References

Barth, K. (1956). *Church dogmatics: The doctrine of reconciliation, Volume 4.1.* G. W. Bromiley & T. F. Torrance (Eds.). Edinburgh, UK: T&T Clark.

Barth, K. (1962). *Church dogmatics: The doctrine of reconciliation, Volume 4.3.2.* G. W. Bromiley & T. F. Torrance (Eds.). Edinburgh, UK: T&T Clark.

Barth, K. (2004). *Church dogmatics: The doctrine of reconciliation, Volume 4.4.* G. W. Bromiley & T. F. Torrance (Eds.). Edinburgh, UK: T&T Clark.

Boersma, J., Gentry, L., & Skaff, E. (2014, April). *Just care: Healthcare on the margins.* Retrieved from http://justhealthcare.weebly.com

Bonhoeffer, D. (1996). *Life together and prayerbook of the Bible.* G. B. Kelly (Ed.). Minneapolis, MN: Augsburg Fortress Press.

Bowser, B., & Longfield, N. (2014, April). Jesustice: A basis and guide for Christian political action. Retrieved from http://jesustice.weebly.com/

Brueggemann, W. (1978). *The prophetic imagination.* Minneapolis, MN: Augsburg Fortress Press.

Clydesdale, T. (2007). *The first year out: Understanding American teens after high school.* Chicago, IL: University of Chicago Press.

Clydesdale, T. (2007, March 28). Grant to aid TCNJ prof's research project. *The Times,* pp. B3. Retrieved from http://clydesdale.pages.tcnj.edu/files/2014/05 /Times-3-28-07.pdf

Clydesdale, T. (2014). Holy grit! The effects of purpose exploration programming on undergraduate engagement and life trajectories exploring purpose and vocation in college. *Association of American Colleges and Universities.* Retrieved from https://www.aacu.org/liberaleducation/2014/winter /clydesdale

Clydesdale, T. (2015). *Calling on purpose: The conversation every campus must have with students.* Chicago, IL: University of Chicago Press.

Cooper, R., & Hienz, J. (2014, December 19). Food + data = great opportunities. Retrieved from http://www.uschamberfoundation.org/food-data-great -opportunities

Douglas, J. D. (Ed.). (1975). Theology and implications of radical discipleship. *Let the earth hear his voice: International congress on world evangelization, Lausanne, Switzerland.* Minneapolis, MN: World Wide.

Duckworth, A. (n.d.). Grit. *Character Lab.* Retrieved from https://characterlab .org/character/grit/

Duckworth, A. (2013, April). The key to success? Grit. *Ted.* Video retrieved from http://www.ted.com/talks/angela_lee_duckworth_the_key_to_success _grit?language=en

Escobar, Samuel. (1975) "Evangelization and man's search for freedom, justice and fulfillment" In *Let the earth hear his voice: International congress on world evangelization, Lausanne, Switzerland.* Minneapolis, MN: World Wide

Green, D., & Larink, A. (2014, April), "Steeple2Sidewalk: connecting the church and community development". Retrieved from http://markhusbands.me/emmaus-scholars-student-research

Grigsby, M. (2009). *College life through the eyes of Students.* Albany, NY: SUNY Press.

Jehle, F. (2002). *Ever against the stream: The politics of Karl Barth, 1906–1968.* Grand Rapids, MI: Eerdmans.

Sabin, J. (1865). *New England's first fruits.* New York, NY: Kessinger Publishing.

Ramachandra, V. (n.d.). What is integral mission? *Micah Network Integral Mission Initiative.* Retrieved from http://www.micahnetwork.org/sites/default/files/doc/library/whatisintegralmission_imi-the-001.pdf

Smith, C., Christoffersen, K., Davidson, H., & Herzog, P. S. (2011). *Lost in transition: The dark side of emerging adulthood.* New York, NY: Oxford University Press.

Stott, J. R. W. (1997). *Making Christ known: Historic mission documents from the Lausanne movement, 1974–1989.* Grand Rapids, MI: Eerdmans.

MILLENNIALS, PARENTS, GRANDPARENTS

Are Families Still Passing on Their Faith?

VERN L. BENGTSON

University of Southern California

Beverly Johnson, now sixty, is an African-American who was twenty-five when this study began in 1970. She was raised by her grandparents, Henry and Eleanor, and still attends the Baptist church that Henry helped to establish in the 1960s when they first moved to southern California. She says her grandfather and grandmother had the greatest influence on her life religiously. She adds that she raised her children as she was raised by her grandparents, with the Ten Commandments at the center of their instruction. Her daughter Erika (thirty-two) says, "My mother still maintains the attachment because my great-grandfather was involved with founding the church." Erika is also a regular church attendee who says she is "very religious."

The focus of this chapter is on members of the Millennial generation, so-called because they were born about 1980 and thus came of age around the turn of the twenty-first century.[1] As they have been growing into young adulthood, much has been written about them, since in many ways they appear to be quite different from their parents' generation, particularly in terms of religion. For example, a highly publicized poll of religious affiliation in the U.S. found that almost one-third of Millennial generation members did not identify with any religious group, in comparison with 21 percent of Generation Xers, 15 percent of Baby Boomers, and less than 10 percent among older cohorts who identified that way (Pew Research Center, 2012).

However, public opinion polls such as this are based on cross-sectional data regarding religious affiliation. In such surveys, questions are asked of individuals who are of different ages—young, middle-aged, and older people—at just one point in time, sampled from those who have land-line telephones. In the case of the Johnson family (above), we get a different perspective. Here we have data about not just one individual but about a family, with several generations of respondents. Moreover, the information they provide spans several decades, from 1970 to 2005. The Johnsons have been participants in the thirty-five-year Longitudinal Study of Generations (LSOG), and they and the other 350-plus families in this study provide a broader perspective by which to view Millennials. We can compare their religious orientations with that of their parents and grandparents, and we can trace religious change not only over thirty-five years of historical time, but also over thirty-five years of the life cycle of individuals. By comparing these trends, we can make some predictions about what Millennials' religious practices and beliefs might be like in the future, as they themselves become parents and grandparents.

[1] This paper is based on material from *Families and Faith: How Religion is Passed Down Across Generations* by Vern Bengtson, with Norella Putney and Susan Harris (Oxford University Press: 2013); Merril Silverstein also collaborated in this research, and he is now principal investigator of the Longitudinal Study of Generations following my retirement. I want to acknowledge their many contributions to this research, which has been supported by grants from the John Templeton Foundation, the National Institute on Aging, and the National Institute of Mental Health. Data are from the Longitudinal Study of Generation's eight waves from 1970 to 2005. These have been archived with the University of Michigan's Inter-University Consortium for Political and Social Research and are available at no cost. We hope other researchers will feel free to conduct their own analyses of these data.

Thus, how different are the religious orientations of Millennials from those of their parents? From those of their grandparents? Moreover, how much has familial religious influence changed over time—across the period of significant social religious changes that we have seen in U.S. culture since the 1960s? These are some questions explored in this chapter.

Millennials and Generational Differences

Many public opinion polls have focused on Millennials recently. They are sometimes defined as a cohort born between 1980 and 1900 (Pew Research Center, 2014), though others categorize them as those currently in their twenties and thirties. Often, popular accounts call them a "generation," though that term is always problematic because it is never clear when a so-called generation begins and ends (Bengtson & Cutler, 1976). In the LSOG, we define Millennials as those who were born from 1980 to 1989, as they became eligible to come into our study at age sixteen. In any case, the defining characteristic for Millennials is that they were adolescents or emerging adults at the turn of the twenty-first century, during a time of significant technological, cultural, and religious change in U.S. society.

Millennials, who made up more than one-fourth of the workforce in 2014, do stand out, and appear to differ from their elders in many ways. In surveys, their responses often reveal a singularly individualistic outlook. Politically, they are more liberal; 29 percent say they are conservative, compared to 41 percent of Americans age 35 or older. Most of them (55 percent) believe that illegal immigrants should receive citizenship, compared to 44 percent of those 35 and older who believe that way. Moreover, they are more ethnically diverse; 57 percent of Millennials are Caucasian white, compared to 72 percent of all of the U.S. population over age 35. In some regions of the country, this generational contrast is even more striking; in California, which comprises almost one-sixth of the U.S. population, over one-third of Millennials and those younger are non-Caucasian whites (Pew Research Center, 2014).

In religion, too, polls show differences between Millennials and their elders. Almost one in three are religious "nones"—that is, they say they are unaffiliated, describing their religion as atheist, agnostic, "spiritual but not religious," or "nothing in particular" (Pew Research Center, 2012). Fewer than 19 percent of those over age thirty-five describe themselves that way. However, when we look further into the data and examine dimensions of religiosity other than religious affiliation, the contrasts are not so dramatic (Pew Research Center, 2012). One-third of the Millennial respondents said they attend worship at least once a week, a figure not that different from the 41 percent of adults thirty and older (including more than half of those sixty-five and older) who say the same. About half of Millennials say they pray every day (48 percent), compared with 56 percent of those thirty to forty-nine, 61 percent of those fifty to sixty-five, and 68 percent of those sixty-five and older. Moreover, the number of Millennials who believe that the Bible is the Word of God is very similar to that of their elders: 59 percent to 64 percent.

How significant are these differences in religion between today's Millennials and older age groups? To what extent is there a "generation gap" in religion? Are families failing to pass on their spiritual and religious values on to their children? And how might the Millennials' own views and practices change as they become parents and grandparents?

Changing Cultural Contexts of Families and Religion

We began the Longitudinal Study of Generations (described more fully below) in the 1960s, during a time of significant political and cultural change in American society. These changes were reflected in social institutions such as religion and the family. Thus, it is important to contextualize research on intergenerational transmission of religion by reviewing some relevant changes in American society and culture over the past half-century.

Changes in American Religiosity.

There have been remarkable changes in American religious culture since the 1950s (especially recently), and often these have been linked to changes in intergenerational relationships. For most of its history, the United States has been a highly churchgoing nation. Affiliation and involvement with church activities increased in the years following World War II, hitting a peak in the mid-1950s (Chavez, 2011; Wuthnow, 1988, 2007). However, the economic prosperity and stability of the 1950s was followed by cultural changes in the 1960s; the first wave of Baby Boomer youth became involved in protests challenging the politics and values of their elders and created what seemed to be a "generation gap" of unprecedented magnitude in American history (Bengtson, 1970). In the 1970s, researchers and social commentators described an increasing secularization of American society, prompting public discourse about the role of religion in education, politics, and mass communication (Bellah, Madsen, Sullivan, Swidler, & Tipton, 1985; Wuthnow, 1978).

More recently, there has been a remarkable increase in the numbers of "nones" in America—those who say they have no religious affiliation. By 2012, the unaffiliated represented over 19 percent of the U.S. adult population, a proportion that more than doubled from the decade before (Pew Research Center, 2012). One of the most sociologically interesting dimensions of this trend concerns its stratification by age. Younger people are much more likely than older ones to report that they have no religious affiliation or never attend services, creating a much greater age gap than observed in previous surveys (Pew Research Center, 2012). Thus, it would be plausible to expect that religious continuity between generations has declined over recent decades—that parent-youth similarity in religiosity is less evident today than it was in 1970.

The Decline of the Family?

American families also have changed over the past half-century, and this too may have led to a decline in religious influence by families. For example, by 1990, one out of every two marriages in America ended in divorce, and by 2000, almost as many children lived in single-parent households as in dual-parent households. Of those children in two-parent households, one-fourth lived in "blended" families with stepparents and step-siblings (Casper & Bianchi, 2002; Cherlin, 2010). In our 1970 survey, only 6 percent of the grandparents had divorced; in 2005, 26 percent had.

Trends such as these led to a growing chorus of public concern about the "decline of the American family." Within sociology, there was support for this position by Popenoe (1993), who analyzed demographic data to conclude that divorce rates and dual-family employment had diminished the influence of parents in the socialization of their children. Such perceptions of declining family influences continue as public and religious issues. For example, in his 2012 presidential campaign bid, Texas Governor Rick Perry proclaimed "a Day of Prayer and Fasting" to focus on "the decline of our culture in the context of the demise of our families" (Sanders, 2012). Catholic scholars have also voiced this view. In a review of the literature, Jesuit psychologist David Vitz (2005) concluded: "When one puts the big picture together, the decline of the family is obvious" (p. 154).

The Increasing Importance of Grandparents

On the other hand, another remarkable development over the past four decades has been the increasing importance of grandparents in American family life. Bengtson (2001) has argued that grandparents have become more important to families than in any previous period of U.S. history. More grandparents are involved in and contributing to their grandchildren's development than ever before, and this is resulting in intergenerational influence far beyond what most contemporary observers recognize. A recent review of research on intergenerational relationships (Swartz, 2009) presents a variety of evidence concerning the importance of grandparents, and additional support is found in the AARP nationally representative surveys on grandparenting (Goyer, 2012; Lampkin, 2012). For example, 52 percent of older grandparents report seeing a grandchild at least once a week; 26 percent say they communicate with a grandchild by e-mail, text, or Skype; 25 percent have spent over $5,000 in providing support for grandchildren recently; and 59 percent feel they play a "very important role" in the lives of grandchildren (Lampkin, 2012).

There are several reasons why grandparents may be more influential today and tomorrow than in the past. First is the growing availability of grandparents due the remarkable increase in life expectancy. Because grandparents are living longer than ever before, grandchildren today have the opportunity to spend a greater proportion of their lives with living grandparents. In 2005, 95 percent of American twenty-year-olds had at least one grandparent alive; at age thirty, almost 79 percent had a grandparent alive. A century ago, in 1900, the figures were 19 percent and 4 percent, respectively (Uhlenberg, 2005, 2009). Second, because today's Baby Boomers had fewer children, they now have fewer sets of grandchildren; there are fewer grandchildren today to share more grandparents.

A third factor is that older people are healthier than in past generations, and as a group they have more resources to provide to grandchildren. In the AARP nationwide survey, 53 percent of grandparents reported providing help to grandchildren with educational expenses, 37 percent with everyday living expenses, and 25 percent with medical expenses. Fourth, a majority of grandparents have retired and thus have more opportunity to interact with and lend support to their grandchildren (AARP, 2012). A fifth factor is technology: for grandchildren living far away, long distance communication is much easier than in the past. Using technologies such as cell phones, Skype and Facebook, there are more ways for cross-generational communication than ever before. Finally, with the majority of mothers with young children in the labor force and with the growing number of single-parent households, more grandparents have been providing care for grandchildren than ever before (AARP, 2012; U.S. Bureau of the Census, 2009).

For these reasons, grandparents today have greater opportunity to play a significant role in the lives of grandchildren than in previous decades. They provide tangible resources, offer both emotional support and useful information about the adult world, and can be transmitters of family and cultural history. Thus, it is not surprising that a majority of grandchildren report being emotionally close to their grandparents, as well as sharing similar views and values with grandparents (AARP 2012; Copen & Silverstein, 2008; Silverstein, Giarrusso, & Bengtson, 2003).

Nevertheless, empirical research on these issues that goes beyond descriptive reporting is as yet underdeveloped. This is not surprising, since it has been only twenty-five years since the first volume with empirical research on grandparenthood was published (Bengtson & Robertson, 1985). Since then, an increasing number of studies have explored the complex roles of grandparents, grandchild perceptions of grandparents, grandparents who are raising grandchildren, and styles of grandparenting (Birditt, Tighe, Fingerman, & Zarit, 2012; Michaleski & Shackleford, 2005; Moserud,

2008; Ruiz & Silverstein, 2007; Szinovacz, 1998; Swartz, 2009). However, no research to date focuses on the *influence* of grandparents on grandchildren's outcomes, such as their religious orientations. This constitutes a significant gap in the research literature because youth today will have greater involvement with their grandparents—and for some, their great-grandparents—than any previous generation of grandchildren in American history (Bengtson, 2001; Mueller & Elder, 2003; Swartz, 2009). Moreover, we know virtually nothing about patterns and processes of grandparent influences—and why some influence efforts are successful while others are not.

A Life Course Perspective

Despite the evidence for family influence reviewed above, some observers of American culture voice the opinion that religious inheritance across generations has declined over recent decades (Putnam & Campbell, 2010; Wuthnow, 2007). Thus, I wanted to explore two questions: To what extent do we see significant religious transmission by families in contemporary American society? And to what degree has this transmission changed over recent decades? I felt it was important to ground this inquiry in social science theory and determined the life course perspective would be the most helpful theoretical orientation in understanding the intersections of families, religion, and time (both historical time and individual aging).

A central dimension of the life course perspective is the concept of "linked lives": as individuals grow up and grow through the course of life, their development is tied to the changing lives of others, particularly parents and grandparents, siblings, then spouses, and eventually children and grandchildren (Bengtson, Elder, & Putney, 2005). This is an important insight: an individual's religious identity develops in ways that are linked to other family members, particularly parents. Expanding on the concept of linked lives, we developed a theory to explain intergenerational continuity in values (Bengtson, Biblarz, & Roberts, 2002). This theory posits conditions and socialization mechanisms by which older generations contribute to transmission of values and beliefs. A prominent mechanism of socialization concerns intergenerational solidarity, particularly emotional warmth. According to the model, intergenerational transmission of values is greater when the child perceives the parent or grandparent as warm and affirming, compared to cold and distant.

Methods

The Longitudinal Study of Generations (LSOG), which began in 1970, involves over 3,500 respondents from 357 three- and four-generation families. Families were recruited from 840,000 members of a health maintenance organization in southern California. The plan primarily served labor union members, but the sample was generally representative of the southern California area (for details, see Bengtson, Putney, & Harris, 2013). There were 2,044 respondents at Wave-1 in 1970. Subsequent surveys took place in 1985, 1988, 1991, 1994, 1997, 2000, and 2005. Response rates averaged 74 percent between waves. Beginning in 1991, the great-grandchildren (G4s) were recruited into the study as they reached age sixteen. In Wave-8, the number of respondents was 1,766, ranging in age from 16 to 102.

Because the LSOG provides four-generation panel data collected over a long period of time, we have been able achieve a "generational-sequential" analytic design (Bengtson et al., 2002), whereby matched cohorts of parents and children, grandparents and grandchildren, at roughly the same ages, can be compared at two different points in time. Such a design allows us to begin to assess the effects of social change (historical or period effects such as religious trends) on socialization and family influence. We constructed family triads consisting of related grandparents, parents, and grandchildren; that is, if grandchildren had siblings, each grandchild was paired with the same parents and grandparents in the sample.

Measures

We use the Millennial grandchildren's religious practices and beliefs as the outcome variable, with grandparents' and parents' religiosity as the key independent (predictor) variables. We analyzed four dimensions of religiosity measured at every time wave. *Religious participation* was assessed with the question, "How often do you attend religious services these days?" (1 = *never* to 4 = *more than once a week)*. For r*eligious intensity,* we asked:

"Regardless of whether you attend religious services, do you consider your-self to be . . . (1 = *not at all religious* to 4 = *very religious*)." Two summed items assessed *conservative biblical beliefs*, reflecting a literal interpretation of the Bible: "All people alive today are descendants of Adam and Eve," and "God exists in the form described in the Bible" (1 = *strongly disagree* to 4 = *strongly agree*). *Conservative civic religiosity*, beliefs about the place of religion in public life, was also measured by two items summed: "This country would be better off if religion had a greater influence on daily life," and "Every child should have religious instruction" (1 = *strongly disagree* to 4 = *strongly agree*).

Factor analysis demonstrated that the above four scales comprise one factor, so, for multiple regression analyses, we constructed a *composite religiosity score* using all dimensions. The scale showed substantial reliability (Cronbach's alpha = .85 for the 1970 survey data; .93 for 2005).

Closeness (Intergenerational Affectual Solidarity)

We conceptualize the strength of emotional closeness between generations, or *affectual solidarity* (Roberts, Richards, & Bengtson, 1991), as having an important mediating or moderating effect on grandchildren's (and adult children's) religiosity and other value outcomes. We use the grandchild's response to the question: "Taking everything together, how close do you feel is the relationship between you and your grandfather (or grandmother) these days?" (1 = *not at all close* to 6 = *extremely close*). This is the item that correlated most highly with the five-item affectual solidarity scale (Mangen, Bengtson, & Landry, 1988).

Results

First, we examined evidence for religious transmission effects from parents to Millennials. We used hierarchical regression to examine factors that predict variations in child and grandchild religiosity. Figure 1 displays the results. Numbers above the bars are standardized coefficients.

These data indicated that parents showed relatively high influence on their Millennial children's religious orientations, even higher than we had anticipated. The degree to which the young adults' religious behavior was related to their parents' was greatest in religious participation and second highest in biblical literalism. It is important to note that high parent-child similarity could come either from both generations reporting they attend church "at least once a week," or from both parent and child saying that they "never attend church."

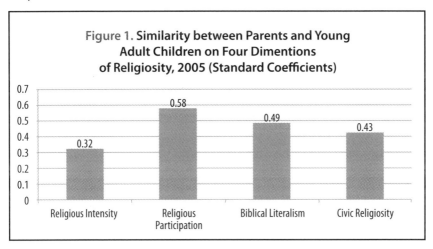

Figure 1. Similarity between Parents and Young Adult Children on Four Dimentions of Religiosity, 2005 (Standard Coefficients)

What about change over time—the contrast between intergenerational transmission in 2005 and in 1970? We expected to see a decline in religious influence by parents over the thirty-five years of the study, given the significant cultural, religious, and familial changes over that time. However, the data did not support this expectation.

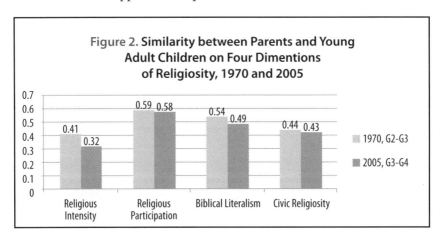

Figure 2. Similarity between Parents and Young Adult Children on Four Dimentions of Religiosity, 1970 and 2005

There does not appear to be a decline in the rate of religious transmission over time. The degree of intergenerational influence in 2005 was similar to that in 1970, at least in our sample of findings. We caution that this is not a large, nationally representative sample, so generalization of these findings to the entire United States is unwarranted. However, these are the only data that exist with which to examine these issues, so we will make the best use of them.

What are the factors associated with intergenerational influence? What might parents do to enhance their effect on children's religious values? Several are significant—for example, parents being role models in religious practice—but perhaps the most interesting variable was the quality of the relationship between parent and child. In Figure 3, we see that there is much greater intergenerational similarity where the child perceives his or her relationship with the parent as "close" compared to those defining their relationship as less close. Figure 4 depicts this in a different way, using a composite measure that combines all dimensions of religiosity. The relationship between high parental warmth and high religious transmission is clear.

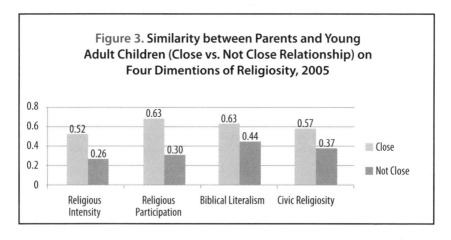

Figure 3. Similarity between Parents and Young Adult Children (Close vs. Not Close Relationship) on Four Dimentions of Religiosity, 2005

Particularly important is the father's warmth. In other analyses (Bengtson et al., 2013), we examined gender differences in transmission and the predictors of transmission. Fathers who were perceived as emotionally close were almost twice as likely to transmit faith to their children as fathers perceived as distant or authoritarian. The same did not apply to mothers; perceived closeness did not make much difference in transmission outcomes.

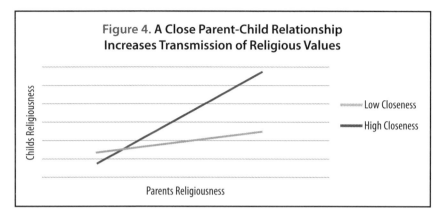

Figure 4. A Close Parent-Child Relationship Increases Transmission of Religious Values

Grandparents and Value Transmission

Are grandparents relevant to religious socialization? If they are, any indication in the literature is almost nonexistent: a search of the literature located only six journal articles published between 2000 and 2014 that contained anything about grandparents and religion. However, as noted earlier, grandparents are of increasing importance to families in the United States, and their influence on grandchildren should be examined. Figure 5 presents data from our study on religious similarity between grandparents and Millennials.

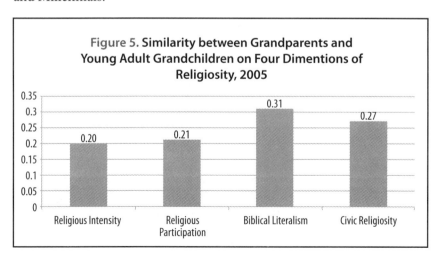

Figure 5. Similarity between Grandparents and Young Adult Grandchildren on Four Dimentions of Religiosity, 2005

Our data show that grandparents are important, and their influence lasts well into their grandchildren's early-to-mid-adult years. The level of influence is not as high as that of parents as shown in Figure 1, (for example, coefficients for religious intensity are .20 for grandparents, .41 for parents) and in statistical models, their effect is mediated through parental effects. However, the grandparent effects are still significant.

Furthermore, when we compare over time, the degree of grandparental influence on grandchildren's religiosity has not declined over recent decades. In Figure 6, we see that the magnitude of coefficients are not less in 2005 than in 1970; in biblical literalism, it is higher, though lower in religious participation.

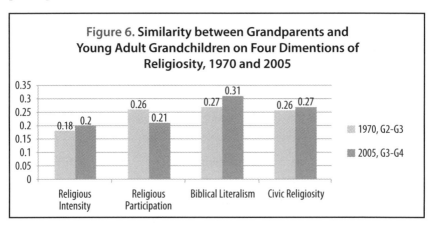

Figure 6. Similarity between Grandparents and Young Adult Grandchildren on Four Dimentions of Religiosity, 1970 and 2005

Discussion and Conclusion

In this chapter, I have examined Millennials and their religiousness through a family perspective. Much has been written about the Millennial generation because they appear in many ways to be so different from their parents' generation. How much of a contrast is there between Millennials' religiosity and that of their parents? How much has family religious influence changed over time, across the period of social and religious changes we have seen in the United States since the 1960s? Are families still passing on their faith?

Data from the thirty-five-year Longitudinal Study of Generations, with information from grandparents, parents, grandchildren, and great-grandchildren who are Millennials, provide information by which to examine these issues.

Is There a "Crisis" in Family Values Today?

No, despite what some politicians, pundits, and religious leaders say. From the data reviewed in this chapter and from other results of this study (Bengtson et al., 2013), we can conclude that family bonds and family influences are strong. In fact, multigenerational bonds may be stronger than ever before in America. The reason is found in "longer years of shared lives" between parents and adult children, grandparents and grandchildren, as people are living longer and maintaining better health.

Is There a "Generation Gap" in Values and Religion Today?

No. In religious values and beliefs, there is significant similarity in spiritual and religious life between parents and children. This is a result that has been repeatedly emphasized by Christian Smith and his colleagues (Smith & Denton, 2005; Smith & Snell, 2009) based on data from their National Study of Youth and Religion. The exception is religious affiliation, where there is less parent-child similarity.

Polls that show large numbers of religious "nones" among Millennials equate religion with belonging to a church. However, there is more to religion than belonging to church: "I'm spiritual but not religious" is what many young adults say. Many youth who reject churches are still religiously oriented, like their parents.

Are Parents Failing To Pass on Their Faith to Children?

No. In religious values and beliefs, a high percentage of young adults are similar to their parents. The quality (closeness) of the parent-child relationship is particularly important to passing on values. Parental religious influence does not appear to have declined over the past few decades; the degree of intergenerational similarity in 2005 is similar to that in 1970.

Are Grandparents Relevant?

Yes. It is important to look beyond the nuclear family. Grandparents are more relevant to family fortunes and functioning than ever before. Grandparents have significant influences on Millennials' religious orientations. Moreover, the extent of grandparents' influence has not diminished since the 1970s.

We must be careful not to overgeneralize from the data just reviewed. These findings are from one study and based on a southern California sample. It may be that results would be different had the sample been nationwide and included families from Alabama and North Dakota, where religious attendance is higher than it is in California. But I am confident that, even with a larger and nationally representative sample, the three major findings of the study would hold. The first is that contemporary parents exert a strong and lasting influence on their children's' religiosity. Second, the magnitude of such parental influence is robust, despite the significant social and cultural changes that have occurred since the 1970s. Third, a great many grandparents exert a significant influence on their grandchildren's religious lives.

Multigenerational bonds are strong in contemporary American society, stronger than often recognized, and what we have seen in this chapter is the strength of what can be called "intergenerational religious momentum" (Bengtson et al, 2013).

References

AARP. (2012). Insights and spending habits of modern grandparents. *AARP Research and Strategic Analysis*. Retrieved from http://www.aarp.org /grandparentresearch/fullreport

Bellah, R. N., Madsen, R., Sullivan, W. M., Swidler, A., & Tipton, S. M. (1985). *Habits of the heart: Individualism and commitment in American life*. Berkeley, CA: University of California Press.

Bengtson, V. L. (1970). The generation gap: A review and typology of social-psychological perspectives. *Youth and Society, 2*, 7–32.

Bengtson, V. L. (2001). Beyond the nuclear family: The increasing importance of multigenerational bonds. *Journal of Marriage and Family, 63*, 1–16.

Bengtson, V. L., Biblarz, T., & Roberts, R. E. L. (2002). *How families still matter: A longitudinal study of youth in two generations*. New York, NY: Cambridge University Press.

Bengtson, V.L., & Cutler, N.E. (1976). Generations and inter-generational relations: Perspectives on age groups and social change. In R. Binstock & E. Shanas (Eds.), *The handbook of aging and the social sciences* (pp. 130-159). New York, NY: Van Nostrand Reinhold Company.

Bengtson, V. L., Elder, G. E., & Putney, N. M. (2005). The life course perspective on aging: Linked lives, timing and history. In M. Johnson, V. L. Bengtson, P. G. Coleman, & T. Kirkwood (Eds.), *The Cambridge Handbook of Age and Ageing* (pp. 493–501). Cambridge: Cambridge University Press.

Bengtson, V. L., Putney, N. P., & Harris, S. C. (2013). *Families and faith: How religion is passed down across generations*. New York, NY: Oxford University Press.

Bengtson, V. L., & Robertson, J. F. (Eds.). (1985). *Grandparenthood*. Beverly Hills, CA: Sage Publications.

Birditt, K. S., Tighe, L. A., Fingerman, K. L., & Zarit, S. H. (2012). Intergenerational relationship quality across three generations. *Journal of Gerontology: Social Sciences, 67B(5)*, 627–638.

Casper, L. H., & Bianchi, S. F. (2002). *Continuity and change in the American family*. Thousand Oaks, CA: Sage.

Chavez, M. A. (2011). *American religion: Contemporary trends*. Princeton, NJ: Princeton and Oxford.

Cherlin, A. J. (2010). *Public and private families*. New York, NY: McGraw-Hill.

Copen, C. A., & Silverstein, M. (2008). Intergenerational transmission of religious beliefs to young adults: Do grandmothers matter? *Journal of Contemporary Family Studies, 38*, 497–510.

Goyer, A. (2012). Study: Grandparents give 'til it hurts. *Generations united: Grandparents investing in grandchildren: The MetLife study on how grandparents share their time, values, and money*. Retrieved from http://blog.aarp .org/2012/09/08/amy-goyer-grandparents-financial-gifts

Lampkin, C. L. (2012). Insights and spending habits of modern grandparents. *AARP: Research and Strategic Analysis.* Retrieved from http://www.aarp.org /research

Mangen, D. J., Bengtson, V. L., & Landry, P. J. (Eds.). (1988). *The measurement of intergenerational relationships.* Beverly Hills, CA: Sage Publications.

Michaleski, R. L., & Shackleford, T. K. (2005). Grandparental investment as a function of relational uncertainty and emotional closeness with parents. *Human Nature, 16,* 293–305.

Moserud, M. A. (2008). Intergenerational relationships and affectual solidarity between grandparents and young adults. *Journal of Marriage and Family, 70,* 182–195.

Mueller, M. M., & Elder, G. H., Jr. (2003). Family contingencies across the generations: Grandparent-grandchild relationships in holistic perspective. *Journal of Marriage and Family, 65,* 404–417.

Pew Research Center. (2008). U.S. religion landscape survey. *Pew Forum on Religion and Public Life.* Retrieved from http://pewforum.org/reports

Pew Research Center. (2012). "Nones" on the rise: One-in-five adults have no religious affiliation. *Pew Forum on Religion and Public Life.* Retrieved from http:/pewforum.org/Unaffiliated/nones-on-the rise.aspx

Pew Research Center. (2014). Millennials in adulthood: Detached from Institutions, Networked with Friends. *Social and Demographic Trends.* Retrieved from http://www.pewsocialtrends.org/2014/03/07/millennials -in-adulthood/

Popenoe, D. (1993). American family decline, 1960–1990: A review and appraisal. *Journal of Marriage and Family, 55,* 527–555.

Putnam, R., & Campbell, D. (2010). *American grace: How religion divides and unites us.* New York, NY: Simon and Schuster.

Roberts, R. E. L., Richards, L. N., & Bengtson, V. L. (1991). Intergenerational solidarity in families: Untangling the ties that bind. *Marriage and Family Review, 16,* 11–46.

Ruiz, S., & Silverstein, M. (2007). Relationships with grandparents and the emotional well-being of late adolescent and young adult grandchildren. *Journal of Social Issues, 63,* 793–808.

Sanders, B. R. (2012, June 18). Texas governor proclaims day of fasting and prayer for lost family life. *Santa Barbara News-Press,* p. A-1.

Silverstein, M., Giarrusso, R., & Bengtson, V. L. (2003). Grandparents and grandchildren in family systems: A socio-developmental perspective. In V. Bengtson & A. Lowenstein (Eds.), *Global aging and its challenges to families* (pp. 75–102). New York, NY: Aldine de Gruyter.

Smith, C., & Denton, M. (2005). *Soul searching: The religious and spiritual lives of American teenagers.* New York, NY: Oxford University Press.

Smith, C., & Snell, P. (2009). *Souls in transition: The religious and spiritual lives of emerging adults.* New York, NY: Oxford University Press.

Szinovacz, M. E. (1998). Grandparent research: Past, present, and future. In M. E. Szinovacz (Ed.), *Handbook on grandparenthood* (pp. 1–20). Westport, CN: Greenwood Press.

Swartz, T. T. (2009). Intergenerational family relationships in adulthood: Patterns, variations, and implications in the contemporary United States. *Annual Review of Sociology, 35,* 191–212.

Uhlenberg, P. R. (2005). Historical forces shaping grandparent-grand-child relationships: Demography and beyond. In M. E. Silverstein (Ed.), *Intergenerational relations across time and place* (pp. 77–97). New York, NY: Springer.

Uhlenberg, P. R. (2009). Children in an aging society. *The Journals of Gerontology, Series B: Psychological Sciences and Social Sciences, 64B,* 489–496.

U. S. Bureau of the Census. (2009). Retrieved from <http://www.census.gov /newsroom/release/archives/facts for features special editions/cb09-f16.htm>

Vitz, P. (2005). Family decline: The findings of social science. In P. Vitz (Ed.), *Defending the faith: A sourcebook* (pp. 1–23). Steubenville, OH: Catholic Social Science Press.

Wuthnow, R. (1988). *The restructuring of American religion: Society and faith since World War II.* Princeton, NJ: Princeton University Press.

Wuthnow, R. (2007). *After the baby boomers: How twenty- and thirty-somethings are shaping the future of American religion.* Princeton, NJ: Princeton University Press.

EDITORS

Timothy W. Herrmann is Professor and Graduate Director of the MA in Higher Education and Student Development program at Taylor University (Upland, IN). Tim has also served in a variety of other roles, including Dean of Assessment, Associate Professor of Psychology, and Associate Dean of Students. In addition to being a former president of the Association for Christians in Student Development, he is also co-founder and co-editor of *Growth: The Journal of the Association for Christians in Student Development*. Tim's publications include the co-authored *A Parents Guide to the Christian College: Supporting Your Child's Mind and Spirit during the College Years* and co-edited *Funding the Future*.

Kirsten D. TenHaken is graduating this May 2015 from Taylor University (Upland, IN) with a Masters in Higher Education and Student Development. She graduated from Whitworth University (Spokane, WA) in 2013 with a B.A. in Mathematics and a certification to teach secondary education, plus minors in Spanish and Music. Kirsten's research interests include purpose and calling development among college students as well as student involvement and engagement in the college experience.

Hannah M. Adderley is graduating this May (2015) from Taylor University (Upland, IN) with a Masters in Higher Education and Student Development. With a passion for academically at-risk students, Hannah is pursuing a career in Learning Support Services at the collegiate level, hoping to earn her PhD in this field in the near future. Her research interests include academic departmental culture, the teaching-research nexus, and college students' dispositions and skills for learning and academic success.

Morgan K. Morris will complete her Masters in Higher Education and Student Development at Taylor University (Upland, IN) in May 2016. She graduated from John Brown University (Siloam Springs, AR) in 2014 with a BSE in Early Childhood Education. With a passion for holistic development, Morgan serves as Taylor University's Graduate Assistant for First Year Experience and hopes to continue to foster student learning both inside and outside the college classroom. Aligning with this vision, Morgan's research interests include campus traditions and learning dispositions.

CONTRIBUTORS

Holly C. Allen is professor of family studies and Christian ministries at Lipscomb University in Nashville, Tennessee, where she holds a joint appointment in the College of Arts and Sciences and the College of Bible and Ministry. She teaches undergraduate courses such as Early Childhood Development and Family Ministry. Holly's areas of research interest include children's spirituality and intergenerational issues. Her most recent book (with Christine Ross) is *Intergenerational Christian Formation: Bringing the Whole Church Together in Ministry, Community, and Worship*. Her first book, an edited volume, *Nurturing Children's Spirituality: Christian Perspectives and Best Practices* was released in 2008.

Vern L. Bengtson is research professor of social work and senior scientist in the Roybal Institute on Aging at the University of Southern California. A past president of the Gerontological Society of America, he is the author of seventeen books and over 250 research articles on families, the life course, and theories of aging. His most recent book, *Families and Faith: How Religion Is (and Isn't) Passed Down across Generations* (with Norella Putney and Susan C. Harris), has been reviewed in the *New York Times, Wall Street Journal, Washington Post, USA Today,* and on National Public Radio.

Guy Chmieleski is the university minister at Belmont University in Nashville, Tennessee, where he has served since 2005. Guy is also the founder and president of Faith On Campus (http:FaithOnCampus.com), an organization committed to exploring the convergence of Christ, culture, and the college experience and to equipping students, parents, and mentors to make the most of the formative college years. He is the author of three books—*Shaping Their Future: Mentoring Students through Their Formative College Years; CAMPUS gODS: Exposing the Idols That Can Derail Your Present and Destroy Your Future;* and *Noise. Hurry. Crowds.: Creating Space for God Amidst the Chaos of Campus and Culture* (forthcoming March 2015).

Perry L. Glanzer is professor of educational foundations at Baylor University and a resident scholar with Baylor Institute for Studies of Religion. Most recently, he is the co-author with Todd C. Ream of *The Idea of a Christian College: A Reexamination for Today's University* and co-editor with Joel Carpenter and Nicholas Lantinga of *Christian Higher Education: A Global Reconnaissance.*

Mark Husbands occupies the Leonard and Marjorie Maas Chair of Reformed Theology at Hope College. Born in Wales, raised and educated in Canada, Husbands is a Christian theologian whose work focuses upon the moral theology of Karl Barth, reconciliation, world Christianity, and political theology. As the founder and director of the Emmaus Scholars Program, his work reflects an abiding commitment to integral mission. He and his wife, Becky, have three children: Olivia, Elliott, and Ethan.

Bill Kuhn serves as campus chaplain at Crown College, St. Bonifacius, Minnesota. He teaches courses in adult ministry, spiritual formation, and leadership and earned a doctorate in education from St. Mary's University in Minnesota.

Aaron Morrison serves as a residential education coordinator at Nebraska Wesleyan University in Lincoln, Nebraska. His research interests include spiritual formation among college students, the nature of church-university relationships, theology of scholarship and the mind, and the history of higher education.

Stephen W. Rankin serves as university chaplain at Southern Methodist University in Dallas, Texas. He has worked in higher education for twenty years, both as a full-time professor and chaplain at two United

Methodist-affiliated schools. He holds a PhD in religious studies from Northwestern University.

Hannah Schundler received an MA in higher education and student development at Taylor University and currently works in the Office of Community Engagement and the Center for Student Development at Gordon College. Hannah is a graduate of Gordon College and believes in the value and formative influence of faith-based higher education. Prior to graduate school, Hannah worked with student groups in short-term missions, which deepened her love of student development and community development. She is interested in the topic of college student spirituality and, more specifically, spiritual struggle. Hannah desires to help college students ask big questions about faith, meaning, purpose, and calling in the world.

Micah B. Weedman is director of outreach and associate university minister at Belmont University in Nashville, Tennessee. He holds an MDiv and is a PhD candidate.